LONG-TERM CARE PLANNING

Assuring Choice, Independence, and Financial Security

ALLEN HAMM

Plan Ahead

The purpose of this publication is to provide accurate information on the subject of long-term care planning and insurance. The publisher and author are not engaged in rendering legal or accounting service. The author's experience is in one narrow aspect of financial planning: long-term care planning and insurance. Because the industry is in constant change, the author recommends seeking professional advice from a competent financial professional trained in long-term care planning, prior to acting on any advice whatsoever given in this book.

The author has made every attempt to give credit where credit is due with regard to material in this book. Much of the material is based on the author's personal experience and opinion. The author and the publisher will not accept liability or responsibility to any person or entity with respect to any loss and/or damage caused directly or indirectly by the information presented in this book.

Any attempt to litigate against the author or publisher with malice will be met with a position of defense and offense that uses the fullest extent of the law to recuperate any damages to the reputation of the author or the publisher, including, but not limited to monetary, time, and emotional resources.

ISBN: 0-9764189-0-8

Published by:	Plan Ahead, Inc.
Editor:	Lyssa Campbell, LCEditing@msn.com
Cover Design:	Andrew Newman, www.newmandesign.com
Interior Design:	Quin Coursey, QuinCoursey@comcast.net
Printed by:	Chromagraphics, www.chromaprinting.com
Interior Photos:	©PhotoDisc/Getty Images

Dedication

Dedicated to my father, who continues to inspire me by example.
And to my sons, Brian and Alex, to whom I strive to do the same.

Acknowledgments

This book would not exist without the contribution of my wife, Eileen. She is so much a part of this project, that the term "we" is used throughout. She not only assisted in writing the book, she constantly motivated me to finish what we started almost two years ago. She also wrote *Chapter 5: Long-Term Care **Is** a Woman's Issue.*

I would like to thank my mentor, Bob Bingham, CFP®, who has inspired me over the years to develop a long-term care educational solution different from any other in the industry. His example of taking the time to build something slow and special has been invaluable to me.

Thank you to attorney Harley Gordon, President of the Corporation for Long-Term Care Certification, Inc. (www.ltc-cltc.com) for permitting us to use material from his writings, derived from many years of experience in long-term care planning.

Thanks to Jesse Slome, editor of *Long-Term Care Insurance Sales Strategies,* (www.ltcsales.com) for permitting us to use material from the magazine.

Thanks to Mark Lapin for the initial research of this project and for assistance with some of the interviews in *Chapter 19.*

I also acknowledge the hundreds of financial planners, estate planning attorneys, and CPAs who have given me advice on how to create a process that assists financial professionals in helping their clients plan ahead for long-term care. They freely gave of their time, and their influence is evident throughout these pages.

A special thanks to Steve Bell, CFP®, for his assistance in developing the Long-Term Care Planning processes found in Part 2. He also made an important contribution by writing *Chapter 18: Long-Term Care Insurance Myths.*

Many thanks to our editor, Lyssa Campbell for her patience as we made many revisions and updates during the project. We also owe much to our graphic designer, Quin Coursey, who stuck with us throughout the entire project when she must have contemplated quitting more than once! Thank you for staying the course, Quin!

TABLE OF CONTENTS

PREFACE
Long-Term Care is America's Real Health Care Crisis

In the next decade, 76 million baby boomers will reach maturity. Ironically, the healthy lifestyles and medical advances that will enable millions of them to live well beyond 100 years may pose the greatest threat to the financial security and retirement plans of this huge and prosperous generation.

Our newest and biggest challenge in health care will be to physically and psychologically care for those who have managed to live well beyond today's life expectancy. It's been estimated that the number of people requiring long-term care will double in the next three decades. This means that more than 14 million people could need help with the basic activities of daily living—tasks such as mobility, which are now performed with ease, will require assistance from others. Unable to live independently, these large numbers of people in need of care will create tremendous demand for new health care solutions in the first half of the 21st century. This new health care challenge—long-term care—will dwarf our current problems of financing physician and hospital care.

Who will provide this care? Where will this care take place? Who will pay the bills? The long-term care industry is busy finding the answers to many of these questions. Soon, planning ahead for long-term care will become as common as making out a will.

One option for paying for the costs of care is long-term care insurance. We devote several chapters of this book to a discussion of this option. You have probably heard about this new type of insurance. If you haven't already purchased long-term care insurance, we encourage you to wait the few hours it will take to read this book. Then, speak with a financial professional—a financial planner, estate planning attorney, or CPA—who has invested the time to become specifically trained in long-term care planning. They will assist you in planning ahead for long-term care by considering all of your options within the context of your current financial situation and goals. This process of integrating your long-term care plan with your total financial objectives is called a *comprehensive planning approach* to long-term care.

If you purchase long-term care insurance without heeding this advice, there is a good chance you'll make a mistake. Why? Because the major distributors of long-term care insurance in America today are insurance agents who know very little about the overall long-term care planning process. Many insurance agents attempt to sell long-term care insurance without regard to your overall financial objectives. This approach of non-integration is called the *single sales approach.*

After you read the information presented in these pages, you will have the knowledge you need to avoid the sales tactics of insurance agents, ask meaningful questions, and make an informed decision about this important area of financial planning.

INTRODUCTION
Long-Term Care is a Family Affair

The following essay recounts my personal experiences with long-term care. Many people have stories that are undoubtedly more painful. My purpose in sharing these personal experiences is to communicate the basis and foundation for my strong belief in planning ahead for long-term care.

For those who are anxious to learn the specifics of planning ahead, I invite you to move ahead to **Part 1: Understanding Long-Term Care.**

LONG-TERM CARE TOUCHES
MOST OF US: A PERSONAL EXPERIENCE

I pondered my family's lack of knowledge about long-term care planning. How could we know so much about most financial issues, but know so little about such an important part of the financial and estate planning process?

— Allen Hamm, *Author*

My family confronted two crises concerning long-term care. These experiences convinced me to choose a career in long-term care planning and to write this book. My experiences aren't much different than those of millions of other American families. In the next few decades, millions more will experience similar scenarios.

I was raised in a traditional American family. As I grew up, I dreamed of going into business for myself, or maybe even buying my grandfather's small construction company. He had built a successful company that supported many of his family members for several decades.

By the late 1970s, when my grandfather was 72, we began to notice a slight change in his mental alertness. Since he appeared to be managing the company without any problems, we paid little attention to it at first. But we began to take it seriously when we received complaints from his suppliers about late invoice payments. Then, one day, we got a call from a close family friend and the owner of one of the businesses that supplied his materials. "Allen," he told me, "your grandfather's check just bounced." There was shock in his voice, and a dead silence on my end of the phone. My grandfather had always been meticulous about keeping his accounts organized.

Over the next few months, my family was subjected to a painful series of discoveries about the state of my grandfather's mental health and his company's finances. We learned that he was suffering from the early onset of Alzheimer's Disease. The condition was causing him to slowly lose control of both his personal life and his business affairs. By the time we discovered the true dimensions of his problems, it was too late. His once thriving company was in financial trouble.

Within two years of his diagnosis, my grandfather required a level of long-term care our family could no longer provide at home. We contacted Medicare, expecting that as a hard-working American businessman who had made a positive contribution to society and the economy, he would be well covered for whatever medical and custodial services he might require. What we learned was almost as upsetting as our original discoveries: neither his Medicare nor his Medicare Supplement policy offered coverage for long-term custodial care in a nursing facility. Although he had lost most of his assets in the demise of his business, he still had too much money to qualify for Medicaid, the welfare program.

Prior to my grandfather's health problems, my parents had been diligently saving for an early retirement. But after my grandfather's funds went completely dry, they were forced to cash in their retirement savings to fund quality care for my grandfather. He spent the last four years of his life in a private pay nursing home.

After the loss of my grandfather's business, I pondered my family's lack of knowledge about long-term care planning. How could we know so much about most financial issues, but know so little about such an important part of the financial and estate planning process? I began to investigate the subject of long-term care and long-term care insurance. I also began thinking seriously about moving to a new part of the country—something that I had been considering for several years.

I moved to California in the mid-1980s. Moving 2,000 miles away from my family was one of the most difficult decisions I've ever made. Dad had always been my mentor. Strong, wise, and patient, he had always been able to say or do just the right thing at the right moment. He had never been wealthy, but he taught us family values and the importance of planning for our financial future. As an adult, I admired his positive attitude and tenacity, especially after experiencing adversity and set-backs. Slowly, with hard work and integrity, he built a separate company of his own. Inspired by his example, and the tragedy that long-term care brought to my grandfather's last years, I fulfilled my own dream of starting a business—a long-term care planning agency.

After becoming a specialist in long-term care planning, I approached my parents about long-term care planning for themselves. I made a special trip to visit them in order to design coverage that would be suitable for their situation. Although we had experienced my grandfather's long-term care situation, I did not expect my parents to react enthusiastically to a conversation about their own potential need for long-term care. Few parents want to discuss the possibility of being dependent on someone else or requiring assistance with their physical care. One evening, however, we all agreed that it made sense to put plans in place that would give them choices we didn't have with my grandfather, and protect the assets they had worked so hard to rebuild after his need for care. I went to bed that night pleasantly surprised that they had agreed to my advice with no resistance.

About three years after his long-term care (LTC) insurance policy went into effect, my father was diagnosed with mild Parkinson's Disease. Had he been diagnosed years earlier or waited longer to purchase LTC insurance, he would not have been able to obtain coverage. As we'll explain later in this book, the ability to obtain LTC insurance is based on a person's health at the time they apply for coverage, and a person with Parkinson's Disease will not qualify for LTC insurance.

My father was in his mid-60s when his symptoms started with a slight tremor in his left arm. The prognosis was progressive neurological deterioration and, over a period of years, severe physical and cognitive disabilities would await him. But in the short term, he remained active with his family, business, and church, and our hopes were high that a cure for Parkinson's Disease would be found within his lifetime.

Busy with my own family and running our company, I tried to keep an objective eye on Dad's condition with frequent phone calls from 2,000 miles away. Fortunately, my brother lives in the same area as my parents, so he is able to keep me updated on Dad's physical health. In my semi-annual visits, I noticed that, physically, his tremor seemed to be slowly getting worse. I respected him too much to pry into his psychological health, but my frequent calls allowed me to monitor his mood for signs of depression or fatigue. By this time, my experience in long-term care planning made me well aware of the signs of many types of health conditions, particularly mental and neurological disorders.

Shortly before Dad turned 70, my wife, two sons and I attended an eagerly anticipated family reunion. Seeing him for the first time in almost a year, Dad seemed unusually tired and melancholy. Even his grandsons failed to spark his usual enthusiasm. Concerned about him, I suggested that the two of us have a private talk in the backyard. We sat down at an old picnic table where we'd had many family cookouts and private talks. I asked him to open up to me.

His eyes began to water, something I'd never remembered seeing. He's a warm person, but has always been very much in control of his emotions. He looked away and began to talk.

"Your mom doesn't know, and I don't know how to tell her. Or even you…but here goes…I'm in debt. We're on the verge of losing it all. We're behind on our house payment and the rental property mortgages. The banks are no longer willing to finance our projects. When I was diagnosed with Parkinson's, I knew that I only had a short period of time to get your mother set-up, to make sure she wouldn't have to worry once the Parkinson's took control. I rushed with some major business decisions; I made some mis-steps; I took on too many projects. I've lost control of where we are financially."

At first, I couldn't accept what he was telling me. I tried to reassure him, the way he had always reassured me. We were in the family backyard, at our familiar picnic table, but I felt as disconnected as if I were watching a movie or having a bad dream. I felt a certain level of panic, followed by—I'm ashamed to say—a sense of betrayal. Could this be my mentor, the man I had always looked up to, allowing something to get so out of control? And how could we repeat something so shockingly familiar to what we had been through years earlier with my grandfather?

It was a heartbreaking moment for us, magnified by the realization and the fear of what could happen to any of us, including me.

In the midst of all those overwhelming emotions, there was not as much comfort as I had expected in knowing that he had an LTC insurance policy in place. As much as the coverage would spare us from the financial consequences of a future long-term care event, I realized for a second time that the worst part of this issue called "aging" is the emotional side—watching how it affects the people we love, and how often it affects their ability to be as emotionally strong as they had been in the past.

A few years have passed since that afternoon when I learned once again how fast a family's financial and emotional situation can change. Fortunately, these past few years have been good to our family: my dad's Parkinson's has progressed more slowly. And after developing a plan of action as a family, the worst of his financial problems have also been resolved. They still have their rental property and their home. He has yet to collect a dime on his LTC insurance policy, as he is very fond of reminding me. The last time we visited him, he seemed like his old self again. Naturally, I still worry about the way Parkinson's will affect his future. But we feel very blessed that he is still able to live an independent and productive life.

My family's experience is one that many families are experiencing this very minute. And one that will continue to affect our society in the coming decades as we learn to respond to this ever-increasing problem of the new health care crisis called long-term care.

PART ONE

Understanding Long-Term Care

1

My father always said,
"We don't want our illnesses
to become your lives."
But of course they had become
that. And in an effort to not
burden us, they didn't want to
talk about anything.

— Beth Witrogen McLeod
Author of *Caregiving: The Spiritual*
Journey of Love, Loss, and Renewal

PART 1:
Understanding Long-Term Care

Most people avoid discussions about long-term care. And who can blame them? Thinking ahead to a time when we might no longer function independently **is** depressing.

We can trace people's reluctance to face the issue of long-term care to the general confusion and misinformation surrounding it. It is easier to address estate planning, for instance, because the issue is black and white—we know we need to plan for the occasion of our death. But planning for chronic illness and frailty? These issues are almost always accompanied by strong emotions of anger and fear.

But planning for long-term care is imperative. Without a plan, the issue might sneak up on us when we're not looking. Decisions must be made about the type of care needed, who will provide these services, where these services will be provided, and who will pay for the care. Planning ahead means not waiting until a long-term care event happens, and then attempting to plan for someone's care. At the time of need, we should be focused on emotionally supporting our loved one.

The five chapters in Part 1 address these key issues and provide you with a foundation for understanding the magnitude of the long-term care crisis.

Chapter 1 What is Long-Term Care?

Long-term custodial care for the chronically ill may prove to be the most challenging and expensive of the several demographic time bombs America faces.

— Stephen Moses
President of the Center for Long-Term Care Financing

Long-term care, in the broadest sense, is defined as a need for assistance from others for an extended period of time. The objective of long-term care services is to assist a person who needs help with the normal activities of daily living. Long-term care can be due to a disability or impairment, whether it is physical or mental in nature. We define true long-term care as care needed for a period of *more than 100 days.* We define short-term care as care needed for a period of *less than 100 days.*

Various definitions of long-term care can be found throughout the industry. For example, many insurance agents will attempt to scare you into believing that care needed for less than 100 days is a huge financial risk. But focusing on short-term care is a financial planning mistake. It encourages a family to insure "small dollars," while placing too little emphasis on the risk of "large dollars" caused by true long-term care. Short-term care is financially inconvenient; long-term care is financially devastating.

ACTIVITIES OF DAILY LIVING

The first part of our long-term care definition states that a person needs "assistance from others." Whether or not a person needs assistance is determined in a variety of ways. Usually, a person's ability to perform basic "activities of daily living" is assessed to determine the need for care. Activities of daily living, commonly called *ADLs,* include the functions most of us perform on a daily basis, without conscious thought: eating, bathing, using the toilet, getting out of bed, and dressing. Performing ADLs can be broadly

FAST FACTS:

- Individuals born during the baby boom generation will begin to turn 60 in 2006.

- In the next few years, older people will outnumber younger people for the first time in history.

- Elder care is on the verge of replacing child care as the number one dependent care issue.

- The over-85 age group is expected to triple as a percentage of the population by 2050.

- Many boomers will need care for the last two decades or more of their life.

- Short-term care is financially inconvenient; long-term care is financially devastating.

defined as "the normal management of daily life without causing harm to oneself or others." Chronic difficulty with performing two or more ADLs independently is the normal definition of "needing assistance."

Incidental Activities of Daily Living

Another important term is "incidental activities of daily living," also known as *IADLs.* Examples of IADLs include such services as cooking, cleaning, and running errands. While ADLs is a medical term used to describe and determine the need for assistance, IADLs is the term used to describe and determine the *convenience* services required as a result of ADL loss or impairment.

MENTAL IMPAIRMENT

The need for assistance may also be due to mental impairment. Memory loss, including conditions such as Alzheimer's Disease, is the most common reason people need long-term care services after age 70.

THE NEED FOR LONG-TERM CARE IS GROWING

The number of people needing long-term care is growing fast, and will continue to escalate over the next three decades. Three major trends that gain momentum as each year passes will have a phenomenal impact on health care in general, and long-term care in particular:

1. **You will live a long life.** According to the Administration on Aging, elder care is on the verge of replacing child care as the number one dependent care issue. In a few short years, older people will outnumber younger people for the first time in history. "The Aging of America" is being driven by the baby boom generation, the largest generation in history. The sheer

numbers—76 million Americans born between 1946 and 1964—have had a significant impact on modern society on every social and economic level. Individuals in this generation will begin to turn 60 in 2006. The implications are profound because the odds of needing true long-term care begin to significantly increase in the years beyond age 60.

2. **Living a long life will almost certainly result in the need for long-term care prior to dying.** This generation of baby boomers is not only large in numbers, they are also the group with the largest percentage of people who are "health conscious." A commitment to a good diet and exercise has a positive effect on longevity. But our bodies and minds will still eventually wear out, only at a much slower pace. Breakthroughs in medical science may contribute to making a life to age 100 a common occurrence. Some experts predict that life expectancy could be pushed to 120 years, and possibly beyond. But longevity does not guarantee independence. Many of the healthy boomers of today will need care for the last two decades or more of their lives.

3. **It is unlikely your family will be able to provide your long-term care.** The changing family structure is having a profound effect on our ability to assist one another. In the past, when a family member needed long-term care, other family members stepped in to fill the role of caregiver. Women, including wives and daughters, became the primary caregiver for immediate and extended family members. But with more women entering the workforce, and careers geographically separating most families, **paid** caregivers are beginning to provide the bulk of long-term care services.

The increase in the numbers of people needing care will also have a profound effect on the cost and availability of long-term care services. And the availability of *quality* long-term care services is likely to be in proportion to the ability to pay for care. For this reason, long-term care services paid for with private dollars, either with personal assets or with long-term care (LTC) insurance, will become more prevalent in future years.

WHEN DO PEOPLE NEED LONG-TERM CARE?

The need for long-term care can arise at any age and at any time. Although we normally think of long-term care as an issue reserved only for the elderly, most of us are aware of younger people who have needed care. Young adults needing assistance are typically victims of accidents or a disabling illness.

Middle-aged people can also suddenly lose the ability to care for themselves. In the pre-senior years, the need for long-term care services normally results from conditions such as heart disease and strokes. Mental health conditions also become more prevalent during middle age.

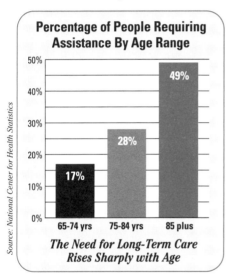

Percentage of People Requiring Assistance By Age Range

The Need for Long-Term Care Rises Sharply with Age

Source: National Center for Health Statistics

But the reality is, the odds of needing long-term care and the duration of the need for long-term care services begin to increase drastically as we age. The vast majority of people needing care for five years or longer fall in the 60-and-older age group.

The biggest leap in the need for long-term care comes when we reach our 80s. Almost half of all people over age 85 require some form of care, either at home or in a facility. Today, this age group is the fastest-growing segment of the American population. The over-85 age group will triple as a percentage of the population by 2050.

WHAT ARE THE ODDS OF NEEDING LONG-TERM CARE?

Statistics illustrating the odds of needing long-term care during our lifetime are not widely available. Most people who have needed care in decades past have received their care from family members and no statistics were recorded. But due to the trends of two-career households and families living in different regions of the country, a widespread need has occurred: the need for long-term care services provided by caregivers other than family members. State and federal governments normally supply statistics regarding services provided to various segments of the population. But prior to the recent acceleration of trends resulting in an increased need for paid long-term care services, the government had little reason to collect statistics on the odds of needing long-term care.

The insurance industry has also been a good resource for statistics regarding certain risks within our society. But only in recent years has the industry begun to collect and analyze information regarding the need for long-term care. With the recent invention of LTC insurance, there will soon be more data available to calculate the true odds of needing long-term care. Within the next decade, the insurance industry will completely analyze the long-term care risk, and will be in a position to provide us with the exact odds of needing care.

Although we lack sufficient data to offer completely accurate statistics at this time, information about the odds of needing long-term care is beginning to emerge. A recent study by the U.S. Department of Health and Human Services gives us some insight into the subject of true long-term care. The study reveals that of all people turning 65 this year, one in four will spend one year or more in a nursing home. And one in eleven will spend five years or more in a nursing home (U.S. Department of Health & Human Services 2003b).

These statistics do not account for people who need home care services. Neither do they account for care received in assisted living communities. Statistics for assisted living care and home care are very difficult to obtain, because no government program reimburses assisted living facility care, and most home care is still provided by family members.

However, since LTC insurance policies do cover home care and assisted-living care, it won't be long before the insurance industry has sufficient data to analyze and provide us with the exact odds of needing long-term care in any environment.

WHAT IS LONG-TERM CARE?

KEY POINTS

- A person who needs long-term care requires assistance from others for an extended period of time, 100 days or more, with little chance for recovery.

- A person who needs short-term care requires assistance from others for a limited period of time, less than 100 days, with an expected outcome of full recovery.

- The need for long-term care is growing due to the aging of America, advances in medical science, and changes in family structure.

- The need for long-term care can arise at younger ages due to an accident or disabling illness.

- The fastest growing segment of our population is the over-85 group. Almost half of all people in this age group require some form of long-term care.

Chapter 2 Where is Long-Term Care Received?

It's nice to be here. At my age it's nice to be anywhere.
— George Burns

A person in need of long-term care can be cared for in a variety of settings, including their home, an assisted living community, or a nursing home. The severity of the condition and the level of care required will directly affect the environment in which a person's care can be received.

The ultimate goal of any type of care is to help the patient maintain comfort, and, if possible, regain their ability to perform ADLs that may have become deficient.

LEVELS OF CARE

There are two broad levels of long-term care: *skilled* and *non-skilled.*

Skilled Care

If the need for care is caused by a condition known as an *acute condition*—such as a stroke or heart attack—intensive medical attention is needed and the patient must be monitored continuously. A patient with an acute condition will normally require a short period of skilled care.

The care being described here would likely fall into the category of short-term care. The duration of the need for care is almost always less than 100 days. Skilled care is sometimes covered by public and private health insurance programs and by Medicare.

The two objectives of skilled care are:
- Help the patient with comfort and assistance, if the condition is terminal. This type of care is also termed as *hospice care.* And/or
- Assist the patient during a recovery period.

For example, the owner of a window cleaning company fell off a roof one morning and broke just about every bone in his body. The

FAST FACTS:

- **57%** of all people with a disability rely exclusively on unpaid care from family or other informal caregivers at home.

- Home care is projected to increase by **178%** by 2030.

- Elderly patients who spend longer than two years in a nursing home rarely return home.

- There was a **48%** increase in the number of assisted living communities built between 1998 and 2002.

- Alzheimer's Disease afflicts about four million Americans; by 2025, this figure is projected to grow by **75%**.

diagnosis given by his physician: full recovery. He did fully recuperate, and his health insurance paid his medical expenses until he was back on his feet. He even went into a nursing home for two weeks and the cost of that care was covered by his health insurance. The level of care he needed was "skilled care" because his prognosis was full recovery, with the need for a short period of rehabilitation.

Non-Skilled Care

The second type of care is non-skilled care, and is the most common level of care. Non-skilled care is commonly known as *custodial care.* It is administered to a person who has a *chronic condition* from which they will not recover. Custodial care is most commonly received at home or in assisted living communities. Conditions such as Parkinson's Disease, Alzheimer's Disease, or simply the aging process can cause the need for custodial care. A disabling accident could also result in the need for non-skilled care—especially in the younger population. This type of care normally lasts for a period of 100 days to several years. This describes true long-term care. Unlike care received for a condition from which a patient will recuperate, custodial care is never covered by regular health insurance or Medicare.

THE LONG-TERM CARE CONTINUUM OF CARE

Many people view "long-term care" as synonymous with "nursing home care." The reality is that most people who need long-term care progress gradually through a continuum of care that may never include nursing home confinement. For example, older people experiencing the frailties of aging may first require only a minimal amount of assistance in their home for a few hours each week. If the condition worsens and they experience problems with maintaining their balance, taking medications, or loss of memory, then a move to an assisted living community may be the next step on the continuum. Unless the condition worsens, or is a terminal illness, the need for more comprehensive care in a nursing home may never be required.

At one time, a nursing home was the first, last and ONLY option available for people who could no longer live independently. Now, nursing homes are just one of many environments in an expanding continuum of long-term care. In fact, due to the more positive preferences of home care and assisted living communities, nursing homes are now utilized less often for true long-term care delivery—a trend that is expected to continue.

This is good news for the burgeoning aging population. New long-term care delivery systems are beginning to meet the individual needs of the people the industry serves. As our population continues to age, it is more likely that delivery systems unknown today will become common tomorrow. Not only will this have the obvious effect of providing the most appropriate level of services, but it will also encourage people to become more comfortable with facing this very difficult issue of planning ahead for long-term care. This trend toward helping the elderly "age-in-place," in the most comfortable setting possible, is a bright spot in the generally somber subject of long-term care.

THE VARIOUS LONG-TERM CARE SETTINGS

The Family Home

The most popular environment for receiving long-term care is not surprising: it has always been and remains today—the family home. Home is where the long-term care continuum normally begins. Most people who find themselves in need of long-term care prefer to remain in familiar surroundings for as long as possible. According to the 1999 National Long-Term Care Survey, 57 percent of all people with a disability relied exclusively on unpaid care from family or other informal caregivers at home. "Even among people with difficulty with up to five activities of daily living, about 41 percent relied entirely on unpaid care [at home]." Currently, over 10 million

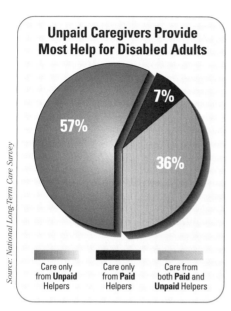

Unpaid Caregivers Provide Most Help for Disabled Adults

7%

57%

36%

Care only from **Unpaid** Helpers

Care only from **Paid** Helpers

Care from both **Paid** and **Unpaid** Helpers

Source: National Long-Term Care Survey

people receive care at home, and home care is projected to increase by 178 percent by 2030 (Congressional Budget Office).

Cost is an obvious factor in the decision to receive care at home. But most people who can afford to pay for formal, institutional care still prefer to stay at home. Medical advances and training have made home care even more practical by allowing home care providers to administer an ever-expanding array of services in a person's own home. The home care industry is a multibillion-dollar industry and exists to support this preferable environment for long-term care services.

When seeking home care services (as with all other long-term care services), the most satisfied consumers are those who are careful, ask the right questions, and shop around. The Joint Commission on Accreditation of Healthcare Organizations has a good list of questions to ask home health care providers. This information is available on the web at **www.jcaho.org** or call the Joint Commission Customer Service Center at 1-630-792-5800.

Services commonly available as a part of home care include:

- **Health Care** — nursing, physical and other rehabilitative services, help with medications, monitoring, and medical equipment
- **Personal Care** — assistance with personal hygiene, dressing, getting in and out of bed, bathing, and exercise
- **Nutrition** — meal planning, cooking, meal delivery, or meals at outside community sites
- **Homemaking** — housekeeping, shopping, home repair services, and household paperwork
- **Social and Safety** — escort and transportation services, companions, overall planning, and coordination of services

Not surprisingly, the home care benefit of an LTC insurance policy has been cited as one of the most important reasons for purchasing LTC insurance. Home care benefits allow family members and friends to remain more involved in the emotional well-being of the policyholder's care, without actually being required to perform all of the exhausting physical caregiving tasks themselves.

When family members are given a choice of whether or not to help with physical care, positive results occur. Studies have shown that even with professional help, friends and family members who can afford paid caregivers continue to be involved in not only the emotional care, but also with some of the physical aspects of care. A study by the U.S. Department of Health and Human Services shows that family members still performed 40 percent of the care themselves, even when their loved one was covered by private LTC insurance (U.S. Department of Health and Human Services 2003b). The insurance coverage paid for the remaining 60 percent of care.

This study proves that formal care delivered by professionals does not necessarily replace the informal care provided by friends and family members. Two-thirds of the informal caregivers continued offering the same level of care even with the presence of professional help. This suggests that people with the ability and determination to remain at home and the funds to hire supplemental help at home may get the best of both worlds: professional help plus the caring support of their loved ones. This combination greatly reduces the stress on informal caregivers and allows them to give more of the emotional care that is so often overlooked by a caregiver who is overwhelmed with the physical tasks of care. "The two systems [formal and informal caregiving at home] seem to be working together to better meet the needs of [patients]," the study concludes.

Adult Day Centers

Staying at home does not necessarily mean staying at home 24-hours-a-day.

Adult day centers provide people with a safe, supportive, supervised place to stay during the day while their informal caregivers are at work or taking a much-needed respite.

Trends in Adult Day Centers

- Nearly **78%** of adult day centers are operated on a nonprofit or public basis.

- **74%** of adult day centers are affiliated with larger organizations such as home care, skilled nursing facilities, medical centers, or multipurpose senior organizations.

- The average age of the adult day center participant is 72; two-thirds are women.

- **50%** of the participants using adult day centers nationwide have some cognitive impairment; one-third require nursing services at least weekly.

- **59%** of the participants require assistance with two or more activities of daily living. **41%** require assistance with three or more activities of daily living.

National Adult Day Services Association

There are more than 3,000 adult day centers in the United States. They provide care for 150,000 people per day, and this number is destined to increase as the population ages.

Studies have shown that adult day centers may also help people stay at home longer. By getting out and interacting socially, people in need of care are more likely to take more of an interest in their personal care and spend less time focused on their disabilities. This socializing aspect has proven to contribute to the overall health of the individual in need.

Most adult day centers provide well-balanced meals and a variety of recreational activities. Many centers can accommodate seniors with relatively severe disabilities. Some even offer preventative health services and therapeutic activities.

Adult day centers are usually open Monday through Friday. Vans may also be available to ease the burden of transporting people who have difficulties with mobility.

The National Adult Day Services Association (NADSA) is a nonprofit association that can help you locate adult day services in your area. Additional information can be found on their website at **www.nadsa.org** or by calling 1-866-890-7357.

Senior Centers

Senior centers are defined as places where "older adults can come together for services and activities that reflect their experience and skills, respond to their diverse needs and interests, enhance their dignity and support their independence" (National Council on Aging, **www.ncoa.org/content**). Several research studies have found that participation in senior center activities has a positive impact on feelings of self-worth, individual growth, and social networking.

There are now 15,000 senior centers across the country. They serve approximately 10 million older adults every year, and are funded in part by the Older Americans Act, the YMCA, and the United Way.

Senior centers typically offer nutrition, recreation, social, and educational services. Their objective is to serve both active and frail elders. Originally intended for social interaction, they are now becoming more comprehensive with a new emphasis on service and community involvement. As a sign of the times, many are adding new services such as training in computer skills.

Multipurpose Senior Centers are a gateway to the National Aging Services Network, which includes more than 29,000 local, regional, tribal, and national service providers for older adults and their caregivers. The National Aging Services Network works to plan, coordinate, and provide home and community-based services to meet the unique needs of older persons and their caregivers. These centers are often the foremost source of vital community-based social and nutritional support that help older Americans remain independent in their communities.

Typical services include:

- Health and wellness programs
- Meals and nutrition
- Education in arts and humanities
- Intergenerational programs
- Employment assistance
- Community action and volunteer opportunities
- Transportation
- Leisure travel
- Financial assistance
- Information and referrals

By using a combination of adult day centers and the services provided by senior centers, thousands of people are able to significantly extend the time they are able to stay in their home environment. But if a person's health declines and the management of day-to-day care becomes more complicated, the cost of care at home rises substantially. At this point on the continuum of care, some other type of residential care environment may become a more realistic option.

Board and Care Homes

For a home-like environment, care from familiar faces, and relatively low cost, board and care can be a good solution for people who simply need help with meal preparation, medication monitoring, and personal care.

Board and care homes are private dwellings where a family or group provides care for a limited number of people with disabilities. The typical number of residents is two to ten. Some converted single-family dwellings are allowed only five or six residents.

A board and care home may be capable of providing residents the services found in an assisted living community, a skilled nursing home or in some cases, an Alzheimer facility. Generally, however, most board and care homes do not offer skilled nursing or medical services, and are therefore not the solution for severely disabled people. But they can provide a safe, supportive environment for people who need help with personal care. At the same time, they encourage residents to maintain as much independence as possible by participating in choices about daily life and health care.

Many board and care homes have their own specialty, and the intensity or type of care needed by residents in a particular home may be similar. For example, some specialize in care of people in the middle to late stages of Alzheimer's. Another may only care for early-stage Alzheimer's patients. Another home may only be licensed to accept those who have mild mental impairment, or need relatively minor help (reminders, meal service, laundry, housekeeping help, and driving services).

Since the federal government does not certify board and care homes, the quality of care and the range of services in board and care homes can vary widely. In some areas, the local government may enforce minimal regulations with periodic inspections for compliance.

Because there are so many board and care homes, hundreds in a populated county, it is also unrealistic to think that licensing can monitor them all. Therefore, it's important to find someone you trust to help you with the decision regarding placing a loved one in a board and care home. It would be wise to have family members, a lawyer, and a trusted financial advisor review contracts before entering into an agreement or paying an entrance fee.

Before placement, it is also important to do some research on the home including:

- Asking for and checking references
- Making unscheduled, unannounced visits at different hours
- Checking with the state licensing agency
- Checking the website: **www.SeniorResource.com**

Assisted Living Communities

In contrast to nursing homes, which have long been viewed as the place where "old folks go to die," assisted living communities are a relatively recent and promising phenomenon. In our opinion, the major long-term care delivery system for the first two decades of the 21st century will undoubtedly be assisted living communities. Choosing to move into assisted living generally means that although you need assistance, you still value your independence and want to remain in a home-like environment. Assisted living offers a philosophy of care that emphasizes values such as individuality, privacy, and choice.

The Assisted Living Federation of America **(www.alfa.org)** defines an assisted living residence as "a combination of housing, personalized support services, and health care designed to meet the needs—both scheduled and unscheduled—of those who need help with the activities of daily living." This association can provide you with an extensive consumer checklist for choosing an assisted living community.

Assisted living is the fastest growing type of senior housing because it meets the needs of people who cannot make it entirely on their own, but do not need or want the skilled nursing care and institutional environment of a nursing home. Over 1 million Americans already live in the 36,399 assisted living communities throughout the country. The demand for space resulted in a 48 percent increase in the number of communities built from 1998 through 2002.

Assisted living communities typically offer the following services:

- Three meals a day in a common dining area
- Housekeeping services
- Transportation
- Assistance with eating, bathing, dressing, toileting, and walking
- Access to health and medical services
- 24-hour security and staff
- Emergency call systems in each room
- Health promotion and exercise programs
- Medication management
- Social and recreational services

A major benefit of the assisted living option is the relief from stress experienced by family members who often find caring for a loved one at home more and more difficult as the loved one's health condition worsens.

The term "assisted living" covers a variety of settings, which can range from remodeled Victorians to high-rise apartments. The typical assisted living residence has from 25 to 120 units, which may vary in size from single rooms to full-size apartments. Most have a common dining room with full meal service, as well as areas for social and recreational activities. Accommodations cover the spectrum from luxurious to spartan, with fees to match.

The costs of care in assisted living communities are less than the cost of nursing homes and, in many cases, can be more economical than home care. For example, assisted living care for a patient with Alzheimer's is 19 percent less than the same care received at home.

Assisted living is paid for with private dollars. Residents or their families pay the bill out of pocket since federal and state governments have no program that will pay for care in an assisted living community. An alternative to paying for these costs with accumulated savings or assets is LTC insurance. Although LTC insurance is a relatively new type of insurance, 1.6 percent of residents in assisted living communities are already paying for care by collecting on their LTC insurance policy.

A typical resident in assisted living is a person in their 70s or 80s. Common health problems of assisted living residents include Alzheimer's, memory loss, incontinence, and loss of mobility.

People in assisted living tend to have fewer ADL limitations than those in nursing homes, and less severe cognitive impairment. Nursing home residents use more medical services, skilled nursing care, nutritional services, and social services than assisted living residents. Assisted living residents are much more likely to receive some of these services by utilizing transportation services available through the community. People in assisted living are about twice as likely as nursing home residents to assess their health as average or good. This difference is mainly one of attitude, and does not strictly correlate with the clinical diagnosis or physical condition of residents. People in assisted living simply seem to feel more positive about themselves and their health than those in nursing homes.

10-Point Philosophy of Care for Assisted Living

1. Offering cost-effective quality care that is personalized for individual needs.

2. Fostering independence for each resident.

3. Treating each resident with dignity and respect.

4. Promoting the individuality of each resident.

5. Allowing each resident choice of care and lifestyle.

6. Protecting each resident's right to privacy.

7. Nurturing the spirit of each resident.

8. Involving family and friends.

9. Providing a safe, residential environment.

10. Making the assisted living residence a valuable community asset.

www.alfa.org/public/articles

Auntie Mae is the perfect example of the typical resident in assisted living. A widow in her 80s, she had lived alone for many years, supporting herself by taking on work as a seamstress. At some point, her eldest daughter noticed that her mother was behaving "strangely," almost as if she were having hallucinations. After a visit to the doctor and a subsequent review of her medications, it was determined that Auntie Mae had been taking too much medication. Her family attempted to organize her medications and schedule so that she wouldn't forget she had already taken the medication and "double-dose." But without someone to remind her, she'd forget to use the reminder system and was once again found in a drug-induced fog.

At this point it was clear that Auntie Mae could no longer live by herself. Since she only needed limited assistance, and was intent on maintaining her independence with no desire to move in with her children, assisted living offered the perfect alternative. She now lives in a community that provides her with her own personal unit with a bedroom, bath, and a small living room and kitchenette. She hasn't had any further incidents of over medicating herself: the staff members monitor her schedule. In addition, her family has found that the social activities available to their mother have made her "blossom" and enjoy life again. Both her physical and mental health have improved significantly with this new living arrangement.

Continuing Care Retirement Communities

Continuing Care Retirement Communities (CCRC) have an awkward name, and a high price tag, but they can offer an excellent approach to aging-in-place for those who can afford the fees. The idea behind continuing care is that people will naturally require higher levels of care and support as they age. Therefore, it makes sense to accommodate the full spectrum of needs on the same campus and within the same community. Assisted living units are normally available in the form of small studio or one-bedroom apartments with scaled-down kitchens. Group dining rooms and common areas for socializing and recreation are often available. A resident of a CCRC signs a long-term (often lifetime) contract when he or she moves on the campus. They may begin their stay in an apartment designed for active, independent living. Choices may include large and small apartments, cottages, cluster homes, or single-family homes. If the resident's health declines, they may move into assisted living in the same community. If their health continues to decline, the community may offer skilled nursing facilities. If the resident recovers, or if their health improves, they can easily move back to a lower level of care.

These are some of the services typically offered in a CCRC:

- Nursing and other skilled medical care
- Meals and special diets
- Housekeeping
- Scheduled transportation
- Emergency help
- Personal assistance
- Assisted living
- Recreational, educational, and social activities

This continuum of care makes a great deal of sense and provides the peace of mind of knowing where you'll be and how you'll be treated regardless of any changes in your health.

If cost were no object, CCRCs might be the wave of the future of long-term care delivery, rather than assisted living communities. Cost, however, is very much an issue and the price of continuing care is well beyond the means of many people. According to the American Association of Retired Persons (AARP), the up-front entrance fees for continuing care communities range from $20,000 to $400,000. Once you pay that lump sum, you still face monthly rent and fees that rival the costs of assisted living communities. But for those with sufficient means, moving into a CCRC can alleviate a lot of the stress and uncertainty that comes from a potential need for long-term care.

The continuing care contract is a legal agreement between the consumer and the community, and it can be complicated. You should familiarize yourself with the following three common contracts if you are considering this option. Then, carefully read the contract to determine the level of service that will be provided.

- **Extensive Contracts** — The most expensive option, extensive contracts offer unlimited long-term nursing care for little or no increase in the normal monthly payments.

- **Modified Contracts** — A middle-of-the road approach, modified contracts cover costs for a specified length of nursing home care (usually three to five years). Beyond the specified limit, you're responsible for your own costs.

- **Fee-For-Service** — An agreement that reduces up-front payments but exposes the resident to potential high costs down the road. Fee-for-service contracts specify that you pay the full daily rate for all long-term care services you require.

CCRCs commonly have a group LTC insurance policy, which a resident is required to purchase when entering the community. People considering moving into a CCRC in the near future are wise to ask the facility about their LTC insurance purchase requirement prior to purchasing private LTC insurance. Some facilities include LTC insurance as part of their payment fees, and may or may not waive the requirement to purchase the group coverage. If you already own LTC insurance, ask if the facility will waive the requirement to purchase their coverage. If they will not waive the requirement to purchase their group coverage, consult your financial advisor prior to canceling your private coverage.

The American Association of Homes and Services for the Aging (AAHSA) provides a consumer directory and additional information about CCRCs. To contact them, visit their website at **www.aahsa.org** or call 1-202-783-2242. The Continuing Care Accreditation Commission (CCAC) at **www.ccaconline.org** lists all communities that have met its standards of certification.

Alzheimer's Facilities

Alzheimer's Disease now afflicts approximately four million Americans, and impacts another 19 million who have a family member with the disease. By 2025, these figures are projected to grow by 75 percent. According to a report published in November 2001, individuals who suffer from Alzheimer's Disease require the longest average duration of long-term care services (U.S. Department of Labor 2001).

Finding and receiving specialized care for those with Alzheimer's Disease can be somewhat difficult. People with Alzheimer's Disease have a different set of needs than those with simpler "age-related" health conditions. In addition to assistance with ADLs, they also require ongoing social stimulation and very close supervision.

Alzheimer's facilities offer a good choice of care for some of these patients. These facilities are specifically designed with smaller spaces for multiple activities. The hallways are designed in a circular fashion, and in many cases, the patient's doors are color-coded.

Other than the specialized services and the design of the facilities, Alzheimer's facilities are very similar in most ways to assisted living communities. The Alzheimer's Association (**www.alz.org** or 1-800-272-3900) is a good source for information and available support services for families of these patients.

Nursing Homes

Nursing homes are the last stop on the continuum of long-term care. **We place nursing homes last for two reasons:**

- Most people will only go into a nursing home if they absolutely are required to do so, *and*
- By planning ahead for long-term care, it's very unlikely that you will need to enter a nursing home for an extended period of time.

Although it's true that nursing homes are the last place that people want or need to go, they still offer a necessary and important role in long-term care. The long-term care continuum of care would not be complete without nursing homes.

Nursing homes are by far the most institutional setting in the delivery-of-care spectrum. They provide mostly medical care to the most physically and cognitively disabled people during their declining months or years. Unlike all the other types of care explained above, a physician must certify a resident's need for nursing home care. The physician must visit regularly and assume responsibility for the patient's overall plan of care.

About 1.5 million people age 65 and older live in nursing homes. The average age of residents is 82 years old. Women residents are in the majority, and the average home has 100-plus beds. A variety of studies have shown that elderly patients who spend longer than two years in a nursing facility rarely return home.

As with any type of long-term care services, the quality of care can vary widely from one nursing home to the next. Unfortunately, one differentiating factor is method of payment. The quality of care provided and the environment in which that care takes place will be determined mostly by our ability to pay for our care. Nursing homes, like any business, must cover their operating costs. This isn't possible with the monies received from Medicaid reimbursements—especially for nursing homes that offer high-quality services *(for more on Medicaid see Chapter 4: Who Pays for Long-Term Care?).* As a result, many nursing homes limit the number of beds available for Medicaid patients. On the other hand, private pay patients will have little trouble with "bed availability" in the facility of their choice. By planning ahead long before there is a need for care, you and your family will have more control over your choice of facility and the quality of care you receive.

WHERE IS LONG-TERM CARE RECEIVED?

KEY POINTS

■ *Skilled care* is provided when intensive medical attention is required. Medicare and most private insurance plans cover Skilled care.

■ *Intermediate care* is provided when recovery and rehabilitation are the primary goals. Medicare and most private insurance plans, under certain very limited circumstances, cover Intermediate care.

■ *Custodial care* is provided when the prognosis is progressive deterioration over a long period of time (100 days or more) with no chance of recovery. Custodial care is never covered by Medicare, Medicare Supplement insurance, or private health insurance.

The long-term care continuum of care includes all the settings in which long-term care services are received:

■ The **family home** has always been, and remains the most popular environment for receiving long-term care.

■ **Adult day centers** provide supervised care during the day as a respite for paid caregivers, or while informal caregivers, such as family members, are at work.

■ **Board and care homes** are private dwellings that offer care in a home-like environment for a limited number of people with disabilities.

■ **Assisted living communities** provide personal assistance and low-level nursing care.

■ **Continuing Care Retirement Communities** offer facilities ranging from apartments for independent and active residents, to assisted living arrangements, and, in some cases, skilled nursing beds.

■ **Alzheimer's facilities** offer specialized care for patients with Alzheimer's Disease.

■ **Nursing Homes** provide mostly medical care to the most physically and cognitively disabled during their declining months or years.

Chapter 3

How Much Does Long-Term Care Cost?

The future, according to some scientists,
will be exactly like the past, only far more expensive.

John Sladde, *Science Fiction Writer (1937-2000)*

Senator John Heinz was an early proponent of the need to plan ahead for long-term care. He understood that if you made a list of potential "big ticket items," you probably wouldn't think to include long-term care. Yet, long-term care expenses may cost more during your lifetime than any other single expenditure.

Specific costs of long-term care services vary widely. **The three major factors that drive the cost of long-term care are:**

> The greatest threat to the financial security of Americans is the cost of long-term medical care. (They) can insure their cars against theft or damage, their houses against flood, fire and earthquakes, their children against the costs of college and braces, and their families against the risks of an early death. But when it comes to insuring the single greatest threat to their life savings and emotional reserves, the costs of long-term care, Americans have no protection. In many ways, it's as if we are all wearing bulletproof vests with holes over our hearts.
>
> The late Senator John Heinz,
> *Select Committee on Aging*

1. **Geographic location:** As with all living expenses, the cost of long-term care will largely depend on where you live.

2. **The place in which the care is received:** The various environments, the levels of care, and the continuum of care were explained in Chapter 2.

3. **Reason(s) for care:** The severity of the condition can cause the costs to vary by thousands of dollars per month.

In this chapter, we'll cover the costs of various common long-term care settings. The statistics and costs given here represent national averages. The specific costs of care in your area can be obtained from a financial advisor trained in a *comprehensive planning approach* to long-term care.

FAST FACTS:
THE SILENT COST OF CAREGIVING

- **88%** of people 50 and older will receive help from family members and other informal caregivers at some time during their lifetime.

- For people with long-term care insurance, that figure is **40%**.

- Women account for **75%** of caregivers 50 and older.

- Among caregivers aged 50–64, **60%** must juggle full- or part-time work and caregiving.

- **58%** had to make changes in their work schedules to provide care.

- **19%** report physical or mental health problems as a result of caregiving.

GEOGRAPHIC LOCATION AND ENVIRONMENT

Home Care

The hourly cost of home care varies more by region than any other form of long-term care service. The national average for a nurse to come to your home is $41 per hour. The average cost for a home health aide, a non-skilled person, to come to your home is $21.50 per hour.

But, in expensive areas of the country, a visit from a Licensed Practical Nurse can cost over $100 per hour. Even a home health aide in expensive areas will charge more than $35 per hour.

Home care costs also involve items other than personnel. When you add up all the average expenses for home care, including personnel, medical equipment, and supplies, the total cost for home care on a daily basis averages $88.

Assisted Living Communities

We believe assisted living communities are the wave of the future in long-term care delivery because they offer a much more pleasant and positive living environment at a lower cost than nursing homes.

Most assisted living communities charge by the month. The average national cost of care per month is $2,490, or about $83 per day. But a recent survey indicated that the cost could vary from a low of $1,800 per month (about $60 per day) to a high of $6,300 per month (about $210 per day).

The above figures do not include any care received beyond the assistance with two activities of daily living. People who need care above and beyond this basic level of care will incur additional costs. Still, compared to nursing home care and, in some instances, home care, assisted living communities offer one of the best values in long-term care delivery.

Nursing Homes

The national average daily rate for nursing home care in 2005 is $192 for a private room. The cost for a semi-private room is $168 per day. That comes to an average *annual* cost of over $70,000 per year for a private room, and more than $61,000 per year for semi-private accommodations.

But the actual cost of care in a nursing home varies almost as widely as home care and is dictated mainly by region. For example, in New Orleans, a private room is a relative bargain at $98 per day, compared to high-cost cities such as Boston at $251 per day, and San Francisco at $280 per day.

While these numbers give you some idea of the cost of care in a nursing home, these averages may be on the low side. Medicaid, the welfare program, is heavily involved in nursing home reimbursement. Analysts point out that most nursing homes lose money on Medicaid patients, because they must accept Medicaid's low reimbursement rates. This results in Medicaid services being delivered at less than true market value. These low reimbursement payments by Medicaid are included in the averaging of nursing home costs, and thus may distort the true average cost of nursing home care. *(For a more detailed explanation of Medicaid, see Chapter 4.)*

REASON(S) FOR CARE

In addition to the geographic area and the environment in which long-term care is received, the reason(s) long-term care is needed also has a direct impact on the costs. Some long-term care services, such as minor assistance with ADLs, can be very reasonable. Other types of treatments, such as treatment for patients with Alzheimer's Disease, are very expensive. For example, the average amount spent over a lifetime of long-term care for an Alzheimer's patient is $204,000. This makes Alzheimer's Disease the third most expensive disease in the United States, behind heart disease and cancer.

THE IMPORTANCE OF CONSIDERING INFLATION

For people planning ahead for long-term care expenses, the most relevant cost figures are not the costs of care today but projections of costs, taking into account inflation, in the years ahead. Once a long-term care plan is put in place, it's wise to consult with your financial professional or long-term care specialist, at least once a year, to make sure the plan considers the newly inflated costs of care.

The rate of increase for long-term care expenses has remained at a reasonable level over the past decade. This is mainly due to the surge in availability and utilization of assisted living communities. That trend is predicted to continue for the next few years. Long-term care expenses are predicted to rise at an annual rate of between 4 and 7 percent between now and 2015. But beyond that, an increase in the demand for long-term care services—due to baby boomers moving into their 70s and 80s—could result in long-term care inflation rates approaching double digits.

THE SILENT COSTS OF LONG-TERM CARE

So far, we've only addressed the costs of long-term care from a line-item standpoint. But these dollar figures do not tell the entire story. The physical, emotional, and psychological costs to care-givers providing care, as well as lost income opportunities, must also be included in any discussion pertaining to the true costs of long-term care.

IMPACT OF CAREGIVING ON EMPLOYEES

40% Unable to advance in careers

75% Affected their health

66% Affected their lifetime earnings

96% Made informal workplace adjustments

84% Made formal workplace adjustments

Family Care: The Loss in Income and Assets can be Tremendous

Most caregivers are family members who attempt to maintain their careers while assuming new caregiving duties for a loved one. Over half of those providing care are employed full-time, while another 13 percent work part-time. We often think of these caregivers as unpaid, but the fact is that those who balance caregiving and employment actually pay a heavy price for their caregiving responsibilities.

In a series of surveys called "The Juggling Act Study," MetLife attempted to measure the financial difficulties encountered by those who balance caregiving with work. A large majority of participants in the survey reported the need for flexible hours—to arrive at work late or leave early—and to take time off during the day. They also had to use sick leave and vacation time to meet caregiving obligations. Other common strategies used by caregivers to juggle career and caregiving include decreasing work hours, taking a leave of absence, switching to part-time work, quitting entirely, or taking early retirement.

By measuring the "cumulative effects from wage reductions, lost retirement and pension benefits, compromised opportunities for training/promotion, and stress-related health problems," the study found that work/care jugglers sacrificed an astonishing amount of earning potential. "The average loss in total wealth as a result of caregiving is estimated at $659,139 over the lifetime (of the individual caregiver)."

Heavy Burdens for Caregivers

In analyzing the role of caregiver, much emphasis is placed on the financial cost and emotional strain from providing care to a disabled or ill family member. Less emphasis is placed on the physical exhaustion experienced by a caregiver trying to care for a full-sized adult—in some cases twice the size of the caregiver. Don't forget to consider the physical aspect, by asking these questions when planning for long-term care for your family:

- Will I be able to help him/her transfer in and out of bed? On and off the toilet?
- Will I be able to roll him/her over in bed to change clothing and bedding?
- Will I be able to help him/her bathe or shower?
- Will I be able to get him/her dressed and undressed?
- Will I be comfortable providing this type of personal care for him/her?

The Average Length of Caregiving is Eight Years

Many of those surveyed never anticipated becoming a caregiver. For those who did consider the issue, few accurately anticipated the number of hours per week they would eventually devote to caregiving, or the months or years the care would be needed. Most estimated they would need to provide care from six months to two years. The actual average length of caregiving is eight years!

Given the stress and time pressures they faced, it's no surprise that three-quarters of the people in the MetLife survey reported that "juggling" had adverse impacts on their own health. More than 20 percent experienced a significant decline in health, and an increase in the number of visits to their own healthcare providers.

Although the majority of family caregivers begin by simply providing occasional assistance to a relative or spouse, most families who experience a long-term care need eventually alter major lifestyle choices, such as postponing or sacrificing career advancement opportunities. A major benefit of planning ahead for long-term care is to ensure that our own lifestyle and retirement goals are not adversely affected in order to provide care to a family member.

The Sandwich Generation:
Spread Too Thin Between Elderly and Children

Trying to juggle a career with caregiving duties is difficult enough. But today, more and more families are finding themselves in the recently coined category of the "sandwich generation": people who are caught in the middle of caring for an elderly relative while still raising their own children.

Raising a family in the best of situations has its own set of challenges. Add to that the financial, physical, and emotional burdens of caregiving, and it doesn't take long to realize that many aspects of family life will be negatively impacted by a loved one's need for long-term care. The attention we once gave our children and spouse may now be diverted to an ailing parent. Our physical energy gradually depletes as we strive to juggle our caregiving duties with maintaining a healthy family life. The time and money we once accrued for family vacations may now be used to supplement the care and services needed by an ill family member.

The costs associated with caregiving are not merely computed in dollar figures. The costs all too often are defined in terms of strained relationships with a spouse, behavioral problems manifested in children, and the emotional and/or physical breakdown of the caregiver as a result of spreading him/herself too thin. These costs are the additional silent costs—costs *in addition* to the direct financial costs of long-term care.

HOW MUCH DOES LONG-TERM CARE COST?

KEY POINTS

- The factors that determine the costs of long-term care are geographic location, environment where care is received, and the severity of the patient's condition.

- Assisted Living Communities charge by the month and can vary in cost from a low of $1,800/month to a high of $6,300/month.

- In a nursing home, the average daily rate is $192 for a private room and $168 for a semi-private room.

- The predicted average rate of inflation for long-term care between now and 2015 is between 4 and 7 percent annually. Beyond that, double-digit inflation is likely, due to the need for long-term care by aging baby boomers.

- The average loss in total wealth as a result of caregiving is estimated to be $659,139 over the lifetime of the caregiver.

- The silent costs of caregiving by family members include changes in current lifestyle and career goals, a delay in retirement goals, stress-related health problems, and strained relationships.

- The phrase "sandwich generation" is often used to define people caught in the middle of caring for an elderly relative while still raising their own children.

Chapter 4 Who Pays For Long-Term Care?

The United States does not have a comprehensive long-term care system. Arguably, it has no system at all. Instead, it relies upon Medicaid, a safety net program designed for persons with low incomes and few assets, as the primary financing source for long-term care.

Mary Jo Gibson
Senior Policy Advisor, Public Policy Institute, AARP

Since long-term care expenses have the potential to dwarf major medical expenses over the next few decades, sources of funding for long-term care expenses are a major concern for our state and federal governments. Long-term care spending is expected to increase almost four-fold by 2050. This strain on state and federal budgets will dwarf our current "health care crisis." Increases in longevity, the size of the baby boom generation, and inflation of health care costs are driving this rapid rise in spending.

With the help of financial advisors, government analysts, and experts on aging, Americans are beginning to realize that long-term care expenses could represent the greatest risk to their financial security. Due to the new awareness of this

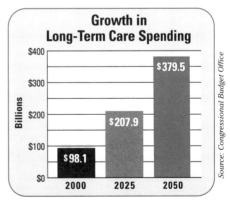

Over the next 45 years, spending on long-term care is expected to increase almost four-fold.

serious risk, many Americans today are making deliberate choices to protect their financial future against long-term care expenses. Unfortunately, however, most Americans are still confused about who pays for long-term care.

FAST FACTS:
WHAT WE DON'T KNOW CAN HURT US

■ **60%** of Medicare recipients mistakenly believe Medicare is a primary source for covering long-term care.

■ Most people mistakenly believe a Medicare Supplement policy will pay for long-term care expenses.

■ **87%** of people under age 65 mistakenly believe their private health insurance will cover the cost of long-term care.

■ Medicaid, our country's welfare program, pays for **45%** of all long-term care expenses.

Unlike services for physician and hospital care, which are covered by Medicare and regular health insurance, families faced with long-term care expenses have limited choices.

There are four sources for paying long-term care expenses:

1. **Personal assets**
2. **Medicaid (Medi-Cal in California), the welfare program**
3. **Family**
4. **Long-term care insurance**

In this chapter, we will discuss these four sources of financing long-term care. Long-term care insurance will only be discussed briefly, as an in-depth discussion is provided in later chapters.

We will also elaborate on other sources normally believed to cover long-term care and provide you with a clearer understanding of what these programs actually do and don't cover.

PERSONAL ASSETS

Americans spend millions of dollars in personal assets annually to pay for long-term care provided at home and in formal settings. Those expenses are expected to rise in the decades ahead due to a reduction in government services and the increased need for long-term care in our aging society. The dollar value of personal assets used to pay for long-term care is predicted to double in the decade ending 2010 (Health Care Financing Administration 1998). These personal assets are normally invested in one or more of three places: personal savings, retirement funds, and home equity.

But many families today are planning ahead for long-term care because they question (1) the wisdom of risking their assets and (2) their ability to accumulate enough assets to pay for long-term care expenses.

Even if you can accumulate the necessary funds to pay for your own long-term care expenses, a long-term care event will likely affect the current standard of living of your family, and also affect your future goals. This may include compromising your legacy and risking assets the family had hoped to leave to their heirs.

Most Americans who spend their own assets on long-term care did not deliberately intend to use their money to pay for care. Planning ahead for long-term care will alleviate any surprises, by deliberately identifying and earmarking where the funds will come from to pay for long-term care.

MEDICAID, THE WELFARE PROGRAM

State and federal governments provide the lion's share of long-term care funding today for those who are unable to pay for their own care. Medicaid, our country's welfare program, pays for 45 percent of all long-term care expenses. But the use of welfare as a means of payment for long-term care may decrease sharply in the decades ahead, due to budget cuts.

Medicaid was enacted in 1965 as a joint program between federal and state governments. To pay for long-term care, the federal government contributes about 60 percent of Medicaid funds and states contribute the remaining 40 percent.

Eligibility for Medicaid

Medicaid was specifically established to care for the poor of all ages, paying for long-term care only after a person has depleted their assets and has no other means of payment.

Rules regarding eligibility for Medicaid are complex: they vary from state to state, and can change from one year to the next. Each state establishes its own standards, determines the scope of services, and sets the rate of payment for services. In order to receive help from Medicaid, the recipient must prove to the government that they are impoverished and that they have no other resource to pay for their own care. Proof is established by completing an application designed to disclose the total assets and income of the applicant. Factors taken into consideration are whether or not the applicant is married and whether or not the assets and income will be "countable, non-countable, or inaccessible," for eligibility purposes.

A person who is eligible for Medicaid benefits in one state may be ineligible in another. The Medicaid program varies so greatly from state to state in the amount and duration of benefits that our country has experienced a growing phenomenon called "Medicaid Migration": the act of moving from state to state in search of the most generous Medicaid benefits. At present, this phenomenon is small, but it shows that when faced with a long-term care event, many people will go to great lengths to receive better care. In most cases, if these families had planned in advance for long-term care, they would have been assured of receiving high-quality care in the locale of their choice.

Medicaid, as a payment source for long-term care, is not a good choice for those who have alternatives. To be eligible to collect benefits from Medicaid, you must receive care by a government-approved provider. The amount of money reimbursed by the welfare program to approved providers of services is far below the actual cost of the care being provided. A 2004 study by the American Health Care Association showed that "the average shortfall in Medicaid reimbursement was almost $10 each day for every Medicaid patient (in a nursing home). In 2003, shortfalls in Medicaid reimbursement exceeded $4.2 billion. This means Medicaid-approved providers are drowning in red ink due to Medicaid reimbursement shortfalls, with no relief in site. In the year 2000 alone, 1,857 of the nation's nursing homes filed for bankruptcy. As Stephen Moses, President of the Center for Long-Term Care Financing **(www.centerltc.org)** so wisely states: "When you're losing money on every customer, you can't make up for it in volume."

Since Medicaid pays providers so much less than market value, many providers do not accept Medicaid beneficiaries, and those that do accept Medicaid allocate only a limited number of beds for Medicaid patients. For these reasons, Medicaid-eligible individuals are frequently refused admission or put on Medicaid-only waiting lists even though beds are available. Many facilities would rather have an empty bed available for a future private pay patient than fill it with a "low reimbursement" Medicaid patient. This practice is common because only a handful of states have enacted laws prohibiting admission practices based on the source of payment.

Quality-of-Care Issues

Since providers who care for Medicaid patients are reimbursed at a lower rate than private pay patients, is there a reduction in the quality of services and care provided to Medicaid patients? This is an ongoing debate. One of my wife's grandparents paid for her own long-term care services until she ran out of money, and then had to rely on welfare *(see insert below)*. The quality of care she received while she was private pay was definitely superior to the care she received once she was on welfare. Evidence that there may be a difference in care provided to Medicaid patients was brought to light in November of 2001 by the ERISA *(Employee Retirement Income Security Act)* Advisory Council with the statement, "Medicaid reimbursement rates are so low that they may compromise quality of care, as well as the financial viability of the long-term care industry."

Having lived through the great depression of the 1930s, Nana and Gramps lived very frugally on my grandfather's salary as a construction worker. As a result of careful planning, after Gramps passed away my grandmother was able to live comfortably on the money they had stashed away under the mattress (literally!). When Nana first went into a nursing home, she went as a "private pay" patient. Allen and I were very impressed with the facility the first time we went to visit her.

By our second visit, a few months later, Nana had "spent down" her savings and was now officially a Medicaid (welfare) patient. No longer on the first floor, Nana was "housed" on the second floor—away from the beautiful lobby with fresh flowers, the library with original works of art, and the community room. Our first impressions of a caring facility were replaced by genuine concern for her care as we noticed a "distinct odor" permeating the hallway. Not long after that, Nana became bedridden and within a few weeks of going on Medicaid, passed away.

Would Nana have deteriorated so fast if she had remained a private pay patient? We'll never know the answer to that question.

– Eileen Hamm

For most people in need of long-term care, receiving care in an assisted living environment is emotionally preferable to moving into a Medicaid-approved nursing home. Although some states have obtained Medicaid waivers allowing patients to enter assisted living communities and be reimbursed by Medicaid, the variety of quality choices and environments included under the umbrella of assisted living are generally reserved for private pay patients and not Medicaid recipients.

Qualifying for home and community care benefits under Medicaid also poses a problem for many families. A 2000 report by AARP and the National Academy on an Aging Society reported that the financial eligibility requirements for home-based care under Medicaid are more restrictive than institutional care, and may force people into institutions, rather than allow them to receive care at home.

Medicaid Planning

You may receive information from attorneys or other organizations or companies that encourages you to transfer assets from your name to the name of someone else, in order to manipulate the Medicaid eligibility requirements. This practice is known as "Medicaid Planning."

Over the years, federal and state governments have sent clear messages that Medicaid is designed to assist those who truly cannot cover their own costs, and that manipulating the system will not be tolerated. In fact, many of the loopholes used by Medicaid Planners in the past have been closed. For example, the Health Insurance Portability and Accountability Act (HIPAA), passed in 1996, makes it a federal crime to knowingly and willfully transfer financial assets in order to qualify for Medicaid. But Medicaid Planners continue to search for loopholes, encouraging people to plan for long-term care by relying on money reserved for the truly poor. Although they may attempt to hide the purpose, the true motive of Medicaid Planners is to make countable assets non-countable and inaccessible, for the sole purpose of allowing an individual to rely on the welfare program.

While Medicaid Planning may actually work in some circumstances, there are many reasons to consider other options when planning for long-term care. The major reason was discussed earlier: quality-of-care issues. But another reason involves the penalties for attempting to hide assets. If Medicaid finds that assets have been transferred for the purpose of qualifying for Medicaid, penalties may apply and Medicaid benefits may be discontinued.

Estate Recovery

Another reason to avoid Medicaid Planning is the problem it may cause for your heirs after you have passed away. While Medicaid Planning may result in expenses being paid with Medicaid dollars at the time of need for long-term care, many heirs have been surprised to find that the government must be repaid for these services. Called "Estate Recovery," this process allows the government to recover a corresponding portion of a deceased person's assets from their heirs for long-term care services provided by Medicaid. The program permits reimbursement from both annuities and property, including personal homes. Federal law requires each state to have an Estate Recovery program. Estate Recovery collections now exceed $250 million annually.

With the continuing escalation of costs for long-term care, the process of collecting money through Estate Recovery is becoming more aggressive. Medicaid is steadily tightening loopholes and increasing their efforts to recover money from beneficiaries of patients who received care paid for with government funds.

Summary of Medicaid

American taxpayers contribute billions annually to Medicaid, the state and federal welfare program designed to pay for long-term care for the impoverished.

But welfare coverage is only available after a family has depleted their assets. When a loved one becomes disabled and needs custodial care at home or in a long-term care facility, our government has made it clear that benefits are only available after a process called "Spend-Down." This is the legal term used to describe the process of depleting your assets, and subsequently becoming eligible for welfare. Once you have spent-down your assets and met other qualifications, long-term care services become available from the welfare program. But using Medicaid as a source for funding long-term care expenses is not the option most families use once they seriously understand that Medicaid was designed as a social safety net for the impoverished. Medicaid simply can't offer the high quality of care most of us expect.

If you have further questions about Medicaid and/or Medicaid Planning, seek the advice of your financial planner, estate planning attorney, or Certified Public Accountant (CPA).

FAMILY

In past decades, it was common to rely on family members to help with the care of an ill or disabled relative. When a family member needed long-term care, other family members stepped in to fill the role. Women, including wives and daughters, normally became the primary caregivers for immediate and extended family members.

In recent times, changes have occurred in our society that make it less likely that our family will be in a position to provide our long-term care. Families today are not only much smaller, but many are also spread across the globe, with two careers needed to support the family's financial obligations. Even relying on a spouse for care may not be an option due to divorce and other changes in the traditional American family structure. In the future, paid caregivers will most likely provide the majority of long-term care services.

Caring for a loved one has become a necessity for many families who failed to plan ahead for long-term care. According to a study conducted by the National Alliance for Caregivers, the number of U.S. households that provide care to adults aged 50 and over has more than quadrupled in the past 13 years. The average caregiver is a married, middle class woman in her mid-40s, caring for her mother-in-law, and/or her own mother, usually in that order. But 28 percent of caregivers are men. Over half of those providing care are employed full-time, and another 13 percent work part-time.

Although well-meaning children insist that they will personally provide for their parents' long-term care, most parents today will do almost anything to keep from becoming a burden on their children. But if you do decide that relying on your family or friends is a viable option to use as your long-term care plan, talk seriously with your spouse and children about the type of care you will expect. This option will require the advice of a trusted financial professional to assure that everyone's responsibilities are clearly outlined. This should be done with your family present, because the need for long-term care often has little impact on the person in need of care, but

WHO PAYS FOR WHAT TYPES OF LONG-TERM CARE?

	Personal Assets	Welfare	Reliance on Family	Long-Term Care Insurance
Home Care	Yes	Limited	?	Yes
Community Based Services	Yes	No	?	Yes
Adult Day Center	Yes	No	?	Yes
Assisted Living	Yes	No	?	Yes
Continuing Care Retirement Communities	Yes	No for Independent and Assisted; Limited for other care	?	No for Independent Living; Yes for all other care
Hospital Care	Yes	Yes	?	No
Skilled Nursing Home	Yes	Yes	?	Yes
Non-Skilled Nursing Home	Yes	No	?	Yes

almost always has a major impact on the lifestyle and financial goals of the rest of the family.

LONG-TERM CARE INSURANCE

Long-term care insurance is the *only* private insurance specifically designed to cover long-term care expenses. Long-term care insurance can pay for care in a nursing home, assisted living community, at home, or in an adult day center setting.

Today, only about 4 percent of the population owns LTC insurance. Part of the reason for this low figure is that this type of insurance has only been available for two decades. Couple this with the general lack of knowledge regarding the overall subject of long-term care, and it's easy to see why most people have not purchased LTC insurance to date. But as Americans become more knowledgeable about the need to plan ahead, LTC insurance is expected to become a major payer of long-term care expenses. By 2025, it's predicted that LTC insurance will pay a larger share of long-term care expenses than any other source, other than welfare.

Long-term care insurance:

- Helps the person in need of long-term care maintain higher quality care
- Offers choices in where their care will take place
- Offers resources and assistance in finding available caregivers for care at home
- Avoids reliance solely on family members
- Avoids depleting assets

In other words, LTC insurance protects and preserves the policyholder and their family's overall financial, emotional, and physical well-being. It is designed to pay for help with the physically and emotionally exhausting caregiving tasks. This allows the family to preserve their energy and resources for the emotional support needed by a loved one.

We devote several chapters of this book to a complete discussion of LTC insurance.

MYTH: OTHER RESOURCES WILL PAY FOR LONG-TERM CARE

Most people are surprised to learn that their Medicare and Medicare Supplement policies do not pay for long-term care expenses. Private health insurance plans also specifically *exclude* coverage for long-term care.

Medicare

Medicare provides health insurance coverage for Americans over age 65 and for some people with disabilities who are under age 65. Studies have shown that 60 percent of Medicare recipients believe Medicare is a primary source for covering long-term care. The fact is, Medicare *does not* pay for long-term care. This may seem odd since people over 65 are generally the ones who need true long-term care. But Medicare was enacted as a benefit to pay for physician and hospital care, and does not cover the expenses associated with the care of people who simply need assistance with activities of daily living or supervision due to cognitive impairment.

The confusion regarding Medicare coverage for long-term care is caused by the wording of information in the *Medicare Handbook (U.S. Health and Human Services 2005)* Under certain conditions,

Medicare covers the first 20 days in a skilled nursing home and another 80 days of care on a co-payment basis. But care with a duration of less than 100 days is short-term care. True long-term care is defined as needing care beyond 100 days.

Medicare's potential "short-term care" coverage is designed to help with rehabilitation from a serious injury or illness. A three-day prior hospitalization is required to qualify for Medicare's short-term care benefit. The care must also be provided in an approved *skilled* nursing home.

Medicare may also cover some home health care for people who need *skilled* nursing care during a recovery period. Custodial care, the most common level of care, is not covered by Medicare.

Even Medicare's skilled home health care benefits have been seriously decreased in recent years. In the one-year period following the enactment of the Balanced Budget Act of 1997 (BBA), nearly 500,000 fewer beneficiaries received Medicare-paid home health care. This downward trend has continued and worsened, with Medicare-paid home health care down by as much as 55 percent.

There are many erroneous statistics stating that "Medicare pays for long-term care expenses." The presumption in these statistics is that "entering a nursing home or needing home care for any period of time," even one day, constitutes a need for long-term care. This myth is caused by the conflicting definitions of "long-term care." True long-term care is care needed beyond 100 days. Medicare pays no benefits for true long-term care.

Private Benefits

■ **Medicare Supplement Insurance**

Medicare Supplement Insurance is designed to supplement services approved, but not totally covered by Medicare. Most people mistakenly believe that a Medicare Supplement policy will pay for long-term care expenses. But because Medicare Supplement policies only cover services approved by Medicare, these policies do not pay for long-term care. Medicare Supplement policies may supplement short-term care. Specifically, Medicare Supplement coverage may co-pay for care by approved providers, beginning on the 21st day, and for up to 100 days of care in an approved nursing home. This skilled care must also be preceded by a three-day hospitalization. Medicare Supplement policies, like Medicare, only pay for short-term care.

■ Health Insurance

Most of us are covered by private health insurance plans, either as a benefit offered by our employer, or with premiums paid out of our own pocket. A survey conducted among people under age 65 concluded that a full 87 percent believe that their private health insurance will cover the cost of long-term care. But health insurance, like Medicare, is only a provider of "short-term care." Our so-called "comprehensive health care programs" that cover most Americans against illness and accidents specifically exclude long-term care coverage. The maximum amount of coverage provided by health insurance plans for any type of care at home or in a facility is 100 days.

WHO PAYS FOR LONG-TERM CARE?

KEY POINTS

- There are four sources for paying for long-term care expenses: personal assets, welfare, family, and long-term care insurance.

- Medicare does not pay for long-term care. Medicare pays for physician and hospital care and does not cover costs associated with care beyond 100 days.

- Private health insurance specifically excludes coverage for long-term care.

- Medicare Supplement policies only cover services approved by Medicare and do not cover long-term care.

- The maximum amount of coverage by health insurance plans for any type of care at home or in a facility is 100 days of care.

- Welfare coverage is only available after a person's assets have been depleted.

- Waiting lists for "Medicaid Only" beds are a reality because few states have enacted laws that prohibit admission policies based on source of payment.

- The Health Insurance Portability and Accountability Act (HIPAA) of 1996 makes it a federal crime to knowingly and willfully transfer financial assets in order to qualify for Medicaid.

- Heirs are surprised to learn that they may be required to reimburse a portion of their inheritance to repay long-term care expenses for their loved ones, through a process called "Estate Recovery."

- Long-term care insurance is the *only* private insurance specifically designed to cover long-term care expenses in adult day centers, at home, in an assisted living community, or in a nursing home.

Chapter **5** **Long-Term Care**
_Is_ a Woman's Issue
by Eileen Hamm

As a woman, a registered nurse, and long-term care specialist, I know that the person who provides the care is generally the female. "We" usually means "she," especially when it comes to taking care of a spouse, parents of a spouse, or one's own parents.

— Eileen Hamm, *RN, MBA*

Long-term care is an important issue for every woman in America. Almost always, the female takes ultimate responsibility for the day-to-day care of a family member who is ill or disabled. This is not sexist. This is not whining. It's a fact. In our years of assisting families with long-term care planning, I have personally listened to the stories of women whose lives have been totally altered due to the long-term care needs of a loved one. Similar stories involving men are also becoming more common. But the great majority of informal caregivers in our country—almost 77 percent of the estimated 7 million—are female.

When I talk with couples about long-term care, they often exchange glances and say, "Oh, we'll take care of one another when the time comes." That pledge of mutual aid between spouses is touching, and without a doubt, sincere. But it normally comes from people who have yet to observe someone in their immediate circle of family and friends move from independence to a need for long-term care. When a long-term care need arises, women notice the distinct disparity in who shoulders the burden. This awareness typically drives a family to seriously consider a long-term care plan, other than reliance on family.

My paternal grandmother, Nana, is a good example. After my grandfather passed away, my father made sure that Nana received the attention she needed. During the many years she was healthy, he took the place of his father by managing her money and offering advice concerning day-to-day living. He joined her during doctor visits, took her shopping, and called every day to make sure she was safe. But when Nana's health declined and she needed assistance with personal care, my father's involvement lessened as my mother took over the major responsibilities of Nana's care. It was my mother, Nana's daughter-in-law, who handled the intimate tasks of helping her in and out of bed, bathing, and dressing her. This is a very typical pattern. As the level of required care grows more personal and intimate, the male caregivers in the family begin to feel uncomfortable, and the women take over the primary role of caregiver. Women tend to be more comfortable, and skilled in this role, especially if they've also had children.

But the prospect of becoming a long-term caregiver should not be the only reason why women initiate long-term care planning for their loved ones—it's also vital that they plan for *their own* care. Women make up the largest percentage of elderly residents in all types of long-term care facilities, with the majority being widowed or divorced. Because women tend to marry men at least a few years older than themselves, by age 85 only 13 percent of women are still married. Add to this the fact that, on average, women live about six years longer than men, and it becomes clear that long-term care truly is a woman's issue. Normally, a wife or daughter helps her husband and parents through to the end. But she may well be left alone and exposed when she needs long-term care herself. Unable to rely on informal, unpaid care from relatives at home, older women are often obliged to seek more formal and costly solutions, such as a nursing home.

Although both my grandfathers lived to a ripe old age, neither of them spent time in a nursing home or other type of senior care facility. As both grandfathers became weaker and more debilitated due to old age or illness, my grandmothers once again found themselves in a mothering role, responsible for their husbands' daily care. By contrast, both my grandmothers spent time in senior care facilities, progressing from senior apartments to assisted living communities, and finally to a nursing home. The trend continues: husbands can generally count on receiving good care in their own home. If their wife can't provide the care personally, she spends their life savings hiring and supervising full- or part-time caregivers. If she provides the care herself, it comes at a heavy price: with the accompanying emotional and physical stress of being a caregiver, she has a 63 percent higher risk of dying earlier than a woman of the same age who does not become an adult caregiver.

It seems that every time I talk with my mother, who is now in her 70s, she tells me about a sister or another friend "having an awful time" taking care of a spouse. These women tell her about the pure physical exhaustion they experience from caring for an adult day to day. They suffer from the depression that comes from shouldering the responsibility alone, and guilt for feeling sorry for themselves. Women often sacrifice their social network and sense of well being to care for a loved one.

Could I do the same thing? Sure, I could. Do I want to? No. Does this mean I care less for my spouse? That I'm a selfish person? No. It means I care enough to plan. To make sure my family and I have choices if someone we love requires long-term care.

My mother, her sisters, and most of her friends grew up in a different era, when the choices for women were limited. Thankfully, women today have access to the knowledge and resources needed to actively participate in planning ahead for their family's well being. We will always be "caretakers," but our role today includes careful planning for the long-term care of our loved ones and *ourselves*. If we don't, the future we envision may be greatly altered, and even cut short, by the sacrifices of administering long-term care.

LONG-TERM CARE *IS* A WOMAN'S ISSUE

KEY POINTS

- The great majority of informal caregivers in our country—almost 77 percent—are female.

- Women make up the largest percentage of elderly residents in all types of long-term care facilities.

- A female caregiver has a 63 percent higher risk of dying earlier than a woman of the same age who is not a caregiver.

PART TWO

The Only Way to Plan for Long-Term Care

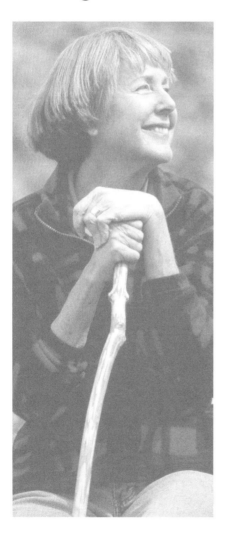

Let our advance worrying become advance thinking and planning.

— Winston Churchill

PART 2:
The Only Way to
Plan for Long-Term Care

Long-term care planning is an integral part of the financial planning and estate planning process. The person in the best position to help you begin your long-term care plan is your trusted financial advisor because they are already familiar with your financial situation, goals, and tolerance for risk. Your advisor, who may be your financial planner, estate planning attorney, or CPA, can help you determine the right long-term care planning option for your unique situation.

This approach to planning within the context of your overall financial situation is called a *"comprehensive planning approach."* Using this approach can be compared to carefully building a home with a blueprint. It takes more time and concentration on the part of your financial advisor because they must become specifically trained in the overall long-term care planning process.

A good example of failing to plan within the context of your family's financial objectives is the *"single sales approach"* commonly used by insurance agents. They promote LTC insurance as the only option for paying for long-term care while ignoring your overall financial objectives. These agents are trained to sell LTC insurance to anyone who will grant them an appointment. This method is disrespectful of you and your time. The major objective of this type of agent is to earn a commission by selling you an insurance policy whether you need it or not. The results of the *"single sales approach"* are always marginal at best. This approach is likely to result in the purchase of LTC insurance from the wrong insurance carrier with benefit levels inappropriate for your family's situation. Using this approach may also cause you to purchase LTC insurance when another long-term care planning option would have been more suitable for your unique situation.

A review of the options for paying for long-term care will assist you in working with your financial advisor to choose your specific plan for long-term care. **The four options for paying for long-term care were explained in Chapter 4:**

1. Personal assets
2. Medicaid (Medi-Cal in California), the welfare program
3. Family
4. Long-term care insurance

When you and your advisor carefully consider the uniqueness of your goals, personal tolerance for risk and current health, the proper long-term care plan for you and your family will become apparent.

Chapter 6 Integrating Long-Term Care Planning with Financial and Estate Planning

With money and financial planning, prudence comes first.
— Benjamin Franklin

T his chapter presents an overview of the financial and estate planning process and illustrates why long-term care planning is an essential component of a secure financial future.

A BRIEF OVERVIEW OF FINANCIAL AND ESTATE PLANNING

Financial planners, estate planning attorneys, and CPAs fulfill their professional roles by advising clients on a variety of financial topics. **The financial and estate planning processes generally address three areas:**

1. Saving and accumulating for retirement
2. Preserving and spending what is accumulated
3. Leaving an estate to heirs and beneficiaries

If money were no object, we would no doubt satisfy all of our financial goals. But for most of us, fulfilling all of our desires and goals would exceed our available resources. As a result, we are required to make choices every day about how we spend our money. In the financial and estate planning process, we integrate daily decisions about money with lifetime financial goals and decide how we will achieve those goals. Financial and estate planning is an overall process of setting financial goals, evaluating where we are with respect to those goals, laying out a plan to achieve them, implementing the plan, and modifying the plans and actions as our current situation and goals change.

Financial planners, estate planning attorneys, and CPAs assist you in reaching your financial goals by advising you in one or more of the following areas:

- **Setting financial and estate planning objectives:** Looks at the complete financial and estate planning process, including budgeting, emergency fund planning, credit and debt management, education funding, insurance planning, and estate management, in order to leave your estate intact for your heirs.

- **Insurance planning and risk management:** Addresses three general areas of risk to the overall success of your financial plan: risk to people you know, risk to your property, and risk to people you don't know and their property. This is a primary area where planning ahead for long-term care fits into the overall financial planning picture.

- **Employee benefits planning:** Looks at the features, advantages, and disadvantages of various types of employee benefit plans. These may include evaluating disability and medical insurance plans, and in some cases evaluating group or sponsored LTC insurance offered through your company.

- **Investment planning:** Evaluates investment risk, objectives, and vehicles such as mutual funds, stocks and bonds, investment strategies, and the tax implications of investing.

- **Income tax planning:** Analyzes the tax consequences of investment planning, insurance planning, retirement and employee benefit planning, and estate planning.

- **Retirement planning:** Integrates all aspects of financial and estate planning into a customized plan for financial independence.

FAST FACTS:

- Men and women who plan for the future—at all ages from 25 to 75 and with household incomes from $0 to $300,000—report increased personal life satisfaction. (Psychology and Aging 2001)

- The National Council on Aging reports that a major worry of Americans about living to age 75 and beyond is that they will be required to spend all of their money on long-term care.

- **66%** of people who created an estate plan felt comfortable with their retirement finances; only **37%** of those without an estate plan felt at ease. (Value of Advice Study by Dalbar and IAFP 1998)

- **Estate planning:** Addresses tax-efficient ways to acquire, preserve, and transfer wealth to other parties both during and after life. Estate planning also addresses planning for incapacity due to a disability or the need for long-term care.

Our goal in explaining the financial and estate planning process is to emphasize that long-term care planning must become an integral part of every financial and estate plan. While planning ahead for long-term care is a major component of the Insurance Planning and Risk Management component of your financial and estate plan, it also overlaps several other areas.

The steps to integrating long-term care planning with your overall financial objectives using a *comprehensive planning approach* is explained in Chapter 7.

**INTEGRATING LONG-TERM CARE PLANNING
WITH FINANCIAL AND ESTATE PLANNING**

KEY POINTS

- Long-term care planning must become an integral part of every financial and estate plan.

- Long-term care planning should always be done within the context of your family's financial situation and goals.

- The financial and estate planning process includes budgeting and saving for retirement, preserving assets during retirement, and leaving an estate to heirs and beneficiaries.

- Insurance planning and risk management is the primary area where planning ahead for long-term care fits into the overall financial and estate planning picture. But planning ahead for long-term care also overlaps several other areas.

Chapter 7 **Planning Ahead Using a *Comprehensive* *Planning Approach***

You got to be careful if you don't know where you're going, because you might not get there.

— Yogi Berra

The only way to assure that a long-term care plan will be effective is to develop it within the context of your total financial picture using a *comprehensive planning approach*. Applying this approach is similar to the carpenter's rule of "measure twice and cut once." It requires that your financial advisor be specifically trained in the area of long-term care planning. It also requires that your advisor be trained in consultative skills—not sales skills.

Many financial advisors limit their role in the long-term care planning process to educating their clients about long-term care and determining the most suitable option for planning ahead to pay for care. They then refer their clients to a specialist to implement the plan. Other financial advisors will assist their clients through the entire planning process, including implementation of the plan.

Regardless of your advisor's method, there are seven steps to achieving the proper long-term care plan for you and your family.

SEVEN STEPS OF A *COMPREHENSIVE PLANNING APPROACH*

1. Learn about Long-Term Care

Become knowledgeable about the issue of long-term care— what it is, where care can be received, and how much it costs in your area. These subjects are discussed in Chapters 1 through 3.

2. Understand Your Resources

This is the heart of a truly effective plan for long-term care. Evaluate long-term care from the standpoint of your personal situation. How will the need for long-term care impact your goals and objectives? Analyze the four resources available to you for paying for a potential long-term care need: using personal assets, relying on welfare, relying on your family, or purchasing LTC insurance. *(This subject is discussed in Chapter 4.)*

3. *Determine Your Preferred Payment and Care Options*

Once you understand the long-term care resources available to you, consider each option by asking, "If I had a need for long-term care tomorrow, where would the money come from to pay for my care, and who would provide my care?" For example, if you plan to rely on your family, discuss this with them and decide who specifically will provide the care. Will you move in with one or more of your children? Or will they move in with you?

If you are considering using LTC insurance to pay for your care at home, in an assisted living community, or in a nursing home, ask your financial advisor to investigate whether or not you qualify for coverage and whether or not you can afford the premium.

4. *Choose the Best Option*

Based on a thorough analysis of the information gathered in steps one through three, choose the best long-term care planning option for you and your family. Each option has its advantages and disadvantages. The proper plan can only be chosen after becoming knowledgeable about the issue, thoroughly understanding your resources, and seriously pondering the fact that any one of us could suddenly have a need for long-term care.

5. *Implement Your Plan*

If you plan to rely on welfare, set up an appointment with an attorney familiar with the process of Medicaid Planning and the new HIPAA Legislation *(see Chapter 4: Who Pays For Long-Term Care?)*. If the plan calls for using your own assets, notify your financial advisor and family that this money is to be reserved to pay for your long-term care needs. If your plan calls for LTC insurance, ask your financial advisor to help you design a customized LTC insurance policy *(see Chapter 11: Choosing the Right Coverage)* or to refer you to a certified LTC insurance specialist trained in a *comprehensive planning approach.*

6. Finalize Your Plan

If using welfare is your plan, finalize the details with your attorney. If LTC insurance is your plan, apply for coverage. Regardless of the plan you choose, make sure you notify your family members. Be specific with them including the location of any policies, account numbers, funds earmarked for care, and the name, address, and phone number of your financial advisor. Remember that it will probably be your family members who handle the details of implementing your plan at the time care is needed. It's also emotionally important for them to know in advance that you didn't leave this important area of financial and estate planning to chance.

7. Monitor the Plan

Long-term care is not a static issue, and any plan put in place today must be monitored. It's important that your plan accomplish the objectives it was designed to achieve—today and in the future. A *comprehensive planning approach* requires that your advisor review your plan with you at least annually, to ensure that it remains the appropriate solution in the years ahead.

WHAT IF YOU DO NOT HAVE A FINANCIAL ADVISOR?

A *comprehensive planning approach* advises that you seek the services of your financial planner, estate planning attorney, and/or CPA for long-term care planning advice. This recommendation presumes that you already have a working relationship with one or more of these professionals. If you have not yet established such a relationship, your efforts at this point should be to locate a reputable and knowledgeable financial professional who is trained in a *comprehensive planning approach* to long-term care. A good place to begin looking for an advisor is to ask your friends, family members, and associates for the name of the financial professionals they use. If they recommend a financial advisor, but the advisor is not trained in this method of long-term care planning, advise the professional to contact our company. We have developed tools, resources, and an educational curriculum to teach financial professionals how to properly use a *comprehensive planning approach* to long-term care.

You may also locate a professional in your area who is trained in a *comprehensive planning approach* by visiting our website at **www.superiorltc.com**.

	A Comprehensive Planning Approach	A Single Sales Approach
Objective	• Determine most appropriate long-term care planning solution for your unique situation	• Sell a long-term care insurance policy
Considerations	• Overall financial goals and situation • Insurance priorities • Risk tolerance philosophy • Cost of care in local area • Health situation • Affordability	• Affordability • Health situation • Whether or not you can be easily influenced to buy long-term care insurance
Approach	• Solutions-based planning • Consultative • Emphasis placed on best overall solution for your unique situation	• Pressure to purchase • "Sales" driven • Agent emphasis on sales commission to be earned
Service	• Monitors plan annually for suitability and makes adjustments accordingly • Helps with claim's process	• Only contact with agent is if you call them and want additional coverage • Agent wants little to do with claims because no commission is earned
People Involved	• Trusted financial professional, which could be a financial planner, estate planning attorney, and/or CPA, or a long-term care insurance specialist recommended by one of these professionals	• A generalist insurance agent with low probable odds of remaining in the business • Most likely contacted you by direct mail, cold call, or with some other direct marketing approach
Agent	• Recommended by your financial advisor • Offers no other financial or insurance products other than long-term care insurance • Graduate of long-term care certification programs • Specifically trained in a *comprehensive planning approach* • Represents only top-rated companies	• General insurance agent selling long-term care insurance plus other types of insurance • Education and training may be as minimal as basic requirements needed to sell long-term care insurance • May represent any company offering coverage regardless of their financial rating

* *This information is for general purposes only. You may meet agents or financial professionals who use a single sales approach, but still offer some of the characteristics and services of a "comprehensive planning approach."*

**PLANNING AHEAD USING A
*COMPREHENSIVE PLANNING APPROACH***

KEY POINTS

- A proper long-term care plan must be developed within the context of your total financial picture.

- A *comprehensive planning approach* requires that your advisor be specifically trained in long-term care planning, and that they possess consultative skills— not sales skills.

- Many financial advisors will simply assist you in identifying the best option for you and your family and then refer you to the proper specialist to implement the final steps of your long-term care plan. Others will not only assist you in choosing the proper plan, but will also assist you in implementing your plan for long-term care.

- Using the seven steps of a *comprehensive planning approach* results in a long-term care plan uniquely designed to fit your family's financial situation and goals.

- Ask your friends, family, and associates to recommend a reputable financial advisor or visit our website at **www.superiorltc.com** for a list of financial professionals in your area trained in a *comprehensive planning approach.*

PART THREE

Planning Ahead with Long-Term Care Insurance

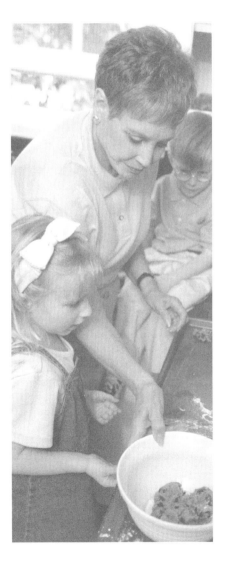

In just two days,
tomorrow will be yesterday.

— Anonymous

PART 3:
Planning Ahead with
Long-Term Care Insurance

INTRODUCTION: HISTORY OF THE
LONG-TERM CARE INSURANCE INDUSTRY

The idea of insurance in general goes back to 3,000 BC when Babylonian merchants began pooling their funds to reduce the economic risks of losing caravans to pirates and thieves.

This ancient idea of *pooling* the financial contributions of a group to reduce the economic *risks* faced by individuals is the same concept used by the insurance industry today. Of course, today's insurance coverage has evolved to a point of sophistication based on well-documented statistics and probabilities.

The LTC insurance industry is in its infancy compared to most types of insurance coverage. The foundation for today's LTC insurance began in 1965, and correlates directly with the enactment of Medicare. Medicare was established to deliver health insurance for those 65 and older and for certain people with disabilities.

Medicare has two parts:
- **Part A** covers Hospital and Skilled Nursing Home Care
- **Part B** covers Physician's Services

In the mid-1960s, creative insurance executives searching for gaps in Medicare's coverage discovered a marketing opportunity presented by Medicare's Part A Hospital and Skilled Nursing Home Care benefit. The nursing home benefit offered by Medicare only pays for the first 20 days of skilled nursing home care. "Skilled Nursing Home Insurance" was invented to pay for skilled nursing home care following Medicare's 20 days of coverage.

These early policies were restrictive in a number of ways. As the name implies, the policies required that a person receive "skilled care" in order to collect benefits. Skilled care is roughly defined as specialized care with doctor supervision and is only needed for the most serious types of health conditions. **Also, to receive benefits**

from these early policies, other requirements had to be met:

- A person was required to first spend at least three days in a hospital, prior to nursing home confinement
- A person then needed skilled nursing home care beyond 20 days

Since a very small percentage of people who need skilled care actually stay in a nursing home for more than 20 days, these policies rarely paid benefits and were thereby deemed worthless by most reputable financial planners and insurance agents.

During the 1980s, our federal and state governments began focusing on the health care issues of our aging population. As data from research on the issue of long-term care became more available, legislators began to understand that Medicare's so-called long-term care benefit was designed for only short-term care and not *true* long-term care. As it became evident that a huge problem loomed ahead for people needing true long-term care, legislators began to focus on encouraging the development of worthwhile LTC insurance as a means of paying for these services.

By the late 1980s, legislators were beginning to pass laws requiring that LTC insurance policies pay benefits irrespective of Medicare benefits and that policies cover all levels of care. Long-term care insurance began to become a real and viable product around 1990.

BILLIONS OF DOLLARS IN FREE PUBLICITY

Despite legislation leading to improvements in coverage, LTC insurance remained an obscure product. For the most part, the only people familiar with the term *long-term care* were those in need of it. The majority of people remained unaware of the subject or the need for coverage.

This lack of awareness abruptly changed in 1991. The term "long-term care" became a well-known term thanks to the Democratic nominee for President that year, Bill Clinton.

Clinton began his election campaign on a platform of health care reform. In speeches to millions of Americans prior to his election, as well as during his first two years in office, he educated Americans about the lack of coverage for long-term care. In a typical speech, he would emphasize that, "This proposed health care reform package will cover you for long-term care." By 1993, we not only knew the meaning of the words *long-term care,* we also had learned more about the subject than any publicity campaign by the insurance industry could have produced for billions of dollars.

We all know the outcome of the health care reform story: in the end, very little progress was made. In an attempt to solve America's entire health care crisis in one single package, President Clinton and Congress were unable to agree on the details of resolving the major problems affecting health care. But at least one positive outcome had been accomplished, even if it was unintentional: we had a new awareness of long-term care. We learned that long-term care is expensive, and we discovered that the government was not prepared to foot the bill.

This new knowledge brought an intense interest in LTC insurance as a means of paying for long-term care expenses. An industry that had been running along on autopilot for several years, with little public interest, suddenly found itself in the limelight with increasing consumer demand for its once obscure coverage. Up to this point, only about 20 insurance companies offered LTC insurance. As a result of the new interest and demand for coverage, over one hundred insurance companies entered the market. Soon, the competition between insurance carriers was fierce.

The LTC insurance industry as a whole responded to this new demand for coverage with some hastily made decisions that benefited the consumer—at least temporarily. First, competition created an overall reduction in average premium rates. Second, eager to gain their share of the LTC insurance market, insurance companies loosened their restrictions on health-disqualifying factors, and began offering coverage to those with major health problems. For the first time, LTC insurance became available to those who were likely to need long-term care sooner rather than later.

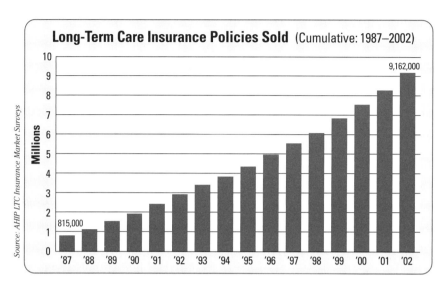

Source: AHIP LTC Insurance Market Surveys

GROWING PAINS FROM INEXPERIENCED UNDERWRITING

But like so many "booms," this one was destined to "bust." Within a few years, insurance companies that had hastily entered the market in the mid-1990s began receiving early and frequent claims from policyholders who were in poor health when the coverage was issued, and even poorer health a few years later. These inexperienced insurance companies, once eager to serve an untapped market, began to feel the pains of improper premium pricing and underwriting. Although they continue to pay their claims, and by law are required to honor all policies issued, most of these inexperienced companies decided to exit the LTC insurance market almost as fast as they entered it.

When an insurance company decides to exit an existing market, it is a major cause for concern for their policyholders. The biggest concern is that premium rates will be raised to levels where they are no longer affordable, due to adverse claims experience *(Adverse Selection is explained in Chapter 17: Group and Sponsored Long-Term Care Insurance)*. To protect consumers who buy LTC insurance, legislators are beginning to enact laws that will stabilize premiums for both present policyholders and future purchasers of coverage.

Today, the market has further evolved. Even though the number of LTC insurance companies in the market is smaller, the companies remaining are much more committed to the industry. By carefully selecting a company offering coverage today, consumers are in a good position to obtain coverage from an insurance company that has a reasonable underwriting and pricing philosophy.

Long-term care insurance protects over 10 million individuals today, with combined coverage protecting over $600 billion in assets. Cumulative claims have reached almost $14 billion, with well over $1 billion paid in benefits in the year 2004 alone. These numbers will increase dramatically over the coming years, as Americans continue to become more aware of the need to plan ahead for long-term care.

Chapter 8 — Why People Consider Long-Term Care Insurance

*Life is pleasant. Death is peaceful.
It's the transition that's troublesome.*

— Isaac Asimov

As emphasized in Chapter 5, the true long-term care planners in America today are women. Their motivation to plan ahead stems from the fact that women provide the majority of long-term care in the United States. Wives and daughters are learning this from firsthand experience, and from the experiences of other women.

The number of American households providing unpaid care has more than tripled over the past decade. Almost 77 percent of these caregivers are women. Their average age is 48. The most likely recipient is her mother-in-law, and/or her own mother.

The effects of long-term care on women are compounded when you consider that:

1. Women tend to outlive men.
2. The largest group of people needing long-term care services are women.
3. Because women most often act as caregivers, the stress of caring for a loved one strains their own health and many times forces them into a need for long-term care themselves.

While women focus on the physical and emotional aspects of a family member's need for long-term care, men tend to focus more on the financial implications of a long-term care crisis. Most men have been taught to be breadwinners, not caregivers. Although this is slowly changing, men generally tend to feel uncomfortable when they attempt to provide the physical and emotional care needed by an ill or disabled relative. Focusing on the financial aspect becomes their outlet and means of coping with the crisis.

Putting a plan in place for long-term care will ease the stress of at least some of the negative aspects that accompany a long-term care

FAST FACTS:

■ **50%** of adult children would be willing to use the money they have set aside for their own children's education to pay for a parent's long-term care expenses.

■ The number of American households providing unpaid care has more than **tripled** over the past decade. Over **75%** of these caregivers are women. The most likely recipient of that care is her mother-in-law.

■ The need for women to take time off work to care for aging parents has increased by **300%** over the past decade.

■ **86%** of long-term care insurance policyholders know someone who was a caregiver at some point.

■ **77%** of adults have planned and saved for their retirement, while only **10%** have planned ahead for long-term care.

(American Society on Aging 2003)

need. Obviously, not all of the emotional, physical, or financial issues of long-term care can be solved with LTC insurance. But as of this writing, it has become the option of choice for over 10 million individuals. Whether it is the right option for you is a personal decision, and depends on your family's unique situation, including how well you understand the impact a long-term care event will have on your family.

Long-term care insurance is like many other forms of insurance: the real beneficiary of the coverage is not the person who is insured; it's the insured's family. The person who ends up needing long-term care services is, in many cases, not even aware of the need. They may be cognitively impaired or so frail at the time of need that they don't actually understand the burden being placed on their family. So as we plan ahead for long-term care, we need to remember that long-term care is not about *us*. It's about the impact our care will have on our family. Long-term care insurance acts as a firewall for your family, protecting them from at least some of the day-to-day care. It also gives your family choices as to where you are cared for, as well as the quality of the care you receive.

MAJOR REASONS FOR PURCHASING LONG-TERM CARE INSURANCE

In the years since LTC insurance has gained widespread acceptance, several surveys have been conducted to determine the major reasons why people purchase LTC insurance. These major reasons are discussed next.

Protect Assets

Long-term care expenses are normally paid for with cash, usually from assets accumulated for retirement. Paying for long-term care with these funds compromises a safe and secure retirement. That's why protecting these assets is the most common reason for investing in LTC insurance. During retirement, many people purchase coverage in order to protect the income their retirement assets provide them. This

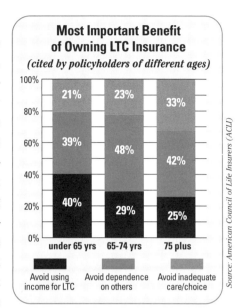

Most Important Benefit of Owning LTC Insurance

(cited by policyholders of different ages)

Source: American Council of Life Insurers (ACLI)

allows a retired couple, for example, to travel or spend their income enjoying retirement without being concerned that a long-term care event with either spouse will alter a well-planned retirement.

Maintain Independence

Many people purchase LTC insurance *after* caring for a loved one. In fact, one study found that 86 percent of policyholders had known someone who has been a caregiver at some point. People who have firsthand experience with the problems surrounding long-term care are by far the strongest advocates of LTC insurance. They have direct knowledge of the overwhelming responsibilities that taking care of a loved one brings. This creates a strong desire to relieve family and friends from the burdens of providing for their own long-term care. Long-term care insurance allows us to maintain our independence by remaining in our own homes, or in the more positive environments of an assisted living community. It also provides options for obtaining the quality of care we need, without relying heavily on family and friends.

These same people also want to be remembered as having lived their lives in dignity and as having been as independent as possible during their entire lifetimes. *"To maintain independence"* gets to the heart of the true issue of long-term care planning. People who purchase LTC insurance are the same people who have carefully planned in other areas of their lives. They're guided by a need to ensure their independence and retain as much control as possible over their own lives. The thought of having to rely on children or friends for lifestyle decisions and personal care is out of the question, and acts as a strong motivator for planning ahead.

Secure High-Quality and Affordable Care

The desire to secure high-quality and affordable care is a major reason for investing in LTC insurance. The underlying goal for many people is to not only maintain independence but to do so in a quality environment, while protecting the financial security of their family.

As baby boomers age, the demand for high-quality care will skyrocket. High-quality care may only be obtainable by those who can guarantee payment with private financing—by using their own assets or owning LTC insurance.

Maintain Current Standard of Living

Long-term care insurance can also help your family maintain their current standard of living. About 15 percent of LTC insurance purchasers cite *"maintaining current standard of living for me and my family"* as the main reason for purchasing LTC insurance.

Although many people still consider LTC insurance "nursing home insurance," the major benefit of the coverage is to pay for care at home, or care in an assisted living community. These environments allow family members to maintain their current living arrangements, minimize disruption, and assist in providing care to their loved ones. While LTC insurance does pay for nursing home care, most policyholders move to a nursing home only as a last resort. Unless you become too ill to receive care at home or in an assisted living community, you will probably never require nursing home care, if you properly plan ahead.

Maintaining the current standard of living is also a major concern for families who have children with physical or emotional disabilities. These families often invest in LTC insurance because they realize that their own need for long-term care could severely affect the care of the disabled child.

CHILDREN AND PARENTS PLANNING AHEAD FOR LONG-TERM CARE

The focus thus far has been on people who are buying LTC insurance for themselves. But what about children interested in purchasing coverage for their parents?

According to a survey conducted by the National Council on Aging (NCOA), parents and children are beginning to feel more comfortable discussing the issue of long-term care (National Council on the Aging 1999). But the survey also revealed that there are distinct generational differences regarding the issue of how a family member's long-term care expenses would be funded.

For example, 50 percent of adult children would be willing to use the money they have set aside for their own children's education to pay for a parent's long-term care expenses. This is clearly contrary to the desires

PAYING FOR CARE
Parents with Adult Children

77% Would **not** want their children's spouse to care for them.

93% Would **not** want money saved for their grandchild's education to be used.

86% Would **not** want children to tap their retirement savings.

91% Would **not** want children to sacrifice job advancement.

Source: Survey of 1,000 American adults. Telephone survey poll by the National Council on the Aging and John Hancock Mutual Life Insurance Company.

of their parents. The survey revealed that 93 percent of parents would **not** want money set aside for their grandchild's education to be used for their long-term care expenses. Long-term care insurance can help both parents and children plan ahead so that education, retirement, income, and inheritance dollars will not be invaded.

In many cases, children and parents are sharing the cost of coverage. Estate planning attorney James Phillips *(see the interview in Chapter 19)* points out that the emotional issue of inheritance, mixed with the topic of long-term care, may provide the catalyst for grown children to consider paying for at least some of the LTC insurance premium for their parents. Many grown children believe that purchasing coverage for their parents is a good investment compared to the cost of care and the potential problems that might arise among siblings once a parent requires long-term care.

The cost of long-term care for a parent may not only deplete an inheritance, it may also affect the children's financial and career goals. A vast majority of households rely on two incomes to make ends meet. Over the past decade the need for women to take time off work to care for aging parents has increased by 300 percent. Long-term care insurance is becoming the peace-of-mind that many families need to ensure that quality care will be provided, without severely altering an existing lifestyle.

Although inheritance and income protection are important, the primary motivation for many grown children to discuss LTC insurance with their parents is the peace of mind of knowing their parents will have options for quality care. For these children, coverage represents a form of security for the relationship they have with their parents. The decision to plan ahead with LTC insurance is made after concluding that the emotional and psychological benefits obtained from the coverage will outweigh the cost of the premiums.

SECOND MARRIAGES

More and more parents in second marriages are involving their children in the long-term care planning process. Since the number of second marriages is growing at a faster pace than ever, the need for long-term care by one partner could cause problems among children of both spouses.

For example, in most second marriages, one partner is considerably younger than the other. Children born of the previous marriage(s) of the younger spouse may be apprehensive that their parent's legacy will be used to care for the older stepparent. The likelihood is high that the older partner will need long-term care services for several years, and this need for care could consume an estate, leaving the children without an inheritance. Prenuptial agreements **will not** prevent the couple from having to *"spend down"* their combined assets to qualify for welfare. Purchasing adequate LTC insurance for both partners of a second marriage can alleviate many of these concerns by assuring that neither spouse will have to spend down assets. This allows both partners to pass their assets down to their own bloodline.

WHY PEOPLE CONSIDER LONG-TERM CARE INSURANCE

KEY POINTS

- The real beneficiary of long-term care insurance is not the person who is insured; it's the insured's family.

- People who consider long-term care insurance want to protect their assets, maintain their independence, secure high-quality and affordable care, maintain their current standard of living, and/or protect their children's income, assets, and inheritance.

- Many partners of a second marriage consider long-term care insurance to assure that neither spouse will have to spend down assets. This allows both parties to pass assets down to their own bloodline.

Chapter **9** **Is Long-Term Care Insurance Suitable for You?**

Ninety percent of the game is half mental.
— Yogi Berra

In considering LTC insurance as an option to pay for long-term care, what is the best age to purchase insurance? Is there a net worth high enough to eliminate LTC insurance as a consideration for planning ahead for long-term care?

These two questions are the most commonly asked questions by people considering LTC insurance. The answers people receive to these questions are varied, and most of the time wrong. Beware of "experts" who offer black-and-white answers like, "If you are younger than X, or older than Y, don't consider coverage," or, "If your assets are under X but greater than Y, don't consider LTC insurance." It is only through a *comprehensive planning approach* that you will be able to determine if LTC insurance is suitable for you and your family.

Your best defense against purchasing coverage you may not need, or going without coverage you should have, is to consult a trusted financial advisor trained in long-term care planning. Working with your financial advisor, or someone referred to you by your advisor, ensures that the plan you put in place is the most appropriate plan for you. That plan may, or may not, include LTC insurance.

Insurance agents who sell LTC insurance with the *single sales approach* will debate the information in this section. They will tell you that you don't need to go through this process prior to considering LTC insurance. But this is an essential part of a *comprehensive planning approach* and has been developed over a period of 16 years with the assistance and advice of respected financial planners, estate planning attorneys, and CPAs. It has a proven track record as the best approach for determining the suitability of LTC insurance.

Remember that the information in this chapter is to be used only as a preliminary guide to having a comfortable discussion of the

FAST FACTS:

- For every year you wait to purchase coverage, your effective premium will be **14-22%** higher.

- The percentage of people able to pass underwriting is considerably less at age 70 than at age 60.

- One in three people between age 75 and 80 will not qualify for coverage because of health conditions.

- The New York State Partnership Program recommends that you allocate no more than **7%** of your annual income to long-term care insurance premiums.

issue of long-term care planning with your financial advisor. It is not meant to replace the more in-depth planning process your advisor will use to determine LTC insurance suitability.

PRIORITIZING YOUR INSURANCE NEEDS

A *comprehensive planning approach* views long-term care planning as an integral part of the financial and estate planning process. Within the seven areas of financial and estate planning discussed in Chapter 6, LTC insurance falls specifically into the area of "risk management." Risk management is the process of deciding how to control financial risk, and whether or not to transfer certain risks to an insurance company.

A discussion of whether or not to consider LTC insurance cannot begin without first addressing the subject of "risk management prioritization." This includes prioritizing your insurance needs. At first, this discussion may seem out of place in a book about long-term care planning. But every family has different insurance needs based on their unique situation. It doesn't make sense to consider LTC insurance unless you have first prioritized your insurance needs.

The following is our list of the most important types of personal insurance coverage, in order of priority:

1. Health Insurance: Anything can happen to our health at any time. For this reason, no one in our country should be without health insurance. There are just too many unexpected illnesses or accidents that carry a hefty price tag. Health insurance helps ensure that a financially comfortable family remains that way, by covering unexpected health expenses that could otherwise devastate their financial future. No other type of personal insurance is more important.

*2. **Disability Income Insurance:*** If you are working and earning an income, disability income insurance can replace a portion of your income if you become disabled and are unable to work and earn that income. For people earning a working income, a risk management plan that replaces the income of the bread-winners is imperative. Disability income insurance is designed to do just that, and should be considered the second most important type of insurance for those earning a working income. What if you are not earning a working income? If you are retired, and/or are living on investment income, disability income insurance is not important. In fact, it's not even available. Disability income insurance replaces a *working income.* If you are not working for an income, this paragraph is not applicable to you.

*3. **Life Insurance:*** If you are earning a working income and have children or others who are dependent upon that income, your death would bring a financial hardship to these people. Life insurance is designed to solve this problem, and is potentially your third most important type of insurance. If your death would not bring a financial hardship to others, life insurance becomes a lower priority, possibly no priority at all. Your financial advisor may have other reasons for advising you to purchase life insurance, such as a vehicle for paying estate taxes. But if your reason for needing life insurance is other than to protect your dependents from hardship, the need for life insurance should be moved to a lower priority on this insurance priority list.

*4. **Long-term Care Insurance:*** LTC insurance falls to as low as number four on our list of insurance priorities. You should consider LTC insurance only after you and your financial advisor have analyzed your need for the above three types of personal insurance protection.

If you have yet to prioritize and plan ahead for your most important types of insurance, we recommend that you put this book aside and address potentially higher priority risk-management topics before you consider LTC insurance.

If you and your financial advisor have analyzed your top insurance priorities, it's appropriate to analyze and evaluate LTC insurance for you and your family.

ANALYZING THE NEED FOR LONG-TERM CARE INSURANCE

Our approach to LTC insurance suitability uses a process of elimination to analyze whether or not to consider coverage. First, do you qualify for coverage based on your current health? If you do not qualify, it makes little difference whether or not you are suitable for coverage based on all the other aspects. Next, can you afford the premium? If you can't afford the premium, again there is no reason to consider the other aspects of LTC insurance. As you review the information below, you may decide that you are "disqualified" at some point. If you come to this conclusion, speak with your financial advisor to confirm your conclusion and to discuss alternative long-term care planning options.

REASONABLY GOOD HEALTH IS REQUIRED

Long-term care insurance is a health-qualifying type of insurance. This means that you must be in reasonably good health in order to obtain coverage. An adage in the LTC insurance industry says, "LTC insurance is purchased with your health; money simply pays the premium." This means that if your health is not good enough to qualify for coverage, no amount of premium you are willing to pay will change the fact that you're ineligible. As with all types of insurance, many times, those who want coverage the most are those who can't qualify for it.

If you decide to apply for coverage, you will go through a process called underwriting. *Underwriting* is defined as "a process of examining, accepting, or rejecting insurance risks, and then classifying those accepted in order to charge the proper amount of premium" (National Association of Insurance Commissioners [NAIC]).

The LTC insurance underwriting process consists of answering questions about your health and may also include a physical and/or a request for medical information from your doctor. *(The entire underwriting process is explained in Chapter 13.)*

If you currently have certain health conditions, you will automatically be ineligible to apply for LTC insurance. The *Disqualifying*

Disqualifying Health Conditions

You will **not qualify** for long-term care insurance if **presently,** or during the **12-month period preceding** the application for coverage, you needed any of the following:

- Assistance with any Activities of Daily Living ("ADLs" include: eating, bathing, dressing, toileting, continence, and transferring)
- Home Health Care Services
- Care in a Nursing Home or Assisted Living Community
- A walker, wheelchair, medical appliance, kidney dialysis machine, or a manufactured source of oxygen
- Treatment for any of the following conditions:

  - AIDS
  - Alzheimer's Disease
  - Acute and unspecified renal failure
  - Acute cerebral vascular disease
  - Congestive heart failure
  - Cirrhosis of the liver
  - Chronic memory loss
  - Chronic renal failure
  - Diabetes Mellitus with complications
  - Mental retardation

  - Multiple strokes
  - Multiple Sclerosis, other bone disease, and musculoskeletal disease
  - Muscular Dystrophy
  - Paralysis
  - Parkinson's Disease
  - Schizophrenia and related disorders
  - Senility and organic mental disorders
  - Severe Emphysema
  - Transient Attack Ischemic

Health Conditions chart above is simply an overview of the most common types of conditions that will exclude a person from obtaining LTC insurance. The list is not all-inclusive. If you can answer "no" to all of these conditions, it does not mean that you will automatically qualify for coverage. Underwriting for LTC insurance is performed on an individual basis, and there may be other conditions, or combinations of conditions, that cause an application to be declined.

The LTC insurance industry is experiencing a trend toward more stringent underwriting. As new health information is released, insurance companies gain more insight into the reasons people need long-term care. For example, a recent study released by Chicago's Rush University Medical Center (Rush University Medical Center 2004) found that participants who had diabetes had a 65 percent greater chance of developing Alzheimer's Disease than those without diabetes. This study will likely prompt other such studies by LTC insurance companies, regarding the link between diabetes and cognitive impairment.

Keep in mind that this discussion is limited strictly to health conditions that you currently have. If you develop one or more of these conditions after your LTC insurance policy is issued, the company cannot deny a claim due to that condition.

AGE IS A FACTOR IN UNDERWRITING

While everyone should plan ahead for long-term care, your current age may be a major factor in whether or not to plan ahead with LTC insurance. From an underwriting standpoint, passing health underwriting for LTC insurance is heavily influenced by age. The older we become, the more likely we are to develop health conditions that will exclude us from obtaining coverage. The chart below illustrates some interesting facts about age and gender. As you can see, the percentage of people able to pass underwriting is considerably less at age 70 than at age 60. The data also show that women are less likely to qualify for LTC insurance in all age brackets, with the exception of the over-75 age group.

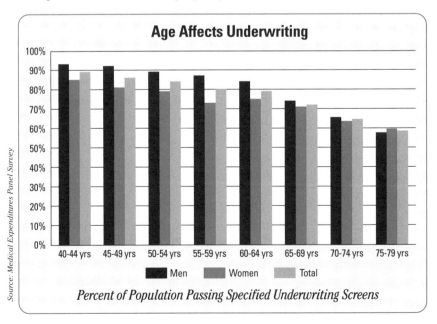

Source: Medical Expenditures Panel Survey

Percent of Population Passing Specified Underwriting Screens

AFFORDABILITY OF LONG-TERM CARE INSURANCE BASED ON AGE

Premium rates for LTC insurance have a reputation for being "high" and may be unaffordable to some people. That's because some people postpone investigating coverage until they are too old. The younger you are when you purchase LTC insurance, the lower your premium will be for the life of the policy. For every year you wait to purchase coverage, your premium will be 8-15 percent higher.

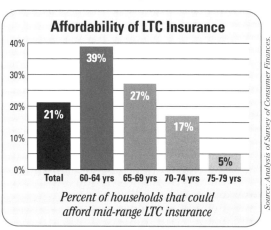

Affordability of LTC Insurance

Percent of households that could afford mid-range LTC insurance

Source: Analysis of Survey of Consumer Finances.

But this percentage does not include the fact that there is an overall upward trend in premium rates in the industry as a whole. When you include this upward trend in premium rates, for every year a person waits to purchase coverage, they will pay an additional 14% to 22% in premium. This means that if a 55 year old who purchases coverage in 2006 would have purchased coverage in 2001, when they were age 50, their premium would have been almost one half as much. It's a mistake for financial advisors to give the common advice to "wait until a certain age" to consider coverage, without first analyzing each person's unique financial objectives. Many people heeding this advice may develop health conditions that disqualify them from obtaining coverage and/or may reach an age where premiums are unaffordable. Remember to always seek advice from a financial advisor trained in a *comprehensive planning approach.*

Most people are surprised to learn that the total *cumulative* premium you will pay the insurance company over your lifetime is lower if you purchase coverage now compared to waiting until you're older. For example, if a 50-year-old purchases coverage today and pays premiums until his life expectancy, he will pay less total cumulative premium to the insurance company than a 60-year-old who purchases coverage today and pays premiums until his life expectancy. In addition, the 50-year-old is more likely to qualify for coverage and be offered preferred rates based on health.

Many financial advisors will point out that this example does not consider that the 60-year-old could save, invest, and earn interest on the premium amount over the 10-year period, instead of purchasing insurance. This is true. But it also does not consider that the 50-year-old could submit an LTC insurance claim and collect benefits on his policy during the 10-year period. This example is purposefully simple, and is designed to point out that waiting until the "perfect age" to buy coverage does not make sense.

For more in-depth discussions of the potential problems of waiting until the "perfect age" to consider coverage, see *Chapter 18: Long-Term Care Insurance Myths.*

Can you afford LTC insurance premiums at your age? As you consider LTC insurance, ask your financial advisor to provide you with a ballpark premium rate for coverage. Keep in mind that this initial figure will be an estimate only and should not be construed as the actual premium rate you will pay if you decide to purchase coverage. However, a ballpark rate should allow you and your advisor to determine whether or not coverage would be affordable for you.

Some people ask, "What percentage of my family's income should I allocate to LTC insurance premiums?" This will vary, depending on your situation. One guideline offered by the New York State Partnership program *(see Chapter 16: Partnership Programs)* recommends that you allocate no more than 7 percent of your annual income to LTC insurance premiums. This is only one guideline and should be used for general purposes only. You and your financial advisor will more than likely adjust any guidelines available based on your unique financial situation.

Remember, we believe everyone in America should have a plan for long-term care. But are people in some age brackets better suited for choosing LTC insurance than people in other age brackets? Yes, mainly due to insurance priorities. The fact that younger people tend to have insurance priorities that rank higher than LTC insurance makes younger people less likely to be able to afford LTC insurance, even if those premium rates are fairly inexpensive.

The following information is based on our experience regarding age and affordability of coverage. Keep in mind that this is general information only. Your unique situation may dictate that you fall into a different circumstance than the ones described.

Under age 40: People under age 40 rarely purchase LTC insurance. People in this age bracket most often fall into the category of having other higher-priority risks that must be covered by insurance. If they have been properly advised to prioritize their insurance needs, LTC insurance may be a type of insurance that they simply can't afford at this stage of their lives.

Another reason people in this age bracket rarely invest in coverage is because they are not aware of the risk. Although many financial advisors are beginning to educate their clients about long-term care, many people under age 40 are simply not knowledgeable about this area of financial planning. This is beginning to change, and as a result, the percentage of people under age 40 who are planning ahead with LTC insurance is on the rise.

Some people in this age bracket purchase coverage through a workplace, group, or sponsored offering. Unfortunately, because a *comprehensive planning approach* is rarely utilized with these types of programs, there is no integration with the insured's total financial objectives. In addition, the policyholder receives no in-depth explanation of his coverage. If you are being offered coverage through your workplace, or any group or sponsored offering, read *Chapter 17: Group and Sponsored Long-Term Care Insurance* and speak with your financial advisor prior to considering coverage.

Between age 40 and 60: This is the fastest-growing age bracket for considering LTC insurance. **People in this age bracket normally have met the three most important criteria for considering LTC insurance:**

1. All other insurance priorities are covered.
2. Their budget can support the LTC insurance premium.
3. They are still young enough to be in good to excellent health and qualify for coverage.

This age bracket is also more aware of aging issues. People in this age bracket have the highest percentage of parents or other relatives and friends in need of long-term care. People who experience a long-term care event in their circle of influence are more motivated to plan ahead for long-term care for their own families.

Between age 60 and 75: People in this age bracket should strongly consider the appropriateness of LTC insurance as soon as possible. The biggest issue facing these people is qualifying for coverage. As illustrated in the *Age Affects Underwriting Chart* (see previous section "Age is a Factor in Underwriting"), people who wait until later years to consider coverage risk not being able to pass the underwriting process.

The second biggest hurdle in this age bracket is the premium amount. Beginning at age 60, premiums can significantly increase with every succeeding birthday—until at some point, coverage is likely to become unaffordable.

Most people in the 60- to 75-year-old age bracket are in one of two situations:

1. They have already investigated LTC insurance and have either purchased coverage, or made the decision to forgo coverage.

2. They are currently investigating, or re-investigating coverage for a specific reason. For example, they or a loved one, or someone close to them, has developed a health condition that has heightened their awareness of the need for long-term care. Hopefully, the person who is experiencing the health condition is not the same person who is seeking coverage. We receive inquiries on a daily basis from financial advisors with clients in this situation. Many times, the person inquiring about coverage investigated LTC insurance years ago, but did not purchase coverage. Now, due to a decline in their health, they are motivated to buy coverage, but are probably uninsurable.

Over age 75: Insurance companies are not overly anxious to issue coverage to people who have waited until age 75 or older to apply for LTC insurance. In fact, fewer insurance companies are issuing coverage to people over age 80.

The average LTC insurance claim is made between age 79 and 85. One in three people between age 75 and 80 will not qualify for coverage because of health conditions. After age 80, odds are better than 50 percent that a person will not qualify for coverage. The premium for people in this age bracket who do qualify for coverage is normally much higher than they are willing or able to pay. If you are in this age group and want to investigate LTC insurance, ask your financial advisor or long-term care specialist to show you some co-insurance options to help make the premium more affordable.

YOUR "RISK TOLERANCE" PHILOSOPHY

Your risk tolerance philosophy is an important consideration when determining whether or not to own LTC insurance. Some people have a high tolerance for financial risk while others believe in a conservative approach and would prefer to transfer an insurable risk to an insurance carrier.

People who plan ahead for their financial security, and have covered their other high-priority insurance needs, usually have a low tolerance for the financial risk of long-term care. Their philosophy is usually to maintain as much financial control as possible and to plan ahead for the insurable event of long-term care.

To understand your risk tolerance philosophy, ask yourself these questions:

- Have I consistently insured my family and myself for the proper types and amounts of insurance coverage such as health, disability, and life insurance?
- If I have, do I tend to transfer the entire risk to the insurance company, or am I comfortable insuring some of the risk myself? This concept is called "co-insuring" and can be a good idea in some instances.

WHY DO THE WEALTHY CONSIDER LONG-TERM CARE INSURANCE?

If you have enough money to pay for your own long-term care needs, should you consider LTC insurance?

Many people are surprised to learn that there is no upper limit for the amount of assets you should own before you automatically choose to self-insure for long-term care. This is evidenced by the fact that thousands of wealthy people have purchased LTC insurance even though they have the financial ability to self-insure.

Often, wealthy people purchase coverage for reasons that are much different than the rest of the population. One of the major reasons many wealthy people purchase coverage is to help their loved ones through major decisions that arise with the sudden need for long-term care. For example, wealthy people are used to hiring others to provide for their needs, and the long-term care coordination benefit included with some LTC insurance policies can help simplify the process of finding providers *(see Chapter 14: Submitting a Claim)*.

Many people, including some well-intentioned financial advisors, analyze LTC insurance from a strictly logical point of view, and place it only in the category of "insurance to protect assets." Although protecting assets is a common reason for purchasing coverage, wealthy people also have a variety of other reasons for buying LTC insurance.

We have asked many high-net-worth individuals and families the following question about why they decided to purchase LTC insurance:

Q. "You have the assets necessary to pay for long-term care without buying insurance. Why are you purchasing LTC insurance?

Here are some of their answers:

A1. "We have always been planners. We've taught our children to plan ahead. Even though we could pay for the cost of care ourselves, we want to leave a legacy that is consistent with our lifelong philosophy of planning ahead."

A2. "All my life, I've used other people's money to succeed. For example, while some of my colleagues avoided borrowing in order to leverage their financial opportunities, I've succeeded by borrowing and then investing that money for our future. I view the purchase of LTC insurance with this same philosophy: long-term care is a high-probability risk, and if I can spend $3,000 per year, in exchange for a potential $70,000 per year in benefits, I view that as leverage."

A3. "By purchasing coverage now, I lock in a lower rate for the rest of my life. Even though I could self-insure for all long-term care expenses today, that could change in the future. If my investments decline in value, I won't have to worry about invading principle in order to pay for long-term care expenses."

A4. "Not only do we believe in insurance coverage, we were also able to write off the premium on our corporate tax return. When our CPA analyzed the bottom line numbers, it made good fiscal sense."

A5. "The 'Care Coordination Benefit' of the LTC insurance policy helps my family find resources to help (us) if we have a claim. This benefit alone is worth the price of the policy."

Planning ahead for long-term care is a personal issue, and the plan you choose has more to do with your emotional make-up than it does the amount of your assets. People who plan ahead for a certain type of lifestyle, and then develop plans of action for attaining those lifestyle choices, are more likely to plan ahead for long-term care. For some, LTC insurance makes sense, even if they have sufficient assets to pay for their own care.

For more insight into why the wealthy consider LTC insurance, read *Chapter 18: Long-Term Care Insurance Myths.*

SEEK ADVICE FROM YOUR FINANCIAL ADVISOR

The only way to investigate LTC insurance is to ask a financial professional trained in a *comprehensive planning approach* to explain your various options for paying for long-term care, and to help you evaluate your suitability for coverage.

If an advisor tells you "No, you don't need LTC insurance" without helping you analyze your unique situation, locate another financial advisor—one who is trained in a *comprehensive planning approach.*

If your advisor tells you "Yes, you should consider LTC insurance," ask them to guide you in the process of obtaining coverage or to refer you to someone who can guide you.

If you need assistance locating a financial advisor who has been trained in a *comprehensive planning approach,* you can visit our website (**www.superiorltc.com**) for a directory of financial advisors in your area.

IS LONG-TERM CARE INSURANCE
SUITABLE FOR YOU?

KEY POINTS

- Before you can consider long-term care insurance, you must prioritize the importance of other types of insurance, based on the unique needs of you and your family.

- The most important types of personal insurance coverage, in order, are health insurance, disability income insurance, life insurance, and long-term care insurance.

- If you are in poor health, no amount of premium you are willing to pay will change the fact that you're ineligible for long-term care insurance.

- The total *cumulative* premium you will pay for long-term care insurance over your lifetime is lower if you purchase coverage now compared to waiting until you're older.

- Beginning at age 60, premiums can significantly increase with every succeeding birthday—until at some point, coverage is likely to become unaffordable.

- The wealthy, even those in a position to self-insure, often purchase long-term care insurance to transfer financial risk, maintain control, and expand their choice of care options.

Chapter 10

The Essentials of Long-Term Care Insurance

*Things which matter most must never be
at the mercy of the things which matter least.*

— Goethe

The essentials of LTC insurance are easier to understand when broken down into the factors that make up the coverage. This chapter is designed to give you a basic education of how LTC insurance works. This will provide you with the foundation you need to have a knowledgeable discussion with your financial planner, estate planning attorney, or CPA about LTC insurance as an option for you.

THE FACTORS THAT IMPACT THE PREMIUM FOR LONG-TERM CARE INSURANCE

In designing an LTC insurance plan, there are seven basic factors to consider. Each factor has a direct bearing on how much you will pay for the coverage. Some of these factors will determine how much you will receive at the time of a claim. There are also a number of optional benefits that can be considered with an LTC insurance policy. These will be discussed after we present the seven basic factors.

THE IMPORTANCE RATING

The importance of balancing and prioritizing the seven factors can't be overemphasized. Although there is no single policy design that is correct for everyone, many people have had the unfortunate experience of purchasing coverage that had them both underinsured and overinsured, all in the same plan. This is because the agent selling the coverage did not properly balance and prioritize the benefits at the time the policy was purchased. At claim's time the importance of proper plan design becomes very obvious, and sometimes painful. We illustrate this with a case study in *Chapter 11: Choosing the Right Coverage.*

FAST FACTS:

- The importance of proper design in a long-term care insurance policy will become obvious, and sometimes painful, at claim's time.

- If it weren't for the home care coverage provided by their long-term care insurance, **60%** of policyholders would not be able to afford to remain in their homes and would be forced to move to a care facility.

- Inflation is the most serious threat to a sound long-term care plan.

Because some LTC insurance factors are much more important than others, we devised a numerical process, accompanied by an icon, to rate the importance of each of the seven factors. We call this assignment an "Importance Rating." A rating of 5 means that the factor is very important in the overall policy design process. A rating of 1 means that it is insignificant. In designing an LTC insurance policy, consider reducing your premium by first adjusting a lower rated factor.

This rating process is heavily based on our opinion and experience. Some will adamantly disagree with our importance ratings. Some will even be quick to point out instances where the recommendations would have been detrimental to a policyholder. In this regard, LTC insurance is exactly like all other types of insurance: if you ever have a claim on a policy of any kind, you'll wish you had purchased the maximum benefits available in every category. But we give these recommendations without the foresight of knowing whether or not you will ever collect on your policy. Based on our 16 years of policy design and claim's experience, we believe these recommendations offer a good balance between coverage choices and premium costs.

THE SEVEN BASIC FACTORS TO CONSIDER IN DESIGNING A LONG-TERM CARE INSURANCE POLICY:

1. How does the policy pay benefits?
2. Where can you go for care?
3. What is your current age?
4. How is your current health?
5. How much will the policy pay in benefits per day, week, or month?
6. How long will the policy pay benefits?
7. What is the policy elimination period?

1. HOW DOES THE POLICY PAY BENEFITS?

Importance Rating:

Long-term care insurance policies have three basic methods of paying benefits:

1. With the ***reimbursement method,*** also known as the expense incurred method, you first pay the care provider, whether it be a facility or the person(s) caring for you at home. Then, you submit a copy of the receipt to the LTC insurance company for reimbursement. Your reimbursement amount will be either the actual amount you paid for services or your in-force "benefit amount," whichever is less. "Benefit Amount" is explained in number 5, below.

2. With the ***indemnity method*** no receipts are needed. The benefit paid to you is the exact amount of your in-force benefit amount, even if your long-term care expenses are less than your benefit amount. This means that indemnity policies may allow you to actually make a profit on your claim.

3. With the ***cash method,*** you are not even required to incur expenses to receive benefits on a legitimate claim. You can collect your full benefit amount, even if someone cared for you free of charge.

These three types of policies are listed in order of least to most expensive in premium cost. They are also listed in order from the least to greatest amount of potential money you receive from an insurance claim. This is where the differences end. When it comes to eligibility for collecting on the policies, all three methods are the same. It's neither easier nor harder to become eligible for benefits based on the payment method of the policy.

Recommendation

On the surface, indemnity and cash method policies appear to have a significant advantage. However, we believe that the opposite is actually true in most cases. The reimbursement, or expense incurred method, is your best value because it does the best job of solving the true long-term care problem—per premium dollar paid—than the indemnity or cash method policies.

Two specific reasons to avoid policies that pay on the indemnity and cash methods are:

1. Your initial premium will be higher—in some cases, significantly higher. This is because these policies make it possible for you to actually earn a profit by paying you a dollar amount higher than your actual costs, or in the case of cash method policies, paying you even if you do not incur expenses for care.

2. Not only will your initial premium be higher, indemnity and cash method policies will also be subject to more frequent and higher rate increases than policies paying claims using the reimbursement method. This is because policies are placed in separate "pools," for claims experience. The method of payment, as well as other factors determines the policies' "pool." Indemnity and cash method policies will always be included in a "pool" that is subject to paying higher and more frequent claims.

Exception to Recommendation: There may be one exception to this recommendation for not considering indemnity or cash method policies. If one spouse is uninsurable, the indemnity or cash policy may be worth considering for the insurable spouse. The insurable spouse could conceivably purchase a benefit amount high enough to pay for care for both spouses. This means that if the insured spouse has a claim, the benefit amount may pay enough in benefits to pay for care for both spouses. This is a complex strategy, and should only be considered with the assistance of your financial advisor or an LTC insurance specialist.

2. WHERE CAN YOU GO FOR CARE?

Importance Rating: **5**

Just as there are three methods LTC insurance policies pay benefits, there are also three different types of policies. The type of policy will determine where you can receive long-term care services. **The three possible LTC insurance policies and their settings are:**

1. *"Home Care Only"* policies pay for care only in your home.
2. *"Facility Care Only"* policies pay for care only in a facility, such as an assisted living community or nursing home.
3. *"Comprehensive Long-Term Care Insurance"* policies pay

for care in any setting, regardless of where the care is received (home, and/or assisted living communities and/or nursing homes).

If a need for long-term care arises, most people want to stay in their own home to receive care. In a national survey funded by the Office of Disability, Aging and Long-Term Care Policy, and the Robert Wood Johnson Foundation, it was learned that in the absence of home care benefits provided by their LTC insurance policy, 60 percent of individuals could not afford to remain in their homes and would be forced to move to a facility *(LTCi Sales Strategies magazine, Vol. 3, No. 2, reprinted with permission, www.LTCSales.com)*. You do not want to be forced to move from your home to an assisted living community, or a nursing home, simply because your policy lacked benefits for at-home care. For this reason, home care benefits are a very important part of an LTC insurance policy.

But in many instances, home care is not an option, and a person must be moved to an assisted living community or a nursing home.

Recommendation

Since you do not know where your care will be received, we recommend only the third option, the *"Comprehensive Long-Term Care Insurance"* policy. Our recommendation that you only consider comprehensive long-term care insurance is **one of the most important points in this book.** Comprehensive LTC insurance offers the best value because benefits will be paid to cover skilled and non-skilled providers in your home, assisted living communities, and nursing homes. These policies also pay for care in community-based settings such as board-and-care homes and adult day centers.

Look for the words *"Comprehensive Long-Term Care Insurance Policy"* displayed prominently on the front of your policy and the forms and materials provided to you at the time you apply for coverage. If you see this term, you are considering the right type of policy because it will pay benefits in any setting. If you see any other term, such as **"Home Care Only Insurance Policy,"** or **"Nursing Home Only Insurance Policy,"** *do not* purchase the coverage unless your financial advisor has given you specific reasons for deviating from this advice.

3. WHAT IS YOUR CURRENT AGE?

Importance Rating:

Your current age will have a major effect on your LTC insurance premium. The younger you are when you purchase coverage, the lower your premium will be for the life of the policy.

When you purchase LTC insurance, you "lock-in" your issue-age premium rate for the rest of your life. This means that a 50-year-old who purchases coverage today will still be paying the 50-year-old premium rate, even when they are 60 years of age.

Although you lock-in your current age rate when you purchase LTC insurance, premium rates *can* increase after the policy is issued. If an insurance company has underpriced their premiums or issued coverage to individuals with health problems that causes a higher than expected number of claims, you could experience rate increases on your policy. But the rate increases will be on the entire "class" of policyholders. This means that everyone in your state who purchased a policy with your "policy form" from the same company will also receive a rate increase. The rate increase will always be a percentage of the amount of your current premium amount. This results in a "real dollar" rate increase that would be smaller if you purchased coverage at a younger age.

When considering LTC insurance, ask your financial advisor or LTC insurance specialist about the company's history of rate increases. Many good insurance companies have a very good record of premium stability, and your financial advisor and/or the LTC insurance specialist should be recommending one of these companies *(for more on this subject, read Chapter 12: Choosing the Right Insurance Carrier).*

Recommendation

Although there are good incentives for purchasing at a younger age, we are not implying that you should purchase LTC insurance simply because you are young and can lock-in a low premium rate. Chapter 9 explains the importance of prioritizing your insurance risks prior to purchasing any type of insurance.

But if you have prioritized your insurance risks, and LTC insurance is being recommended by your financial advisor, purchasing coverage at the earliest possible age is a wise decision.

4. HOW IS YOUR CURRENT HEALTH?

Importance Rating: **5**

Your current health not only has a direct effect on the premium, but a direct effect on your eligibility for LTC insurance.

Long-term care insurance is a health-qualifying type of insurance. You must be in reasonably good health to qualify for coverage. While most of the general population qualifies for coverage, there are specific factors about your health that will determine your exact premium, including your height and weight, and whether or not you smoke. *(For more on this subject, see Chapter 9: Is Long-Term Care Insurance Suitable for You?)*

Those in good to excellent health will likely qualify for preferred rates. Generally, preferred rates are available to people who are average height and weight, are non-smokers, and have not experienced any negative physical or mental health conditions in recent years.

A person with a history of minor health conditions that are well-controlled, such as high blood pressure, will likely qualify for coverage, but will receive a standard premium rate. The difference in premium rates between a preferred premium rate and a standard premium rate is in the range of 15 percent with most insurance companies.

If you currently have significant health problems, you may have difficulty obtaining LTC insurance. While some smaller, lower-rated insurance carriers may accept your application, we advise extreme caution in purchasing coverage from companies that do not pass the carrier evaluation process we outline in *Chapter 12: Choosing the Right Insurance Carrier.*

Recommendation

All things being equal, consider LTC insurance while your health is good to excellent.

5. HOW MUCH WILL THE POLICY PAY PER DAY, WEEK, OR MONTH?

Importance Rating: **5**

The **benefit amount** is the ongoing amount of money the insurance company will pay if you have a claim on the policy.

The benefit amount is the most important decision to make in designing LTC insurance coverage. It is also the most influential factor in determining what your premium will be. The benefit amount is expressed in a dollar amount per day, week, or month. For example, if you purchased a policy with a daily benefit amount of $150, you would collect about $4,500 per month when you become eligible for benefits.

Choosing the proper benefit amount is imperative. A *comprehensive planning approach* includes knowing the cost of care in your area and using that cost as a benchmark. Then, by defining your insurance philosophy, your goals, and your budget, a customized solution is developed to select the proper benefit amount for your unique situation. This process includes determining whether to purchase coverage that will pay the full cost of care, or whether to co-insure by electing coverage that pays for some, but not all, of the average cost of care in your area.

In using a benchmark for the cost of care in your area, it's important for you and your advisor to use the specific cost of care in your city or immediate area, and not the average cost of care in your state. Designing coverage based on the average cost of care in your state will not produce accurate results. For example, costs of care in New York State can range from a low of $135 per day to a high of $268 per day.

Recommendation

Most people who purchase LTC insurance wish later that they had purchased a higher benefit amount. Start by considering the premium for a benefit amount that covers the entire average cost of care in your area. Then, if applicable, adjust it downward based on your risk-tolerance philosophy and the amount of money you are budgeting for LTC insurance.

6. HOW LONG WILL THE POLICY PAY BENEFITS?

Importance Rating:

The **maximum lifetime benefit** is the factor that determines the maximum amount of money your LTC insurance policy will pay in dollars once you have a claim and begin to receive benefits. The concept is similar to a bank account on which you can withdraw money. Once you have a claim, you can withdraw the daily, weekly, or monthly benefit amount explained in number 5, above. Once your maximum lifetime benefit is reached, the policy will not pay any further benefits.

You will choose the maximum lifetime benefit when you apply for coverage. As soon as you collect your first dollar of benefits from the policy, the clock starts ticking on your maximum limit.

You can choose a maximum lifetime benefit of as little as $50,000, or about one year of long-term care services. Or, on the upper end, you can choose a maximum lifetime benefit with "no limit." The no limit choice is also known as the "unlimited benefit maximum," or a "lifetime benefit period." This option means that benefits will continue to be paid for as long as you need care, even if the care is needed for several decades or even for the rest of your life. These two examples are the extremes in the available options; many options exist between these two extremes. As you would assume, the higher the maximum lifetime benefit, the higher the premium.

The maximum lifetime benefit is one of the most difficult choices to make in designing an LTC insurance policy. Accurate statistics regarding the odds of needing long-term care and the average length of a long-term care need are difficult to obtain. **There are two major reasons for this:**

1. Until the past two decades, there has been little reason for our government or the insurance industry to keep records of how long people need long-term care. People in earlier generations lived much shorter lives and the average duration of a long-term care need was shorter.

2. When long-term care services were needed, people were cared for at home by a loved one, prior to entering a facility. Statistics for care received at home prior to admission to a facility are difficult to obtain even today.

It may be feasible for you to estimate how long you might need long-term care services by analyzing your family health history. This might help you decide the best maximum lifetime benefit for you and your family. **You may want to consider a longer benefit period if:**

- There is longevity in your family.
- There is a history of Alzheimer's Disease or other types of dementia in your family.
- There is a history of neurological conditions, such as Parkinson's Disease in your family.

Recommendation

If you are fortunate enough to be investigating LTC insurance at a fairly young age (60 and below), the difference in premium between the unlimited benefit maximum and a limited benefit maximum is fairly negligible. We recommend the "unlimited benefit maximum" if the premium is affordable.

But if affordability is a factor, consider coverage with a limit that would cover you for roughly 5 or 10 years of care. Some statistics indicate that the vast majority of people do not need long-term care for more than 5 years, and a very small percentage need care for more than 10 years. However, we recommend never choosing a maximum lifetime benefit that would pay benefits for less than 3 years of care.

7. WHAT IS THE POLICY ELIMINATION PERIOD?

Importance Rating:

Also known as a deductible, the **elimination period** is similar to deductibles with other types of insurance coverage, such as your automobile or health insurance. However, instead of being defined as a dollar amount, the elimination period with LTC insurance is defined in *days between the time you begin to need care and the time the policy begins to pay benefits.* For example, if you need long-term care services, and you purchased coverage with a 100-day elimination period, on the 101st day of your need for care, your elimination period would be satisfied.

The more days that you are willing to pay for care yourself before your policy begins paying benefits, the lower your premium rate will be. You can choose a variety of elimination periods, ranging from a zero-day elimination period, which would pay benefits from the first day you needed long-term care services; to elimination periods as high as 730 days or more.

There are various ways that insurance companies calculate the elimination period. Some companies use a calendar day process, whereby your elimination period begins on the day you begin to need care and every day counts, even if you do not receive care every subsequent day thereafter. Other companies use a "days of service" method, whereby an elimination period day must be a day that care was actually received. Many insurance agents will attribute a great deal of importance to which method a company uses. But we do not place significant emphasis on the details of how the elimination period is calculated. In the overall picture of LTC insurance policy design, this is a minor point.

The elimination period is the simplest and most practical way to save money on your premium. Without sacrificing significant benefits, an elimination period in the range of 100 days can save you a significant amount of premium dollars over a lower elimination period.

To determine the elimination period that fits your situation and how that translates into out-of-pocket dollars, you and your financial advisor should discuss two important issues:

1. Your insurance philosophy and whether or not you believe in co-insuring a small or large amount of your potential long-term care needs.

2. The cost of care in your area. This allows you to see your out-of-pocket dollar risk for various elimination period choices. Multiplying the elimination period options you are considering by the cost of care per day in your area will give you your potential out-of-pocket risk during the elimination period.

Throughout this book we have explained that true long-term care is *needing assistance for a period beyond 100 days.* Short-term care, care needed for less than 100 days, can normally be paid for without significant hardship to the person or family receiving the care. Although it's not common, in certain instances a percentage of short-term care may even be paid for by your health insurance or Medicare.

Insurance agents normally recommend elimination periods between 0 days and 100 days. This is because they don't understand the definition of true long-term care.

On the other extreme, some people view LTC insurance as a highly catastrophic type of insurance, and choose elimination periods much higher than 100 days, sometimes up to 730 days or more. We caution however, that this strategy could cause unexpected problems: if a policy's benefits cannot be accessed until several months or years after the need for care, a policyholder and their family may be required to delay quality caregiving that could have been received earlier. As mentioned throughout this book, long-term care planning is more than just a topic about money—it's also about quality of life and choices—for both you and your family members.

Recommendation

We recommend that you concentrate your premium dollars on true long-term care. This means choosing an elimination period in the range of 100 days. In some circumstances, you may wish to choose an elimination period higher than 100 days, but choices beyond 100 days do not offer significant savings in your premium amount.

RIDERS AND EXTRAS: BELLS AND WHISTLES

Long-term care insurance can be purchased with an array of extras that can be added to the basic policy. These bells and whistles are called *riders.*

These riders increase the premium on the policy. In our opinion, most of them fail to add significant value to the coverage. But some are worth considering.

INFLATION PROTECTION

Importance Rating:

The costs of long-term care services will definitely increase in the coming decades. An inflation protection rider will help hedge against these rising costs. This rider should be an essential part of almost every LTC insurance policy.

An inflation protection rider automatically raises the benefit amount on your policy each year. Without having to think about it, or pay an additional premium each year, the rider helps ensure that your long-term care planning objectives continue to be met, years after the policy was purchased.

Long-term care insurance inflation protection riders normally offer a 5 percent simple or 5 percent compound inflation benefit. The compound inflation protection benefit is more costly, but is the best choice because it is more realistically tied to predicted inflation rates. This means that if your policy has a maximum monthly benefit of $4,000 when you purchase it, in the 13th month of your coverage, your monthly benefit would rise to $4,200 per month. The compound inflation rider will double the benefits of your policy about every 14 years. If you purchase the simple 5 percent inflation benefit, your benefits will double every 20 years.

You will still want to monitor the cost of care in your area to make sure your plan is meeting your objectives. In an annual review provided by your financial advisor or LTC insurance specialist trained in a *comprehensive planning approach,* you will be advised of the new current costs of care compared to your current inflation-adjusted coverage.

Recommendation

The reason we include this benefit in the riders section of this chapter is because it is possible to purchase LTC insurance without inflation protection. But inflation will always be with us, with a high probability that the inflation rate for long-term care services will be higher over time than the overall inflation rate.

For this reason, we recommend the following:

- Everyone who purchases coverage at age 70 and under should purchase the compound inflation protection rider.

- If you are purchasing coverage between ages 71 and 75, and the compound inflation rider adds too much to the premium, consider the simple inflation protection rider.

- If you are purchasing coverage after age 75, and both the compound and simple inflation riders add too much to the premium, consider increasing your benefit amount to act as a cushion against inflation. It may be a better value at these ages to purchase an additional 25 percent in benefit amount, instead of an inflation protection rider. This should be analyzed, and explained carefully by your financial advisor or LTC insurance specialist.

RESTORATION OF BENEFITS

Importance Rating:

This rider states that if you buy a policy with a "limited benefit maximum" and you use a portion of your policy benefits, the entire pool of benefits in the policy will be restored if your health returns and you go without care for a specified period of time (usually six months or more).

Recommendation

The likelihood is very low that a person will receive long-term care for more than 100 days, and then fully recover, to later receive care again for more than 100 days. This rider is not a good value.

NONFORFEITURE BENEFIT RIDER

Importance Rating:

This rider states that if you cancel your LTC insurance policy, a minimal amount of "paid up" insurance will remain in force, to slightly compensate you for premium payments paid into the policy. The amount of "paid-up" coverage is normally equal to the amount of premium you paid into the policy. For example, if your annual premium is $3,000, and you canceled the policy after five years, you would have "paid up" coverage of $15,000 if you had purchased the nonforfeiture rider. The $15,000 would be your lifetime benefit maximum. In this example, you could collect the benefit amount, up to a maximum of $15,000, if you qualify for long-term care benefits on the policy in the future.

Recommendation

Since LTC insurance becomes more valuable the longer it's in force, it should rarely, if ever, be canceled. In fact, only 4 percent of LTC insurance policyholders have canceled their policies after having them in force for 10 years. This rider is not a good value.

SURVIVORSHIP OR PAID-UP SURVIVOR BENEFIT

Importance Rating:

This rider states that if a husband and wife have coverage with the same company, and one passes away after the policies have been in force for a certain number of years with no claims paid on either policy, the surviving spouse's policy will be "paid-up," and no further premium payments will be due. The typical number of years that both policies must be in force and claim-free in order to benefit from this rider is 10 years.

Recommendation

In the overall LTC insurance planning process, this rider is insignificant. We recommend that you not invest in this rider and concentrate your LTC insurance planning dollars in the more important factors rated 3 or above.

SHARED-CARE RIDER

Importance Rating:

This rider allows couples who are insured with the same insurance company to use one another's LTC insurance coverage. For example, if a couple purchases "limited benefit" policies, and one spouse goes on claim and depletes their benefits but still requires care, this rider would allow them to access the benefits of their spouse's policy.

Recommendation

We recommend first considering the "Unlimited Benefit Maximum" coverage. Following this recommendation negates the need to spend extra money on the shared care rider.

However, there may be a few instances in which this rider could make sense. Couples who are over age 65, and cannot afford the "Unlimited Benefit Maximum" may consider this rider a good value. If you are older than 65 and applying for coverage with your spouse, ask your financial advisor or LTC insurance specialist about the feasibility of this option.

GUARANTEED INSURABILITY OPTION

Importance Rating:

This rider, also known as "The Future Purchase Option," allows you to purchase additional LTC insurance in later years, without going through the health-qualifying process again. In other words, if you develop a health condition that would normally exclude you from purchasing additional coverage, this rider will allow you to purchase a pre-determined, limited amount of additional coverage after the policy has been in force.

These riders normally offer the option to purchase additional coverage at various intervals during the life of the policy. For example, the insurance company may allow you to exercise this option every two years. This offer would come in the form of a letter from the company, asking you if you would like to exercise the Guaranteed Insurability Option of your policy. If you elect to exercise the option, your premium for the additional coverage will be based on your new "attained age"—not at the age when you initially purchased the policy. But if you had developed new health conditions during that time, you might be glad to purchase the coverage, even at the higher age rate.

Recommendation

Depending on the cost, this can be a worthwhile rider at advanced ages, due to the increased susceptibility for developing health conditions as we age. But if you are under 65, and have been in good to excellent health all your life, we recommend investing your premium dollars in factors rated 3 or above. If you are over 65, ask your financial advisor or LTC insurance specialist about the feasibility of this option.

THE ESSENTIALS OF LONG-TERM CARE INSURANCE

KEY POINTS

- Seven long-term care insurance factors affect the premium. Some of these factors also affect the amount you will receive at the time of claim.

- Long-term care insurance policies pay benefits under the reimbursement method, indemnity method, or cash method.

- Policies are specific as to where you'll receive care: home, facility, or any setting of your choice.

- Choose a benefit amount using a benchmark based on the cost of care in your immediate area, not based on the average cost of care in your entire state.

- Of all the policy riders available to policyholders, the inflation protection rider is the most important one to consider.

Chapter 11

Choosing the Right Coverage: A Case Study

*Every well-built house started in the form
of a definite purpose plus a definite plan
in the nature of a set of blueprints.*

— Napoleon Hill (1883-1970)
American Writer

If LTC insurance is determined to be the best solution for you, the next step in a *comprehensive planning approach* is to design coverage customized for your particular situation and goals. Your financial advisor, estate planning attorney, or CPA may assist you in the design of your LTC insurance plan. Or, they may refer you to an LTC insurance specialist.

DESIGNING A LONG-TERM CARE INSURANCE PLAN

Your financial advisor or LTC insurance specialist will guide you through six steps in designing the proper long-term care insurance plan:

1. **Review** the analysis that led you to the conclusion that LTC insurance is the best alternative for you. This analysis is a result of using a *comprehensive planning approach,* as explained in Chapter 7.

2. **Customize** the coverage. Focus on your current financial situation and goals, your health, the cost of long-term care near you, and your ability and willingness to pay for some of your long-term care expenses out-of-pocket. The end result will be a policy design with benefits tailored to your unique situation.

3. **Select** the insurance carrier. Identify the top-rated insurance carriers that offer coverage within the parameters of the customized coverage determined in Step 2, and select the best company for you and your family.

4. **Apply** for LTC insurance.

5. **Communicate** the information in the steps above to your financial advisor, if they are not already personally involved in the plan design. This information is normally communicated to the advisor by the LTC insurance specialist.

6. **Monitor** the LTC insurance solution by reviewing the plan at least annually with your financial advisor and/or your LTC insurance specialist.

As you can see from Step 5, if your financial advisor does not actually offer coverage, communication between the LTC insurance specialist and the financial advisor is imperative. This ensures that the LTC insurance plan you have implemented is fully integrated into your total financial plan.

A CASE STUDY IN CHOOSING THE RIGHT COVERAGE

The importance of using a *comprehensive planning approach* instead of a *single sales approach* is explained throughout this book. The steps in the process are explained in Chapter 7.

To illustrate the potential results of the two opposing approaches, the following case study gives a real-life example of a woman who became involved in the LTC insurance purchasing process while we were writing this book. She first worked with a traditional insurance agent and later with an LTC insurance specialist who was referred to her by her advisor and is trained in a *comprehensive planning approach*.

For illustrative purposes, we'll call this woman Betty Anderson. Betty was first solicited about LTC insurance by the agent who handles her automobile insurance. Using a *single sales approach,* the agent presented her with options from the standpoint of an insurance purchase, rather than with options from the standpoint of a financial planning solution. **Consistent with a *single sales approach*, the agent omitted the following areas:**

- He did not educate her about the four ways to pay for long-term care
- He did not educate her about the cost of care in her area
- He did not discuss her risk-tolerance philosophy
- He did not have any knowledge of her finances and did not

volunteer to assist her with analyzing how much she should budget for LTC insurance

The entire process was aimed at making a sale, with the client's financial objectives almost completely ignored.

The agent did ask about her health, but only because this is a necessary part of the LTC insurance application process. He discovered that she had high blood pressure. The one insurance carrier the agent represented would consider issuing coverage to Betty, but only at a standard rate, not a preferred rate.

The agent attempted to persuade her to sign an application during their first conversation about LTC insurance. But she resisted, remembering that her financial advisor had recently mailed her a letter suggesting that they discuss LTC planning during the upcoming annual review of her financial plan. She took the LTC insurance proposals given to her by the generalist insurance agent and sought further advice from her financial advisor.

Her financial advisor does not sell LTC insurance, but has been properly trained in a *comprehensive planning approach*. He was able to educate Betty about the need to plan ahead for long-term care and answered important basic questions about the issue of long-term care planning. After doing so, Betty's advisor recommended that she consider LTC insurance. The financial advisor referred the client to an LTC insurance specialist who was trained in a *comprehensive planning approach*.

Some Facts About the Client

Before we get into the specific recommendations given by each agent and the potential results of those recommendations, it's important to know more about the client.

Betty is 48 years old. She is in excellent health, other than high blood pressure, which is under good control. She is a divorced mother of twins who have just graduated from college and live in different parts of the country. There is longevity in her family, but her family also has a history of needing long-term care: her father needed long-term care services beginning at age 76. His care continued for the last eight years of his life. He spent most of his assets paying for care in an assisted living community.

Betty owns her own employment agency, which does business as a C-Corporation. Her annual income is $85,000. She has a total net worth of $350,000 and liquid assets of about $125,000.

The average cost of long-term care services in Betty's area is $120 per day.

She has given little thought to her risk tolerance philosophy with regards to long-term care planning.

The Generalist Insurance Agent's Recommendation

The generalist insurance agent focused his efforts on what he believed Betty could afford for LTC insurance. He based his affordability assumption on what "most of his clients who buy coverage can afford to pay."

Since the agent was attempting to make an insurance sale, and not develop a plan, many facts about Betty's situation were not discussed. **He had no specific knowledge of the following areas, and thus was unable to utilize this information in designing a plan for Betty:**

- **Affordability:** His knowledge of her specific finances were not discussed, so he simply estimated that Betty could afford a premium of about $2,000 per year.

- **Cost of care in the area:** He had a general idea about the costs of long-term care, but he had no specific knowledge of the exact costs of care in Betty's area.

- **Betty's risk-tolerance philosophy:** He did not offer to assist her in determining her risk-tolerance philosophy.

Many of the other steps in a *comprehensive planning approach* were ignored, including answering one of the most important questions of all: How was it determined that LTC insurance is the best solution for Betty's plan for long-term care? Without a complete understanding of the impact that a long-term care need can have on a person, both emotionally and financially, as well as the other educational steps involved in the planning process, purchasing LTC insurance becomes no more than another casual insurance purchase.

The agent made the following plan design recommendations:
- Benefit Amount: $100 per day
- Elimination Period: 0 Days
- Maximum Lifetime Benefit: Lifetime, Unlimited
- Inflation Protection? No
- Guaranteed Insurability Option? Yes
- Underwriting Class: Standard
- Policy Premiums Payable: For Life
- Annual Premium: $1,986
- Effective Premium after Tax Write-off: $1,450

These recommendations contain an imbalance of benefits that has the client both over-insured and under-insured, all in the same plan. **Let's analyze each specific area of the above recommendation:**

- **The Benefit Amount:** The benefit amount is the most important consideration in LTC insurance policy design. The agent is unaware of the exact cost of care in Betty's area, and is recommending a benefit amount that is dangerously low.

- **Elimination Period:** The recommendation of an elimination period of 0 days makes little sense, since true long-term care begins after 100 days of care. Betty can afford to pay for the first few weeks or months of care herself, but neither Betty nor the agent understand the issue of true long-term care yet. They also do not know her risk-tolerance philosophy at this time.

- **Maximum Lifetime Benefit:** The Unlimited Benefit Maximum is a good recommendation.

- **Inflation Protection:** The lack of inflation protection is the biggest mistake made in the policy design recommended by this agent. The odds of needing long-term care are significant beyond age 75. But, by the time this client reaches that age, the policy would pay just a small fraction of the total costs of long-term care, due to the effects of inflation and the policy's lack of inflation protection.

- **The Guaranteed Insurability Option:** This rider is best considered for people who are age 65 and older. Betty will not likely benefit by spending premium dollars on this option.

- **Underwriting Class:** Since the agent only represents one insurance company, he was unable to shop the market and attempt to locate a company that might offer Betty a preferred health rating.

- **Policy Premiums Payable:** This recommendation has Betty paying LTC insurance premiums for the rest of her life, even during her retirement years. This is acceptable in most cases, but based on the information given during a subsequent *comprehensive planning approach* analysis by an LTC specialist, this approach is not in the best interest of Betty's unique situation.

- **Effective Premium After Tax Write-off:** Although this has not yet been explained to Betty, she can save $536 annually by writing off the premium as a tax deduction.

Potential Outcome at Claim's Time

This plan design could potentially result in enormous out-of-pocket expenses for long-term care for Betty at claim's time. Let's take a look at a hypothetical example:

Let's presume that Betty purchased the above policy and followed the path of her father, developing Alzheimer's Disease and entering an assisted living community at age 76. Let's also presume that, just like her father, she ends up needing care for 8 years. Between the time of purchase and the time of claim, let's presume that inflation has risen at a rate of 5 percent compounded annually. Let's also presume a very common scenario when it comes to whether or not people exercise the Guaranteed Insurability Option: because of the rising costs of LTC insurance premiums during the years after her policy is issued, Betty elects not to exercise any of the options available to her with the Guaranteed Insurability Option. This means her daily benefit remains at $100 per day.

Here is the cost/benefit scenario for Betty at age 76, when her hypothetical claim begins:

Cost of care in her area: The original cost of care in her area was $120 per day. Even though the agent was only short by $20 per day in his recommendation of the $100 benefit amount, the lack of inflation protection will severely harm Betty at claim's time. The cost of care in her area at the time of need, due to a 5 percent compounding inflation rate, will have quadrupled to $480 per day!

The policy will begin to pay for care from the very first day of need, due to the zero-day elimination period.

The eight-year duration of care equates to 2,920 days. Using the daily cost of care of $480, the total long-term care bill would come to just under $1.4 million. The policy would pay for 2,920 days of care at a rate of $100 per day. The total benefits paid by the policy for those eight years of care would be $292,000. The out-of-pocket expenses to Betty would be over $1.1 million. This deficit is entirely due to poor plan design using a *single sales approach.*

Even though a claim of this nature would have Betty paying only $56,000 in premiums for a return of $292,000 in benefits, the poor plan design will cost her a large portion of her estate.

The Long-Term Care Insurance Specialist's Recommendation

Before meeting with Betty, the agent using a *comprehensive planning approach* consulted with her financial advisor to learn about Betty's situation, and how it was determined that LTC insurance was the best option for her.

During her first meeting with Betty, this agent continued to educate her about the issues of long-term care that were not specifically discussed by the financial advisor. These areas included the specific cost of care in her area, an analysis of her risk-tolerance philosophy, and her financial objectives as they related to a possible need for long-term care.

This agent supported her facts about the cost of care in the area ($120 per day) with information from various assisted living communities and home care providers in the area.

After becoming further educated on the issue of long-term care, and how it relates to her risk-tolerance philosophy, Betty came to understand that her philosophy is to protect large dollars. She was not interested in covering relatively small amounts of money, and was willing to pay for short-term care herself.

The effects of inflation were discussed, and the agent emphasized that purchasing LTC insurance at age 48 without inflation protection would be foolish. The agent informed Betty that inflation rates for long-term care expenses were currently around 3.5 percent, but that this rate was predicted to double during some years, and would likely average at least 5 percent over time.

The agent also gathered information about Betty's health, but went beyond the basic information needed for an application. She also asked for more specific information about the high blood pressure, and learned that it had been well-controlled for almost six years.

Since the agent represents a number of top-rated companies, she was able to recommend a company that would offer Betty preferred rates based on the fact that her blood pressure had been under control for many years. This would save Betty about 15 percent in premium over the standard health rating offered by the first, and only carrier represented by the agent using the *single sales approach*.

The agent also learned about Betty's retirement goals. Betty informed the agent that she planned to work for about 15 more years, and would sell her company at the time of retirement.

The process of being guided through a *comprehensive planning approach* helped Betty understand the significance of planning for long-term care, and the importance of doing so within the context of her total financial objectives.

Determining how much she could afford to pay for the premium was an important aspect of the plan design. But even more important was creating a plan design that accomplishes the results she wants. Through this analysis, Betty learned that she had an opportunity to write off the premium for her coverage through her corporation. She also learned that she had the opportunity to purchase LTC insurance that could be "paid up" by the time she entered her retirement years.

With this information in hand, the agent worked with Betty and made the following recommendations for plan design:

- Benefit Amount: $120 per day
- Elimination Period: 100 days
- Maximum Lifetime Benefit: Lifetime, Unlimited
- Inflation Protection: Yes
- Guaranteed Insurability Option: No

- Underwriting Class: Preferred
- Policy Premiums Payable: For 10 years
- Annual Premium: $3,511
- Effective Premium After Tax Write-off: $2,563

This recommendation reallocates some premium dollars from the traditional agent's proposal to a customized plan design that will come much closer to ensuring that Betty will achieve her desired objectives. **Let's analyze each specific area of the above recommendation:**

- **Benefit Amount:** The recommended benefit amount pays for the average cost of care in her area today.

- **Elimination Period:** Betty saves premium dollars by choosing a comfortable elimination period and will pay for "short-term care" herself—the first 100 days of care.

- **Maximum Lifetime Benefit:** The policy will pay benefits for as long as the coverage is needed.

- **Inflation Protection:** Adding the inflation protection rider is the most important difference between the approaches used by the two agents. This rider offers a hedge against the most serious threat to a sound LTC plan—inflation.

- **Guaranteed Insurability Option:** This rider is not recommended to Betty at her age because most young people never use this rider once it's purchased. It's better to invest premium dollars in higher-priority areas.

- **Underwriting Class:** Because this agent represents several top-rated companies, she was able to shop and find a company that would offer Betty a preferred health rating.

- **Policy Premiums Payable:** By knowing Betty's goal of retiring in 15 years, this agent recommended a policy that would have her paying no premiums during her retirement years.

- **Annual Premium:** Because the policy is payable for only 10 years, instead of for life, the premium for this policy is higher than the policy that requires premium payments for life. But by carefully analyzing affordability, Betty realized that she could afford the extra premium and that it was worth the pay-off of having no LTC insurance premiums during retirement.

- **Effective Premium After Tax Write-off:** Because Betty is in a 27 percent tax bracket, her effective premium rate is reduced by $948.

Potential Outcome at Claim's Time

The potential outcome of this more balanced recommendation will allow Betty to receive benefits at claim's time that will preserve much more of her estate. This plan considers her total financial objectives as well as the future inflationary conditions that will affect the cost of care in years ahead.

Using the same scenario of needing care for eight years beginning at age 76, this recommendation would have the following outcome:

- The cost of care in her area at time of claim is $480 per day. Due to the inclusion of the inflation protection rider, the policy will pay the entire cost of care.

- The elimination period of 100 days means that Betty pays for the first 100 days herself. This equates to $48,000 in out-of-pocket expenses at the beginning of the need for care.

- The policy would pay benefits for 2,820 days (8 years, minus the 100 days paid by Betty) for a total policy benefit payout of $1.35 million.

SUMMARY

By choosing the coverage recommended from using a *comprehensive planning approach,* Betty's policy will pay an extra $1 million in benefits over the policy recommended using a *single sales approach.*

The above example is a real life example of a client who purchased LTC insurance. It is for illustrative purposes only from the standpoint of claim's experience, since the client has yet to file a claim.

To make sure your long-term care plan accomplishes the desired results, we recommend that you review your plan at least annually with your financial advisor and/or your LTC insurance specialist.

CASE STUDY: SUMMARY OF PLAN DESIGN AND POTENTIAL RESULTS

	Single Sales Approach	Comprehensive Planning Approach
Education and Advice	Only enough to make the sale	Complete understanding of long-term care including: • Four options to pay for long-term care • Cost of care in area • Analysis of risk-tolerance philosophy
Consideration within Financial Objectives	Minor Emphasis	Major Emphasis
Carrier Comparison	None	Several top-rated carriers
Underwriting Class	Standard	Preferred
Benefit Amount	$100 per day	$120 per day
Elimination Period	0 days	100 days
Maximum Lifetime Benefit	Lifetime, Unlimited	Lifetime, Unlimited
Inflation Protection	No	Yes
Guaranteed Insurability Option	Yes	No
Policy Premiums Payable	For Life	For 10 Years
Annual Premium	$1,986	$3,511
Effective Premium After Tax Write-off	$1,450	$2,563
Cumulative Premium Paid at Hypothetical Claim's Time	$55,608	$35,110
Potential Policy Benefit Payout	$292,000	$1.35 Million
Potential Out-of-Pocket Expenses	$1.1 Million	$48,000

CHOOSING THE RIGHT COVERAGE: A CASE STUDY

KEY POINTS

■ Carefully consider the premium/benefit trade-off to make sure your premium dollars are used to design a plan that is well balanced and is likely to result in achieving your financial objectives.

■ For the best long-term care insurance plan, consult with a financial advisor or a long-term care insurance specialist trained in a *comprehensive planning approach.*

Chapter 12 Choosing the Right Insurance Carrier

We cannot direct the wind but we can adjust the sails.
— Vince Lombardi

Choosing the right LTC insurance carrier is the most important consideration in the LTC insurance planning process. All the other details of coverage discussed elsewhere in this book, including benefits, premium rates, tax advantages and more, are irrelevant if you do business with the wrong insurance company. That's because an insurance policy is no more and no less than a contract between the insurance carrier and the policyholder. At the time of claim, all the other components that make up the LTC insurance policy are insignificant compared to the commitment, integrity, and financial strength of the insurance company.

To better understand the importance of insurance carrier selection, we encourage you to read the Introduction to Part 3, *"History of the LTC Insurance Industry."* In that section, we offer a chronology of the LTC insurance industry and the problems that can arise when insurance carriers enter an area of risk they have not fully researched.

COMMITMENT TO THE MARKET

In recent years, a record number of insurance companies that had entered the LTC insurance market in the mid-1990s have decided to exit the market. Companies that exit the market must, by law, honor their current policyholders by keeping their coverage in force and paying claims.

Since an insurance company must honor all its existing policies even if it exits the market, it would seem that selecting the right insurance carrier would simply be a matter of choosing the company with the best benefits and the lowest premium. The danger in this approach lies in the fact that an insurance company will only remain

FAST FACTS:

■ When it comes to long-term care insurance, it's best to do business with the larger, more diversified companies.

■ Consider insurance carriers that have been in the long-term care insurance market for 10 years or longer.

■ Reasonableness of premium rates is a factor in selecting the proper carrier. Reasonable premium rates mean not too high, or too low.

■ Reasonableness in underwriting is one of the most important factors to look for in a carrier.

in markets that are profitable for the company. If an insurance company exits the LTC insurance market, the likelihood is very high that they underpriced premiums and issued coverage with underwriting standards that were too liberal. To compensate, the insurance company will usually begin to impose frequent and sometimes substantial rate increases on its existing policyholders. Since a high percentage of these existing policies have been in force for years, many policyholders may have developed health conditions that prohibit them from obtaining coverage from an alternate insurance carrier. These policyholders may now find that what was initially the lowest premium on the market is now the highest. Their choices are limited at this point: risk the likelihood of paying an increasingly higher premium in the future, or cancel the coverage and go without the insurance protection they had planned to use to pay for their long-term care expenses.

EVALUATING INSURANCE CARRIERS

History proves that most insurance companies that enter the LTC insurance market will not remain in it for an extended period of time. Therefore, the majority of insurance companies offering LTC insurance should be avoided. It's best to narrow your choice to only those companies that are highly committed to the industry and offer excellent service in today's market. Following are guidelines for choosing such companies.

Longevity in the Long-Term Care Insurance Industry

The longer a company has been in the LTC insurance business, the more likely they are to remain in the business. As a general guideline, it's best to do business with an insurance company that has been in the market for 10 years or longer.

Financial Ratings

Some insurance agents will tell you that financial ratings are not important. To the contrary, a strong financial rating is vital to the future of your investment in the coverage.

As a general guideline, if you are in excellent health you should only purchase coverage from a company with an **A Plus or higher** rating by the A.M. Best financial rating service. If you have minor health conditions and cannot be issued coverage with such a company, consider coverage with an **A** rated company. Never do business with an insurance company rated less than **A** by A.M. Best.

Although A.M. Best is one of the oldest and most common rating services, you may also want to ask your financial advisor and/or LTC insurance specialist about a company's rating with one of the other rating services listed at the end of this chapter.

Name Recognition of the Insurance Company

Recognizing the name of the insurance company being recommended is another indicator that the insurance carrier will remain committed to the market. While small companies with good financial ratings *may* be a safe place to invest your LTC insurance dollars, why take the chance? We recommend purchasing coverage from one of the larger, well-recognized names in the insurance industry. Insurance companies that have built name recognition and have protected a brand name over a number of decades are more likely to continue protecting the reputation of their name. These large name brand companies rarely make short-term decisions, such as casually entering and exiting a particular insurance market.

Rate Increase History

Long-term care insurance premium rates can be increased on existing policies if an insurance carrier can justify the rate increase to your state's insurance department. However, these rate increases cannot single out any individual policyholder. Premium rates can only be increased on a "class basis." This means that any premium rate increase must affect everyone in the state who purchased the same policy "form" from the insurance carrier requesting the rate increase. Rate increases are always issued on a percentage basis.

Since policies are subject to rate increases, always ask about the rate increase history of the insurance carrier being recommended. Some excellent insurance carriers have done such a good job with underwriting and pricing that no premium rate increases have ever been issued on existing policyholders. We recommend choosing a carrier that has had no rate increases on existing policyholders. If this is not an option, consider carriers that have had only one rate increase of 20 percent or less.

How Does the Premium Compare to the Premium of Other Insurance Carriers?

An insurance company should be chosen based on its ability to pay your future claim, not on its ability to market insurance.

This means that doing business with a company that has a lower-than-average premium rate could spell disaster for your future LTC insurance plan. This is one of the few industries in which shopping for the lowest price, combined with the greatest benefits, is not wise.

Why should you be concerned about a company with a lower-than-average premium rate? Because history shows that insurance carriers with rates lower than the average market premium will raise rates substantially in future years. Since no company operates in a vacuum, buying from the lowest price company will soon have you paying premium rates that are much higher than the industry average.

But we also do not recommend that you purchase coverage from an insurance carrier with the highest premium rates. "Reasonableness in premium rates" is a good indicator for determining which insurance carrier to trust with your LTC insurance plan.

Ask your financial advisor or LTC insurance specialist to show you premium rates from several companies. A general guideline is that the company being recommended should have rates that are within 15 percent of the other top-rated carriers.

How Easy is it to Get Coverage with this Company?

Underwriting is the "process of examining, accepting, or rejecting insurance risks, and then classifying those accepted in order to charge the proper amount of premium" (NAIC).

For people in good to excellent health, it's best to select an insurance carrier that is very stringent in their underwriting. Since you have maintained your good health, you should be rewarded by being insured in a "risk pool" of people who have also maintained their good health. Doing business with an insurance carrier with a stringent underwriting philosophy offers you the best strategy for stable LTC insurance coverage for decades to come. Stringent underwriting is a strong indication that the insurance carrier will be in an excellent position to pay your claim in the future and will be less likely to substantially raise your rates along the way.

Unfortunately, stringent underwriting guidelines present bad news for people in poor to fair health. But people in poor health are very fortunate if they can obtain LTC insurance at all. If current trends continue, it won't be long before people with health problems will not be able to obtain long-term care coverage from any insurance carrier.

RATING SERVICES

A.M. Best
Ambest Rd.
Oldwick, NJ 08858
908-439-2200
www.ambest.com
Provides ratings for insurance companies. No charge for company ratings. Full written reports are available for $35 per report. Free rating information is available via the company's website.

Demotech, Inc.
2941 Donnylane Blvd.
Columbus, OH 43235
1-800-354-7207
www.demotech.com
Provides financial stability ratings for insurance companies. There is a small fee to the insurance company being rated; information is free to consumers. Information needed: insurance company name. Free rating information is available via the company's website.

Fitch
55 E. Monroe St., Suite 3500
Chicago, IL 60603
1-800-853-4824
www.fitchratings.com
Provides ratings for 1–5 insurance companies over the phone at no charge. Information needed: insurance company name. A fee is charged to the insurance company being rated. Free rating information is available via the website.

Moody's Investors Services
99 Church St.
New York, NY 10007
212-553-0377
www.moodys.com
Provides ratings for 1–5 insurance companies per call at no charge. Information needed: insurance company name. Rating information is available via the company's website.

Standard and Poor's Corporation
55 Water St.
New York, NY 10041
212-438-2400
212-208-1527
www.standardandpoors.com/ ratings
Provides ratings for 1–5 insurance companies per call at no charge. Information needed: insurance company name. There is a small fee to the insurance company being rated. Free rating information is available via the company's website.

Weiss Research, Inc.
4176 Burns Rd., P.O. Box 109665
Palm Beach Gardens, FL 33410
1-800-289-9222
www.weissratings.com
Provides ratings for insurance companies. There is a $15 charge for a verbal rating (over the phone) for one company.

CHOOSING THE RIGHT INSURANCE CARRIER

KEY POINTS

- Choosing the right insurance carrier is the most important consideration in the long-term care insurance planning process.

- An insurance carrier must honor all existing policies for as long as premium payments are paid, even if the company exits the long-term care insurance market.

- Consider insurance companies that have been in the long-term care insurance market at least 10 years.

- Never do business with an insurance company rated less than an **"A"** by A.M. Best.

- Purchase coverage from one of the larger, well-recognized names in the insurance industry.

- Ask your financial advisor or long-term care insurance specialist to show you the rate increase history for the company they are recommending.

- Select an insurance carrier that issues coverage with stringent underwriting guidelines.

Chapter 13 The Application and Underwriting Process

Happiness is nothing more than good health and a bad memory.
— Albert Schweitzer (1875-1965)

Once you and your financial advisor or LTC insurance specialist have determined that LTC insurance is the best planning option for you, the next step is to apply for coverage. **The following information will explain the process for applying for coverage, and what to expect in the LTC insurance application and underwriting process:**

- **Complete the application.** The application includes personal information such as your name, date of birth, height, and weight. But more importantly, the application includes a series of health questions. The answers to these health questions, and the remainder of the process explained below, will determine whether or not you will be issued coverage, and if so, the premium rate you will pay.

  The application and a refundable deposit (usually one month's premium) are submitted to the insurance company's underwriting department. The underwriting department reviews the information on the application and determines your insurability.

- **Wait for the decision.** The insurance company may simply issue or decline the policy based on the information on the application. Although it has been common for underwriting to be this simple in the past, the underwriting process today is generally more complex and requires additional steps.

- **Verification of information on your application.** The next step is normally a telephone conversation between a member of the company's underwriting department and the applicant, to verify the information on the application. The company also uses this call to confirm that the applicant understands the type of coverage and benefit amounts for which he or she has applied.

- **Complete a physical exam.** After the phone interview, the underwriter may request a face-to-face physical. While it is becoming more common for companies to request physical exams, most companies limit the request to applicants above certain ages, usually age 65. Physical exams on younger applicants are normally requested at random.

  During the physical exam, a memory test for cognitive impairment will also be performed. This is a simple test, designed to assure that a person is not already developing memory problems, prior to the issuance of coverage.

FAST FACTS:

- Physical exams are normally performed on applicants 65 and older.

- The physical exam is paid for by the insurance company.

- The underwriter may request a written statement from your doctor or your actual medical records.

- If your application is declined with one company, you may still have alternative options with other companies.

The physical exam is paid for by the insurance company, and is scheduled at a place and time that is convenient for the applicant. No disrobing is required.

- **Request your medical records.** A last step in the underwriting process may include a request for a statement from your doctor, and/or a copy of your medical records.

Based on some or all of the information above, the underwriter will determine whether or not to issue coverage. If coverage is to be issued, the underwriter will also determine the premium amount. This means that the premium rate quoted by your financial advisor or LTC insurance specialist may be revised. The quotes provided by these professionals are based on "general underwriting guidelines," using the preliminary information you give to them about your health. While an LTC insurance specialist or financial advisor specifically trained in a *comprehensive planning approach* is usually able to accurately quote the premium amount, the underwriting process must be completed prior to knowing the final premium rate.

If the policy is issued, the agent or financial advisor once again explains the benefits and the final premium amount.

If you agree to the conditions of the policy, including the final premium amount, the coverage will be accepted and go into force. You have 30 days to decide whether or not to accept the policy—this is called the "free-look period." This 30-day period begins on the date you actually receive the policy. If you decide not to accept the policy within this 30-day period, the insurance company must refund the initial deposit submitted with the application and the policy is null and void.

If you accept the policy, you will be asked to select the frequency of your premium payments. Premium payments to the insurance company can be made on an annual, semi-annual, quarterly, or monthly basis. Generally, discounts are available for selecting longer durations between premium payments.

If your application is declined, you may still have alternative options to obtain coverage with other insurance companies.

THE APPLICATION AND UNDERWRITING PROCESS

KEY POINTS

- Physical exams are typically performed on applicants over age 65.

- The underwriting process must be completed in order to know the exact final premium rate.

- The "free-look period" gives you 30 days to decide whether or not to accept the policy once it is issued and received.

- Generally, discounts are available for selecting longer durations between premium payments.

Chapter 14 Submitting A Claim

Old age is not so bad when you consider the alternatives.

— Maurice Chevalier, *Actor*

HOW DO YOU BECOME ELIGIBLE FOR BENEFITS?

Like most insurance coverage, LTC insurance is coverage you hope to never use. But if a long-term care need does arise, you'll certainly appreciate having taken the time to plan ahead. It will then be time to collect benefits from the investment you made in coverage.

Just as with all types of insurance, LTC insurance pays benefits when an "insurable event" occurs. The insurable event with life insurance, for example, would be the death of the insured. The insurable event with an LTC insurance policy has to do with "needing assistance."

Specifically, there are two ways to become eligible for benefits with LTC insurance: Inability to perform the ADLs and/or cognitive impairment.

> ## ADLs
>
> People who have lost the ability to perform activities of daily living, also known as **ADLs,** may require long-term care services.
>
> **The list of ADLs includes:**
> - Bathing
> - Dressing
> - Toileting
> - Continence
> - Transferring (from bed to chair, etc.)
> - Eating

Inability to Perform ADLs

People who need long-term care services have lost their ability to live independently. Many times this is due to their inability to perform the activities of daily living, also known as ADLs. The need for ADL assistance can result from the frailty of aging, a deteriorating health problem, or an accident.

The ADL list shown above is listed in the order in which we typically lose them. This is the reverse order in which we learn them from birth.

FAST FACTS:

■ There are two ways to become eligible for benefits: 1) The inability to perform ADLs and/or 2) Cognitive impairment.

■ Care coordinators are independent of both insurance carriers and direct-care providers, so they can be objective and unbiased.

■ Care coordinators recommend care based on the insured's needs and develop a plan of care that coordinates available services.

At the time of claim, an ADL assessment will be performed. This process is used to determine the extent of your inability to function without assistance.

Recommendation

The best policies pay benefits if you are unable to perform only two or more ADLs without assistance. Never consider coverage that requires you to need help with more than two ADLs to become eligible for benefits. Especially beware of and avoid policies that might require you to lose three or more ADLs prior to collecting benefits for home care, or care in an Assisted Living Community, but only require you to lose two ADLs for nursing home confinement.

Cognitive Impairment

If loss of short-term or long-term memory or other cognitive impairment—such as judgment relating to safety—are severe enough that a person can no longer live independently, the policyholder may file a claim for benefits. This is regardless of whether or not a person is able to perform ADLs. Conditions such as the onset of Alzheimer's Disease are included in this category of cognitive impairment. If this is the reason for the claim, a cognitive assessment will be performed to determine the extent of the condition.

Once an ADL or cognitive impairment assessment is performed to determine eligibility, a "plan of care" is developed. This is such an important part of the process that we explain it in detail later in this chapter, under Care Coordination.

If you become eligible for benefits, your LTC insurance policy may also pay for "homemaking services" such as cooking, cleaning, and running errands. These services fall under the category of "Incidental Activities of Daily Living," or IADLs.

Important: You cannot receive IADL services unless you first become eligible for benefits by either losing your ability to perform

ADLs, or by cognitive impairment. LTC insurance will not pay for someone to clean, cook, and run errands for you unless you first have an insurable event and become eligible for benefits.

POLICY EXCLUSIONS

All LTC insurance policies contain exclusions. Exclusions include conditions which will prevent a policyholder from collecting benefits from the policy, even if they would have otherwise qualified for benefits.

Typical exclusions found in most policies include:

- Treatment or services for which no charge was made, with the exception of a cash method policy *(see Chapter 10: The Essentials of Long-Term Care Insurance).*
- If your care was paid for by another type of coverage. For example, if Medicare or your regular health insurance paid for your care, your LTC insurance policy would not pay duplicate benefits. Remember, Medicare, Medicare supplement insurance, or your regular health insurance do not pay for true long-term care—care provided beyond 100 days. But if you choose an elimination period of less than 100 days, and one of these sources *did* pay for your care during that time, your policy would not normally duplicate payment.
- War or acts of war.
- Alcoholism or drug addiction.
- Self-inflicted injuries or attempted suicide.

Beware of Mental Exclusion Clause

Some LTC insurance policies contain an exclusion that states that mental and nervous disorders will not be covered, unless the disorder is "Organically Demonstrable." Although most states have banned this exclusion in policies being issued today, be sure to read the policy exclusions section of any policy being recommended, to make sure this clause is not included. Avoid any policy that contains an exclusion of any kind for mental or nervous disorders.

SEEK ASSISTANCE WITH THE CLAIM'S PROCESS

The policyholder is rarely the person who must deal with the claim's process. It is normally the family. The family always learns at claim's time whether or not the policy was designed and priced to pay claims, or simply to make a sale. **Most insurance agents who sell LTC insurance want nothing to do with the claim's process for two reasons:**

1. It earns them no direct compensation, and
2. They must face a client, and become accountable for the outcome of the sale they made.

The agent, agency, or financial advisor who works with you when the LTC insurance policy is issued should always become involved in the claim's process. In fact, they should assist with the entire claim's process for the family, relieving them from as much of the paperwork and other claim details as they can. Prior to purchasing coverage from any financial advisor or agent, ask for evidence, in writing, that they have assisted other policyholders through the claim's process. Ask for references of those they have assisted, including phone numbers, and permission to call the policyholders. Then take the time to call these people who have had claims and received assistance from the agent, agency, or financial advisor. If the financial advisor or agent cannot supply you with such information, do not do business with this person. Anyone who cannot provide you with references of those who have had claims and claims assistance should not be involved in the LTC insurance planning process.

The claim's process requires that information from three sources be recorded onto the claim's forms: information from the policyholder, information from the provider (home care provider or facility), and information from the policyholder's physician. The information from these three sources must match perfectly or the claim will be delayed or denied. Your agent or financial advisor should assist in the collection of this information from these three sources, collect the claim forms, and confirm that the information matches before he or she submits the claim to the insurance company. Human beings make errors, and the last problem you and your family need to face at claim's time is a clerical error delaying payment of your claim.

WHAT IF YOUR CLAIM IS DENIED?

The likelihood of a legitimate LTC insurance claim being denied is rare today, because most states have passed laws mandating high penalties for insurance companies caught denying legitimate claims. If your financial advisor or LTC insurance specialist has been properly trained in a *comprehensive planning approach,* they will be aware of these laws. Additionally, their involvement in the claim's process will be extra assurance that the insurance company will not deny a legitimate claim.

However, if you feel a legitimate claim has been denied, ask your advisor or LTC insurance specialist for assistance in contacting your state insurance department where you can file a complaint against the company. The person who sold you the coverage must, by law, supply this information to you upon request.

CARE COORDINATION

A little known benefit to owning LTC insurance is the Care Coordination benefit. Care Coordination is a value-added benefit that provides assistance to family members at a very critical time. This benefit has increasingly become standard in most policies, but be sure to confirm that any policy you purchase includes this benefit. All other aspects being equal, LTC insurance policies that offer a Care Coordination benefit are far superior to policies that do not. In addition to relieving family members of the burden of trying to juggle multiple caregivers, the Care Coordination benefit may also extend the benefits of an LTC insurance policy by developing a coordinated plan for efficiently utilizing informal and formal care.

Care Coordination is defined as *a service that helps manage the coordination of a person's care among all the parties involved.* These parties may include the people currently in the policyholder's circle of support: a spouse and close relatives, including sons and daughters, neighbors, and friends. It may also include paid caregivers, facilities, health care practitioners, and social workers. Care Coordinators are usually health care practitioners who are able to quickly and comprehensively assess the individual needs of a patient, identify the level of care needed, and assist the family in obtaining that care.

One of the major benefits of using a Care Coordinator has to do with their experience in the practical aspects of long-term care. Because the Care Coordinator is familiar with long-term care providers in the area, they can help reduce the time it takes a family and policyholder to screen and select qualified provider(s) that fit the personal needs of the patient. This frees up family members to provide the emotional support needed by their family member in need of care, instead of spending their time researching and interviewing potential providers.

A Care Coordinator is sometimes known as a *Care Manager.* Your insurance company may recommend a Care Coordinator or Care Manager to you, or you may seek the services of an independent agency specializing in care management.

Care Coordination should not be confused with "managed care." The services recommended by a Care Coordinator are strictly optional and not required. The insured and/or their family may choose to hire providers other than those recommended by the Care Coordinator *(for more specifics on the difference, see the experts interview in the last section of this chapter).*

The Care Coordination process involves two main steps:

1. **Conduct an initial assessment.** Visit and interview the person needing care, their circle of support, and the patient's physician to determine the patient's needs. This evaluation may include a physical and cognitive assessment, assessment of social and emotional state of mind, functional capabilities, and living arrangements.

2. **Develop a Plan of Care.** After assessing the policyholder's needs, the Care Coordinator will look at the current resources available and link the patient to a full range of appropriate services. A **plan of care** will become a written description of the formal and informal needs of the patient, the frequency and duration of the care, and the cost of care. This **plan of care** is developed with the participation of the policyholder, the policyholder's family, and the policyholder's physician. **The plan of care specifically documents the following information:**

    • The type of care that is needed

- Where the care can be received
- A recommendation of quality providers
- How much the care will cost
- Any other available alternatives

In addition, the Care Coordinator may perform other functions such as:

- Provide the certification required to satisfy potential requirements from the doctor or insurance company.
- Provide ongoing monitoring of services and the plan of care, and provide reassessment as needed. This would include development of transitional plans. For example, providing assistance if a patient must be moved from their home to an assisted living community.
- Document and maintain records
- Intervene during a crisis
- Manage nutrition and diet
- Coordinate bill-paying services

A MAJOR BENEFIT TO OWNERS OF LONG-TERM CARE INSURANCE

At claim's time, the services of a Care Coordinator may turn out to be an LTC insurance benefit that is just as important as the monetary benefits paid by the policy.

Insurance companies offering LTC insurance are beginning to locate and contract with providers who have demonstrated high-quality work and ethics. It's very likely that a provider approved and recommended by an LTC insurance company will provide better care than one who is not. In fact, in the future, a lack of quality providers in the general population may be a major benefit of owning an LTC insurance policy. Policyholders may have better access to high-quality providers who wish to maintain relationships with insurance companies because the work and payment processes are more secure.

This will become increasingly important in future years, as the baby boom generation reaches maturity. In 1970, as the baby boomers first began to reach adulthood, there were 21 potential caregivers for every 1 person potentially in need of care. By 2030, this number is estimated to be 6 potential caregivers for every 1 person potentially in need of care (The Institute for Health and Aging, University of California).

LONG-TERM CARE COORDINATORS: AN INTERVIEW WITH EXPERTS

Featured Experts:
- **Susan Westerman,** *HIA (Claims Manager)* and
- **Pat Pannone, RN, BSN, MPH, CMC** *(Care Coordination Manager)* with ERC Long-Term Care Solutions, Third Party Administrator and LTCI Reinsure

This is a paraphrased interview conducted by Jesse R. Slome, CLU, ChFC, Publisher/Editor in Chief, **Long-Term Care Insurance Sales Strategies Magazine, Vol. 4, No. 4, www.ltcsales.com** *and reprinted with permission (Slome 2002).*

SLOME: Why are some people concerned when they hear about the Care Coordination feature of an LTC insurance policy?

PANNONE: It is natural to be concerned because many associate the LTC insurance coordination feature with medical case management common to health insurance. Many people have experienced a hospitalization where they were introduced to someone called a case manager who basically is a discharge planner. Or, they've had contact with a case manager associated with their health insurer who is in a utilization review role. These functions are distinctly different from the geriatric Care Coordinator's role associated with LTC insurance. But, it is natural for consumers to be unfamiliar or initially uncomfortable with the process of Care Coordination because of the similarity in the names "care management," also known as "Care Coordination," and "case manager."

SLOME: So, the Care Coordination component of LTC insurance is different. How so?

PANNONE: Long-term care insurance Care Coordination is a benefit to the insured, and is stated as such in the policy. It is a consumer-focused service that links and coordinates assistance from both formal and family/community service providers to enable policyholders with chronic functional and/or cognitive limitations to reach optimal independence for their conditions.

The coordinator has special long-term care experience and knowledge to guide chronically ill people and their families to needed care. They are licensed health care professionals such as a registered nurse or medical social worker. They are skilled in conducting a face-to-face "best practice" comprehensive assessment and sensitively working with both the insured and family members. They will develop a needs-based plan of care, arrange services, monitor and revise the plan over time, and periodically complete a face-to-face reassessment. The coordinator who meets with the insured can also complete certification of the individual as being chronically ill.

Care Coordinators are independent of both insurance carriers and direct care providers, so they can be as objective and unbiased as possible. They do not determine or pay benefits. The claim analyst interprets the policy and determines benefits based upon the Care Coordinator's recommendations.

SLOME: When is the Care Coordinator engaged?

WESTERMAN: From the beginning of the claim. Typically, a spouse or family member calls the administrator at the insurance company to file a claim. The administrator arranges for the Care Coordinator company to contact the insured for a face-to-face assessment appointment. This is done at a time that is convenient to the insured and family members who wish to be present. The initial assessment is typically done at the insured's home. But at the request of the policyholder and family, the visit could take place in any setting.

SLOME: If you were paying for these care coordination services on an independent basis, what would it cost?

PANNONE: A geriatric Care Coordinator/Care Manager typically charges anywhere from $85 to $100 an hour, depending upon expertise and region of the country. So, the total cost of these services, including assessment, care plan development, service arrangement, monitoring, and periodic on-site reassessment could cost several hundred dollars a year.

WESTERMAN: And, it's important to note that the cost of Care Coordination is part of the LTC insurance benefit. It's an incredibly valuable benefit for the LTC insurance policyholder.

SLOME: Do Care Coordinators know the provisions of the claimant's LTC insurance policy?

PANNONE: No, the Care Coordinator does not know the individual's policy information prior to the initial assessment. They recommend care based on the insured's needs, regardless of the policy benefits. But if the Care Coordinator learns that there is a recommended setting or type of care not covered under the insured's policy, the Care Coordinator may assist in creating an alternate plan of care as the policy allows, or find other payers or cost-conscious alternatives to preserve the insured's resources.

SLOME: Can you share an example of how a coordinator assisted the insured or the family?

PANNONE: A lot of what the Care Coordinator does is to support or empower family caregivers, to prevent fatigue and burnout that can lead to the insured's premature move to a facility.

One case was a stressed 81-year-old woman caring for her husband with Parkinson's and heart problems. He had ADL deficiencies with bathing and dressing, and also was memory-impaired. They didn't want to have strangers come to their home. The coordinator recommended they consider an adult day center, explaining the available local resources that could help their situation.

In some cases, the coordinator might also recommend safety bars in the bathroom or a life-call system. If the insured requires a skilled-care facility, the coordinator can see if there are viable ways to have the individual return home as soon as possible to receive care.

Care Coordination is a benefit that the policyholder can receive during the elimination period. The Care Coordinator often works with the insured or family members during the elimination period to find options that could be less costly. Accessing this benefit during the elimination period is a value-added benefit of LTC insurance.

SUBMITTING A CLAIM

KEY POINTS

- The best long-term care insurance policies pay benefits if you are unable to perform only two ADLs without assistance.

- Policy exclusions that prevent a policyholder from collecting benefits include treatment for services for which no charge was made, and self-inflicted injuries.

- Your financial advisor or long-term care insurance specialist should always become involved in the claim's process. Ask for references of people who have placed claims and used the services of the advisor or agent you are working with.

- You can file a complaint through your state insurance department if you feel a legitimate claim has been denied.

- Care Coordination is a service that coordinates a person's care among all the parties involved.

- Long-term care insurance policyholders might have better access to high-quality, high-demand caregivers because these providers wish to maintain relationships with insurance companies who can provide them with steady work and guaranteed payment.

PART FOUR

Incentives for Purchasing Long-Term Care Insurance

To me, old age is
fifteen years older than I am.

— Bernard M. Baruch (1870-1965)
Presidential Advisor

PART 4:
Incentives for Purchasing
Long-Term Care Insurance

As our government, employers, professional organizations and financial institutions begin to fully recognize the coming long-term care crisis, we will see more and more incentives to plan ahead for long-term care. Planning ahead with LTC insurance offers incentives through tax-qualified plans, state-sponsored Partnership Programs, and group and sponsored LTC insurance plans offered through employers, associations, financial institutions and other groups. You can learn more about these programs—their advantages and disadvantages—in the following three chapters.

Chapter 15
Tax Advantages of Long-Term Care Insurance

I feel very honored to pay taxes in America.
The thing is, I could probably feel
just as honored for about half the price.

— Arthur Godfrey

Rarely does a year pass without our federal and state governments experiencing budgetary constraints. These budgetary challenges will only get worse as the aging population grows due to increased life expectancies, combined with the expected trend of baby boomers taking early retirement.

In recent years, federal and state governments have been sending stronger messages that public programs to pay for the costs of long-term care will decrease in the years ahead. The federal government continues to commission studies to research ways to finance the long-term care needs of our current senior population, and 76 million aging baby boomers.

But there is a pervasive fear among legislators that the baby boom generation does not understand that public programs cannot be relied upon to pay for long-term care. To help alleviate part of this problem, incentives are being put in place to encourage people to purchase private LTC insurance. Our legislators are convinced that LTC insurance must play a major role in financing long-term care.

Hoping to encourage more people to invest in coverage, the federal government and some states have granted tax advantages to the owners of certain types of policies.

Before explaining these tax advantages, it's important to understand the difference between policies that have been granted guaranteed tax status and those that have not.

HIPAA OF 1996 DEFINES TAX-QUALIFIED LONG-TERM CARE INSURANCE POLICIES

Prior to 1996, the lack of standardization in LTC insurance policies made them very difficult for the average consumer to understand. **While many consumers did purchase coverage, an equal number of people failed to purchase LTC insurance for two major reasons:**

1. A lack of understanding about long-term care in general; and
2. The confusing language and eligibility requirements of LTC insurance policies.

In 1996, much of the confusion was eliminated. The Health Insurance Portability and Accountability Act of 1996 (HIPAA) was signed into law and became effective on January 1, 1997. HIPAA created a long-needed standardization of LTC insurance policies, by creating policies known as tax-qualified (TQ) insurance.

Passage of this legislation also had many positive effects on other areas of the health insurance system. But many experts believe the most significant impact of the legislation was the legitimization of LTC insurance. HIPAA sent clear messages that (1) our government believes that it cannot finance long-term care and (2) LTC insurance will play a major role in financing long-term care.

FAST FACTS:

■ The number of people receiving Social Security benefits between now and 2050 will rise by **100%** while the number of workers will only increase by **22%**.

■ In 1940, there were 42 workers for every retiree; today, there are only 3 for every retiree. By 2050, this ratio is expected to be 2 to 1.

From a practical standpoint, the HIPAA legislation created LTC insurance policies that were much easier to understand. Tax-qualified policies contain clear, easy-to-understand language with standardized consumer protections that are a part of every policy. At the time of claim, TQ policies contain the most standardized and objective criteria for determining eligibility for accessing benefits.

Equally important is the standardization and clarification of the tax advantages of TQ policies. HIPAA clarified that the benefits collected on TQ policies are guaranteed tax-free. In addition, it also grants tax deductibility of premiums. Prior to HIPAA legislation, the tax consequences of collecting on an LTC insurance policy were unclear and premiums were not tax deductible.

NON-TAX-QUALIFIED POLICIES DO NOT MEET HIPAA DEFINITIONS

It is possible to purchase LTC insurance that is non-tax-qualified (NTQ). These policies do not meet HIPAA definitions for LTC insurance. They are less standardized and the tax treatment has not been firmly established.

Since HIPAA legislation, there has been an ongoing debate about the differences between NTQ and TQ long-term care insurance policies. Although some insurance agents claim that NTQ policies are less restrictive at the time of claim, we do not believe this is the case, especially for true long-term care needs—care needed for more than 100 days.

In our opinion, because of the lack of standardization, NTQ policies should be avoided. NTQ policies may contain language that allows an insurance company too much discretion in determining eligibility for benefits. In fact, most reputable insurance companies today only offer TQ policies.

If you purchased an LTC insurance policy prior to January 1, 1997, when HIPAA legislation went into effect, your policy was "grandfathered in" to tax-qualified status. This means that policies issued prior to this date enjoy HIPAA protections with regard to the tax advantages, even though the legislation was not in force at the time the coverage was purchased. This is true as long as you make no *material changes* to your policy. An example of a *material change* would be making application to the insurance carrier to increase the benefits of your existing policy.

CAUTION: Never replace or request a modification to an LTC insurance policy you purchased in the past without consulting your financial advisor and/or LTC insurance specialist *(for more information on replacing an existing policy, see Part 5: Questions and Answers).*

The remainder of this section will focus on the specific tax advantages of TQ long-term care insurance policies.

FEDERAL TAX ADVANTAGES TAKE THE FORM OF A TAX DEDUCTION

As of 2005, the federal government does not offer a tax *credit* to owners of LTC insurance. This has been seriously discussed in

Congress, and is being encouraged by prestigious organizations such as the American Medical Association. Most experts believe a federal tax credit will be offered in the future.

The federal government does offer tax advantages for owners of TQ long-term care insurance in the form of a tax *deduction.* Your filing status determines the rules for your federal income tax deduction.

Individuals (Non-Self-Employed) Use Form 1040 Schedule A

For individuals, premiums for LTC insurance may be deducted as a medical expense on your federal tax return, but only if you itemize on Form 1040 Schedule A. The total amount of medical expenses added to your LTC insurance premium must exceed 7.5 percent of your adjusted gross income. The amount in excess of 7.5 percent can then be deducted from your adjusted gross income, up to a maximum eligibility amount *(see the Maximum Eligibility chart on the next page).*

Few individuals benefit from this tax break. A person spending as much as 7.5 percent of their adjusted gross income on medical expenses is not likely to be healthy enough to pass LTC insurance underwriting and be issued LTC insurance. However, if a policyholder's health declined after the policy was issued, and they began to incur significant health care expenses, this deduction could become beneficial.

Self-Employed Individuals, S-Corporations and LLCs

Self-employed individuals, S-Corporations, and LLCs enjoy more favorable tax advantages. These entities can deduct LTC insurance premiums for policies purchased for owners, employees and others. For example, they can deduct premiums paid for LTC insurance for a spouse or other tax dependents, such as parents. If the parents are not dependents, the business owner may still enjoy a tax deduction if the parents are employees of the company. A tax deduction can also be made for premiums paid for any employees working for the company, and the employees' relatives.

The deduction is taken as a health insurance premium expense (Internal Revenue Code section 162(I) on line 30, Form 1040). This means that the premium is deductible, regardless of whether or not you itemize deductions. Premiums are subject to self-employment tax.

Although premiums are deductible for these business entities there are limits to the tax deduction. The amount of the deduction is based on the age of the policyholder. The *Maximum Eligibility* chart at right shows the age ranges and amount of deductible premium as of 2005. This amount increases annually.

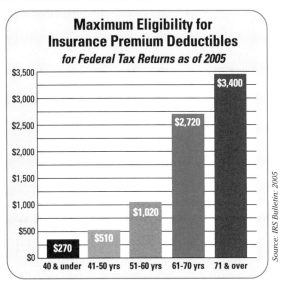

Maximum Eligibility for Insurance Premium Deductibles
for Federal Tax Returns as of 2005

40 & under: $270 · 41-50 yrs: $510 · 51-60 yrs: $1,020 · 61-70 yrs: $2,720 · 71 & over: $3,400

Source: IRS Bulletin: 2005

C-Corporations

Many employers are searching for ways to reward key employees and reduce the caregiver workload for employees caring for loved ones. LTC insurance is one way to provide this dual benefit, and the tax advantages to C-Corporations are substantial.

C-Corporations can pay all or a portion of LTC insurance premiums for employees selected to receive this benefit. The tax advantage to the employer is the deductibility of the full amount of the company's portion of the premium paid as a reasonable and necessary business expense. If the employee pays part or all of the premium, the employee is subject to the rules discussed above for "non-self-employed individuals" for his or her portion of the premium paid.

LTC insurance can be beneficial from a tax standpoint for both the employer and the employee. The employer creates a tax-deductible benefit for the company; and if the employee has a long-term care claim, the benefits paid from the policy are not counted as part of the employee's compensation. Many companies have also found that offering LTC insurance as an additional benefit can help attract and retain good employees.

Employers who wish to purchase LTC insurance for their employees are allowed to choose which employees receive the benefit. There is no requirement to purchase coverage for every employee.

Coverage purchased with a "Limited Pay" option is a popular choice for business owners and corporations of all entities. This option is explained in *Part 5: Questions & Answers.*

Caution: Anyone considering offering LTC insurance as a benefit to employees should first read *Chapter 17: Group and Sponsored Long-Term Care Insurance.*

STATE TAX INCENTIVES FOR LONG-TERM CARE INSURANCE

Many state governments are beginning to offer tax incentives to owners of TQ long-term care insurance policies. Unlike the federal government, some states do offer a tax credit, while others simply offer an income tax deduction. Credits can be substantial because a tax credit directly reduces the amount of taxes you owe. When a state offers a tax credit for owners of LTC insurance, the tax credit is normally a percentage of the total premium paid.

A chart of the current tax advantages by state can be found in the Appendix. States not listed on the chart do not currently offer a tax advantage, but that can change from year to year.

We advise you to consult with your financial advisor and/or tax advisor to fully understand the tax ramifications that LTC insurance will have on your specific situation.

TAX ADVANTAGES OF LONG-TERM CARE INSURANCE

KEY POINTS

- Lawmakers are concerned that Americans are not doing enough to plan ahead for long-term care.

- HIPAA of 1996 defined tax-qualified policies and standardized long-term care insurance policies.

- Most reputable insurance companies today only offer tax-qualified long-term care insurance policies.

- Policies purchased before January 1997 were granted tax-qualified status and will remain tax-qualified unless you make a material change to your policy.

- All federal tax advantages for long-term care insurance premiums are in the form of a tax deduction.

- Some states offer a tax deduction for long-term care insurance premiums; others offer a more powerful tax incentive: a tax credit.

Chapter 16 Partnership Programs

*The significant problems we face
cannot be solved at the same level of
thinking we were at when we created them.*

— Albert Einstein

In addition to tax incentives available from state and federal governments, four states are currently offering an additional financial incentive to purchase LTC insurance. The incentive is known as the **"Partnership for Long-Term Care Program."** It is aimed at solving at least part of the budgetary problems caused by the need for long-term care.

The four states currently offering Partnership Programs are: California, Indiana, Connecticut, and New York. If you live in one of these four states, ask your financial advisor or LTC insurance specialist to explain the details of the Partnership Program to you, and to recommend whether or not a Partnership policy would be suitable for you. In most cases, Partnership policies are a very good value, and if one is available in your state, you should definitely investigate the details of the program if LTC insurance is the option you chose for planning for long-term care.

Although legislation is being discussed that would make Partnership policies available in most states, for the time being, the Omnibus Budget Reconciliation Act of 1993 (OBRA 1993) is severely restricting the expansion of the Partnership Program into other states. However, the success of the Partnership Program in the original four states has encouraged several states to seek waivers to those restrictions that would allow them to offer Partnership policies.

If you do not live in one of the states listed above, ask your financial advisor or LTC insurance specialist if a Partnership Program has become available in your state since the publication of this book.

HISTORY AND OBJECTIVES OF THE PARTNERSHIP PROGRAM

In 1986, the Robert Wood Johnson Foundation, a charitable organization instrumental in the development of the Partnership Program, generously gave grants to 10 states to fund the study of long-term care delivery and financing. A major objective of the grants was to assist states in developing solutions to the problem of funding long-term care for an increasing number of aging Americans. The outcome of these grants and studies was the creation of the **Partnership for Long-Term Care Program.** This program uses a combination of public and private dollars to pay for long-term care.

The Partnership Program has the following objectives:
- To make LTC insurance more readily available to consumers.
- To reduce consumers' fears of impoverishment due to long-term care.
- To improve consumers' understanding of the challenges of financing long-term care.
- To cap the use of public expenditures in financing long-term care.

HOW DOES EACH PARTNERSHIP PROGRAM WORK?

Partnership Programs allow people to shelter some or all of their assets by combining the purchase of private LTC insurance with future eligibility for Medicaid, the welfare program (Medi-Cal in California). If a person owns an LTC insurance policy certified through the Partnership Program, qualifying for Medicaid would not require the usual "spend-down" rules that normally impoverish a family. Some of these Medicaid rules are discussed in *Chapter 4.*

In all states where a Partnership Program is in place, the programs conceptually work the same way. Purchasing a Partnership policy allows the policyholder to keep some or all of their assets, instead of totally depleting them to pay for long-term care expenses. The Partnership Program policies are private LTC insurance, underwritten by a select few, high-quality insurance companies. When a person needs long-term care, they first use their Partnership policy coverage to pay for long-term care expenses. When the benefits of the policy are depleted, the policyholder may then become eligible for Medicaid—without having to spend-down all their assets.

All other things being equal, Partnership Program LTC insurance is more valuable than traditional LTC insurance. This is true, even if the policyholder elects to purchase the "unlimited benefit maximum." In our opinion, the fact that the Partnership Program insurance companies must go through a stringent approval process in order to offer Partnership policies indicates a major commitment by these companies to the LTC insurance industry.

The Partnership Programs in California, Connecticut, and Indiana are based on a **dollar-for-dollar** model of coverage. Under this model, for every dollar of LTC insurance coverage that the consumer purchases under the Partnership Program, a dollar of assets is protected from the spend-down requirements for Medicaid eligibility. Connecticut offers an extra incentive, by requiring that facilities offer Partnership policyholders a five percent discount off their published daily room rates.

The New York Partnership Program is based on a different model: the **total-assets protection** model. Partnership Certified policies must cover at least three years in a facility or six years of home care, with minimum daily benefit amounts that are raised annually. Once the Partnership policy benefits are exhausted, the Medicaid eligibility process will not consider the policyholder's assets. Protection would be granted for an unlimited amount of assets. However, an individual's income must contribute to the cost of care.

Like Partnership Programs in the other three states, the goal of the New York Partnership is to help people finance long-term care without impoverishing themselves or losing their life savings. At the same time, the program will also help to reduce New York's massive Medicaid tax expenditure. Twenty percent of all purchasers of LTC insurance in New York are taking advantage of the Partnership Program.

Example of How a Partnership Policy Might Work

If a purchaser wants to protect $250,000 in non-exempt assets, he or she might purchase a Partnership Program policy with a maximum lifetime benefit of $250,000. When the policyholder becomes eligible for benefits, the insurer will cover long-term care expenses up to $250,000, plus any inflation-adjusted benefits due to the inflation protection benefit of the policy. After that sum is paid out by the insurance company, the policyholder would then receive Medicaid benefits, but still protect assets up to the dollar amount paid by the policy. This essentially allows Partnership Program participants to receive government assistance without losing all of their assets, *if* they purchase a Partnership LTC insurance policy first.

Standardized Requirements of a Partnership Policy

The Partnership Programs also have standardized requirements that make them a unique consideration:

- All Partnership Programs must include inflation protection.
- All agents who offer the Partnership Programs must be specifically trained and receive Partnership Certification.
- Partnership Programs in most states are required to include Care Coordination, which may assist the policyholder in locating services *(see Chapter 14: Submitting a Claim).*
- Claims may be made on Partnership policies even if the policyholder leaves the state in which the policy was issued. However, in order to access the asset protection component of the policy, the claimant would need to move back to the issuing state. The exception is Indiana and Connecticut: in 2001, these two states adopted a reciprocity program.
- Most Partnership Programs offer protection against unreasonable rate increases.
- If for any reason a state decides to discontinue the Partnership Program, all in-force policies will remain in force for as long as premiums are paid.

At the time of this publication, over 150,000 people have purchased policies under Partnership Programs. Many experts believe that programs similar to the Partnership Program, ones that combine private insurance with public financing, offer the most promising solution to the huge challenge of providing long-term care for an increasing number of aging Americans.

For more insight into the philosophy and future of the Partnership Program, see *Chapter 19* for an interview with Dr. James Knickman, Vice-President of Research and Evaluation at the Robert Wood Johnson Foundation.

PARTNERSHIP PROGRAMS

KEY POINTS

- At the time of this publication, Partnership Programs are offered by only four states; however, legislation may soon make them available in more states.

- Partnership Programs use a combination of private and public dollars to pay for long-term care.

- Under a Partnership Program, policyholders can keep some or all of their assets and still qualify for Medicaid. Long-term care insurance is used first to pay for long-term care expenses. When the policy benefits are depleted, the policyholder becomes eligible for Medicaid without having to spend down all their assets.

- Many experts believe that programs such as the Partnership Program offer the most promising solution to the long-term care crisis.

Chapter 17
Group and Sponsored Long-Term Care Insurance

Nothing assures disaster like the group mentality.

— Allen Hamm

Many companies and business owners are voluntarily educating their employees about the need for long-term care planning and even offering LTC insurance as a benefit. Some companies have learned that offering LTC insurance to key employees can help attract and retain good employees. In a study conducted by LifePlans, Inc, it was learned that LTC insurance benefits clearly reduce the caregiver workload for employees caring for loved ones.

LTC insurance can be obtained not only through your employer, but also through an association, financial institution, or other group. **Coverage offered through a "group" falls into one of two categories:**

- **"True"** group LTC insurance
- **"Sponsored"** LTC insurance

Some people in the industry promote the myth that group and sponsored coverage is a good value in every situation. We believe

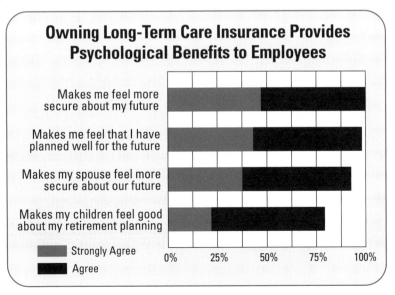

Owning Long-Term Care Insurance Provides Psychological Benefits to Employees

FAST FACTS:

- **62%** of employers solicited by agents about offering long-term care insurance to their employees believed that agents do not truly understand the issue of long-term care.

- The number one reason for purchasing group long-term care insurance is the employee's belief that they face a greater-than-average risk of requiring long-term care.

that there are some people who can benefit from group and sponsored programs, but that LTC insurance marketed with this approach should never be *automatically* purchased. In many cases, you will receive a better value by purchasing individually issued, non-sponsored LTC insurance. Prior to considering coverage offered at your workplace, association, bank, or any other type of group or sponsored promotion, we encourage you to read the information in this chapter, and to seek the advice of your financial advisor.

TAX ADVANTAGES

In Chapter 15, we discussed the tax advantages of LTC insurance and the fact that there can be significant tax advantages for employers who offer coverage as an employee benefit. For example, some companies may deduct 100 percent of the premium, while the benefits paid on a claim are not subject to taxation.

The most significant tax advantages available to employers are for benefits that qualify for Section 125, "Cafeteria Plan" status. Unfortunately, long-term care insurance **DOES NOT** qualify as a benefit under Section 125. This means that LTC insurance cannot be purchased with pre-tax dollars under an employer-provided cafeteria plan. This is a significant shortfall in LTC insurance as an employee benefit and explains one of the reasons why offering coverage is not as attractive to employers as you might expect.

Still, group and sponsored coverage may be a good benefit under certain circumstances. This chapter will discuss the advantages and disadvantages of considering such programs.

LONG-TERM CARE INSURANCE THROUGH YOUR WORKPLACE

Long-term care insurance can be offered through the workplace either through a "true" group program or a "sponsored" program.

Group Long-Term Care Insurance

The basic factors that affect the premium of individually issued LTC insurance *(explained in Chapter 10)* are also true with group LTC insurance. However, group LTC insurance contains some distinct disadvantages compared to individually issued coverage.

These disadvantages include:

1. People most suited for LTC insurance are learning to integrate the long-term care planning process into their total financial plan. The group market is championed by traditional insurance agents who are normally not familiar with financial planning. Most often, they sell LTC insurance as a stand-alone insurance product, outside the context of your total financial objectives. As explained throughout this book, your financial advisor is in the best position to help you with long-term care planning, and the best approach is to use a *comprehensive planning approach.* Many company decision-makers are aware of the fact that traditional agents are not the best resource for long-term care planning. According to a study conducted in 2001, 62 percent of employers who are solicited by agents about LTC insurance for their employees believe that agents do not truly understand the entire long-term care planning process, but are simply trying to sell insurance.

2. Group coverage normally uses a "cookie-cutter" approach to coverage. In order to assist agents in making sales, insurance companies many times narrow the benefit choices to a few simple options, leaving little possibility for a customized plan that addresses your unique situation.

3. Unlike most types of group insurance coverage, group LTC insurance is usually more expensive, not less expensive (when comparing identical benefits), than individually issued coverage.

Adverse Selection

Disadvantage number three is due to a problem called **Adverse Selection.**

Group LTC insurance is normally issued with health underwriting standards that are not as strict as individually issued coverage. This results in group LTC insurance being issued to many people who are already in poor health.

Specifically, group LTC insurance is normally issued on either a **Guaranteed Issue** basis, or a **Modified Guaranteed Issue** basis. **Guaranteed Issue** means that any employee, regardless of health, will be accepted for coverage without being required to pass any underwriting requirements. **Modified Guaranteed Issue** means that some people in very poor health may not qualify, but as long as a person can certify that they are not currently needing long-term care services, or as long as they have not been diagnosed with a major health condition that will likely require long-term care in the near future, they will likely be issued coverage.

Adverse Selection results in the issuance of LTC insurance to individuals who would not normally pass typical underwriting requirements. This results in a substantially higher than normal number of claims than in a pool of policyholders who were issued coverage under strict underwriting requirements. Healthy people who purchase coverage through the group offering may end up subsidizing the premiums of people in poor health.

Adverse Selection results in group LTC insurance usually being more expensive than individually issued policies. It also increases the likelihood of premium rate increases in the future.

Adverse Selection is made worse because group LTC insurance is normally offered on a voluntary basis. Group programs largely attract individuals who are already in poor health and know they can't obtain LTC insurance any other way. A study conducted in 2001 among buyers and non-buyers of group LTC insurance revealed that the number one reason for purchasing group coverage was the employee's belief that they face a greater-than-average risk of needing long-term care. (HIAA 2001) This is not good news for healthy people who purchase coverage through the group.

If you are in good to excellent health, you are normally wise to avoid group LTC insurance because:

1. You may be subsidizing a higher premium for those who are not healthy.
2. The poor health of many participants increases the chance of premium rate increases in future years.

3. You will obtain better results using a *comprehensive planning approach.* The insurance agent offering the group program will likely use a *single sales approach.*

For most people, an individually issued policy results in a better value than a group issued LTC insurance policy. But there is an exception.

When to Consider Group Long-Term Care Insurance

There is one situation when group LTC insurance is worth considering. If your financial advisor has recommended LTC insurance, but your health is not good enough to qualify for individually issued coverage, you may want to carefully consider group coverage. It's important to work with your financial advisor when evaluating the pros and cons of such a decision. If you and your advisor decide the group offering is appropriate, work with your advisor to select the most appropriate benefits within the "cookie cutter" group policy options, so that the result is as close as possible to a customized solution.

When evaluating this decision, it's imperative that you consider the financial rating of the insurance company issuing the group coverage. As explained in Chapter 12, it's important to have coverage with a company rated **A** or higher with A.M. Best. An insurance company with a rating lower than **A** that offers a Guaranteed Issue or Modified Guaranteed Issue group LTC insurance policy has higher odds of experiencing financial problems. This could compromise your ability to receive benefits after paying the premiums for a number of years. Almost as detrimental, the carrier is more likely to impose such frequent and substantial rate increases that the coverage becomes unaffordable.

But, for those with health conditions and no other choices for obtaining LTC insurance, group coverage may be worth considering.

SPONSORED LONG-TERM CARE INSURANCE

As an alternative to *true* group LTC insurance, your employer or other group may offer a *sponsored* program.

Sponsored programs offer a better value for healthy people than group LTC insurance policies. Since they use the same strict underwriting guidelines as individually issued policies, sponsored programs are not likely to experience the adverse selection problems of group LTC insurance programs.

Insurance companies offer sponsored LTC insurance policies that are marketed by agents, or through marketing campaigns over the phone, by internet, or through the mail.

Sponsored LTC insurance programs may also be offered by your financial institution, such as a credit union or bank, Chamber of Commerce, professional association, senior association, or some other group. These programs work the same way as sponsored programs offered by your employer.

One advantage of a sponsored offering is a possible discount on the premium. These discounts are normally in the range of 5 to 10 percent.

There are several disadvantages of sponsored LTC insurance:

1. There is normally only one insurance company involved in the offering. This means that you forfeit the opportunity to compare and choose coverage offered by several different insurance carriers.

2. You're limited to the narrow coverage options offered by that one company. A plan offered by another carrier might give you more appropriate coverage options for your unique situation.

3. The discounted premium offered through a sponsored program may actually be higher than the normal premium rate with an alternative insurance company. Ask your financial advisor or LTC insurance specialist for premium rates and benefits among several top-rated insurance carriers, prior to considering a sponsored offering.

4. Sponsored offerings are normally promoted by insurance agents who sell LTC insurance using the *single sales approach* rather than a *comprehensive planning approach.* If an agent is not involved, it means that the insurance company is offering coverage directly, either over the phone, by internet, or through the mail. This kind of purchase could be even worse than purchasing from a traditional insurance agent. Dealing directly with the insurance carrier means that you will also be dealing directly at the time of claim.

When To Consider Sponsored Long-Term Care Insurance

Sponsored LTC insurance offerings are rarely a good value. But there is one exception to this general rule: when the employer, association, or other organization uses the services of a financial advisor, or *independent* LTC insurance specialist trained in a *comprehensive planning approach*. **In this situation, you may get the best of all worlds:**

1. The ability to choose coverage among several different insurance carriers.

2. The advantage of having your LTC insurance integrated into the total context of your financial objectives.

3. The possibility of receiving a discount on the premium.

If your employer, organization, association, or group wishes to consider a sponsored program, remember that the financial advisor or LTC insurance specialist chosen to administer the program directly affects the reputation of your company or organization. **Decision makers in your organization should ask the following questions when interviewing potential financial advisors or LTC insurance professionals:**

1. What criteria do you use to choose the insurance companies you recommend? How can our (company, association, bank, or other organization) be assured that the recommended insurance companies will pay claims properly? How can we be sure the companies are reasonable in their underwriting? How can we be sure they will still be in business at the time of claim? *(See Chapter 12: Choosing the Right Insurance Carrier.)*

2. Will you provide our (members, clients, or employees) with assistance at claim time? *(See Chapter 14: Submitting a Claim.)*

3. Can you provide us with the names and phone numbers of others you have assisted who have had LTC insurance claims?

Whether your group currently has a program in place or is considering sponsoring an LTC insurance offering, these questions should be adequately answered by the financial advisor or LTC insurance specialist prior to continuing or committing to having them work with your group.

GROUP AND SPONSORED PROGRAMS

	ADVANTAGES	DISADVANTAGES
GROUP	Guaranteed/Modified Issue coverage may allow people in poor health to obtain long-term care insurance when they would otherwise not qualify for an individually issued policy	Long-term care insurance sold with the *single sales approach* and not integrated within total financial objectives **Adverse Selection** may result in higher premiums and a greater risk of premium rate increases in the future Limited to the coverage options offered by the one insurance company chosen for the offering. This eliminates any opportunity to compare coverage and premium rates among different carriers
SPONSORED	Possible discount of 5–10% Working with an agent or financial professional trained in a *comprehensive planning approach* may offer additional advantages: • Choice of multiple top-rated carriers • Long-term care insurance planning occurs within the context of total financial objectives	Long-term care insurance sold with the *single sales approach* and not integrated within total financial objectives Even with a discount, premium may be higher than coverage offered by an alternative carrier Limited to the coverage options offered by the one insurance company chosen for the offering. This eliminates any opportunity to compare coverage and premium rates among different carriers

GROUP AND SPONSORED LONG-TERM CARE INSURANCE

KEY POINTS

- Group long-term care insurance is typically issued with lenient underwriting standards, causing the healthy policyholders to subsidize the premium of people in poor health.

- Group plans offered on a voluntary basis attract people already in poor health who cannot obtain long-term care insurance any other way.

- Adverse Selection results when the pool of policyholders includes more people in poor health and fewer in excellent health; thus, the insurance company experiences a higher-than-normal amount of claims and charges higher premiums.

- Long-term care insurance does not qualify as a Section 125 Cafeteria offering.

- Sponsored long-term care insurance policies are offered through employers, associations, financial institutions, and other groups.

- Sponsored policies are superior to true group policies because they are individually issued, and use the normally strict underwriting guidelines. But sponsored programs usually limit you to a choice of one insurance company and narrow coverage options. The exception is a sponsored program using the services of an independent financial advisor or long-term care insurance specialist trained in a *comprehensive planning approach.*

PART FIVE

Questions & Answers about Long-Term Care Insurance

5

A fulfilled life evolves from an eternal childlike curiosity.

— Eileen Hamm

PART 5:
Questions & Answers about
Long-Term Care Insurance

Over the years, we have been asked hundreds of questions about long-term care insurance. We've answered the majority of those questions in the previous pages. But several questions would be difficult to answer by including them in the general text. The following questions and answers section provides a practical format for answering these miscellaneous questions.

GENERAL QUESTIONS ABOUT LONG-TERM CARE INSURANCE

Q. A financial advisor on television continuously states that LTC insurance should only be considered by people over a certain age. This advisor has used two ages as "ideal" for purchasing coverage: age 54 and age 59. What are your thoughts on this?

A. This topic is discussed in several areas of this book, and specifically in Chapter 9. The advice given above is the most prevalent and dangerous myth in LTC insurance planning.

Whether or not to purchase LTC insurance has nothing to do with your age. It has to do with whether or not you have prioritized your insurance needs, whether or not you can afford the LTC insurance premium, and your philosophy in regards to risk tolerance. **There are a number of reasons why "blanket advice" to wait until a certain age before considering LTC insurance is dangerous to both consumers and to financial advisors giving such advice:**

1. Long-term care insurance premiums are on the rise in general, and continue to rise with each year a person waits to purchase coverage.

2. While waiting until the "perfect age" to purchase coverage, many consumers will become uninsurable, and some may even begin having a need for long-term care services.

3. Financial advisors who give this advice may find themselves involved in litigation with clients and consumers who heeded

their advice, and later find they can no longer afford coverage, or no longer qualify for coverage.

Long-term care planning should be done with the assistance of a financial advisor who has become completely educated in the long-term care planning process. A knowledgeable financial advisor will guide you through your options after thoroughly analyzing your unique situation. They will help you plan within the context of your total financial objectives, and not advise you based on generalizations.

Q. *Are policies that combine life insurance and LTC insurance a good value?*

A. These types of insurance policies are referred to by different names, including "Combination Products," "Bundled Products," or "Accelerated Death Benefit Products."

The policy is a life insurance policy with an LTC insurance rider that can be used to pay for long-term care expenses. Using this rider is called "Accelerating the Death Benefit." In other words, instead of having to die to receive benefits, the policy would pay benefits to cover the cost of the policyholder's long-term care expenses.

These policies are sold as a conceptual sale, to people who dislike the idea of paying for insurance coverage they may never use. The sales pitch explains that the policyholder can own insurance coverage, and always be assured that a benefit will be paid. If long-term care is not needed, at least the beneficiary will receive benefits from the life insurance portion of the policy.

The sales pitch is enticing and the agent normally makes it seem so simple. But don't be fooled into believing you are getting something for free. You are paying for two types of insurance coverage, whether you need both types or not: long-term care insurance and life insurance. If you use the long-term care coverage within the policy, the benefits for the life insurance are reduced proportionately.

For example, if you bought a $100,000 accelerated benefit life insurance policy, with an LTC insurance rider, and then collected

$75,000 for long-term care expenses, your beneficiary would collect only $25,000 at your death. But you've paid a premium for $100,000 in life insurance benefits, as well as a premium for the insurance company's estimate of its at-risk exposure for a long-term care event.

Ask your financial advisor to analyze each of your insurance needs separately. If life insurance is appropriate, purchase the best life insurance value for your particular situation, and do not bundle it with another type of insurance. If life insurance is not appropriate, then don't purchase it at all.

The same is true with LTC insurance. Ask your financial advisor to analyze your options and make a recommendation. If LTC insurance is appropriate, purchase the best LTC insurance value for your particular situation, and don't bundle it with another type of insurance. If LTC insurance is not appropriate, don't purchase it at all.

Q. *Do LTC insurance policies build cash value?*

A. No. Since the enactment of HIPAA legislation in 1996 *(see Chapter 15)*, the only type of cash return permitted in Tax Qualified policies is in the form of a "return of premium upon death." In other words, the premiums paid can be refunded to a beneficiary, but not to the insured directly. Insurance companies offering this benefit will deduct the amount of any claims they have paid to you prior to death from the premium paid to your beneficiary. This additional option, known as a "return of premium" rider, can add from 20 to 40 percent to the premium. We do not recommend this rider.

Q. *Can a person who would qualify for Medicaid, the welfare program, purchase LTC insurance?*

A. No. People who qualify for Medicaid do not need LTC insurance because the welfare system will pay for their care. In fact, it is illegal for an insurance agent to solicit, or an insurance company to issue an LTC insurance policy to an individual who is likely to qualify for Medicaid benefits. Every LTC insurance application includes a specific question about whether or not an applicant is Medicaid-eligible.

Q. *Explain the difference between Guaranteed Renewable and Non-Cancelable LTC insurance.*

A. Guaranteed Renewable policies guarantee that the policy must be renewed for life, as long as premium payments are paid on time. However, the insurance company reserves the right to increase the premium—as long as the premium increase is implemented on a class basis—not an individual basis.

Non-cancelable policies guarantee that (1) the policy is renewable for life if premium payments are paid on time, and (2) the insurance company can never increase the premium rates, even on a class basis. Although insurance companies have experimented with non-cancelable policies in the past, there are none available at the time of this writing. You may, however, purchase a rider with many companies that guarantees your premium rate will not be increased for a specified number of years.

Q. *Can you reach an age where LTC is unattainable because of age?*

A. As of 2005, some insurance companies issue coverage to age 84. A very limited number will issue coverage to age 89. However, most carriers restrict the benefit choices for applicants above age 80. This means that even if the applicant qualifies for coverage, the benefit options offered will be limited. Even though it may be available, LTC insurance is rarely issued at these older ages, due to the likelihood of poor health and high premiums.

Q. *Can a person purchase an LTC insurance policy for a parent, or someone else, without them knowing that the coverage has been purchased?*

A. No. The person who will be insured must consent to the coverage by signing an application. They must also be fully aware of the purpose of the application, understand the policy benefits, and understand the underwriting process.

However, a person may pay for the premium for another person. In many cases, children pay the premium for their parents' LTC insurance coverage. *(This is explained in more detail in Chapter 8: Why People Consider Long-Term Care Insurance.)*

Q. *If a person already owns an LTC insurance policy, should they replace it with a more "modern" policy?*

A. The decision of whether or not to replace a current policy should be taken very seriously and analyzed by your financial advisor. In most cases, you have more to lose than gain by replacing an existing policy. But each situation is unique, and should be analyzed by considering the following factors and questions, in addition to your objectives and goals:

- The first factor is your current insurance carrier. Are they stable? Do they increase your premium rates frequently?

- The next factor is your health. Has it changed for the worse since you purchased the policy? If so, you may not qualify for coverage if you applied today.

- The final factor is how long ago the policy was purchased. A policy purchased more than five years ago probably has a fairly low premium compared to the premium on newly issued coverage today. This may be true even if your current carrier has increased your premium rate.

Q. *Is it important to work with an agent, agency, or financial advisor that can offer coverage with multiple carriers?*

A. More than important, it's absolutely essential. We recommend that you never purchase LTC insurance from a "captive agent"—an agent or financial advisor who only represents one LTC insurance company. Instead, you should trust one independent advisor specifically trained in a *comprehensive planning approach* who will work on your behalf, not the insurance company's behalf. Working with an independent advisor who represents several top-rated carriers allows you to compare benefits and rates from a number of carriers without spending time with several different advisors.

An agent or advisor who only represents one company has a very strong allegiance to that company. They may have difficulty being unbiased when the time comes to file a claim. We recommend purchasing coverage from your independent financial advisor or someone referred to you by your advisor.

Q. *Is there a safety net in place for policyholders who have coverage with insurance companies that become insolvent?*

A. We devote Chapter 12 to the subject of choosing an insurance carrier. By following the guidelines in that chapter, your chances of having to face this issue are greatly reduced.

But there are protections in place if the company insuring you becomes insolvent. States operate "Guaranty Funds." These programs are designed to become the insurer for policyholders who have purchased coverage from carriers that become insolvent. The specific benefits of Guaranty Funds, and the way they work, vary from state to state. Ask your financial advisor or contact your state's insurance department for more specifics on the Guaranty Fund in your state.

Q. *What happens if I buy an LTC insurance policy, and the insurance company later decides to stop offering LTC insurance to new applicants?*

A. All individually issued policies sold today are guaranteed renewable. This means that the company cannot cancel your policy as long as you pay your premium on time. This is true even if the company decides to no longer offer coverage to future applicants.

Policies issued in earlier years, including group coverage, may or may not be "guaranteed renewable," and thus may be cancelable. If you currently own an LTC insurance policy, look for the words **"Guaranteed Renewable"** on the front of the policy. If your policy is not guaranteed renewable, you may want to consider replacing the policy. As with our recommendation throughout this book, seek the advice of a financial advisor prior to canceling, replacing, or making any modifications whatsoever to a currently in-force LTC insurance policy.

Q. *What recourse does a policyholder have if they believe they have a legitimate complaint to file against an insurer or an agent?*

A. Your best defense against a problem with an insurance company or an insurance agent is to follow our advice in Chapter 12 about choosing an insurance carrier, and our advice about working with an advisor who is trained in a *comprehensive planning approach.* You will also want to make sure your advisor proves that they offer assistance at the time of claim, by providing you with the names and phone numbers of policyholders who have had claims.

But if you purchased coverage from someone you believe has not served you well, or will not assist you with claims, or from an insurance company that you believe has not treated you fairly, you should contact the Insurance Department in your state. Each state's insurance department has a formal process for filing a complaint.

Q. *Is there an insurance product that covers "Short-Term Care?"*

A. Yes. Short-term care insurance policies cover you for less than one year of care. In order for a policy to be called "long-term care insurance," the benefit limit must have a benefit period of at least one year.

Short-term care insurance is not a good value. These policies are designed for people who can't afford LTC insurance. It's unlikely that people who can't afford LTC insurance will benefit from a short-term care policy. These policies are mainly an insurance industry profit center, designed to help insurance agents make sales to consumers who can't afford LTC insurance.

Q. *What is your opinion of the Federal LTC Insurance Program (FLTCIP)?*

A. When a new law went into effect in 2002 creating the Federal LTC Insurance Program, the federal government sent a clear message that long-term care financing will not be available through government entitlement programs. *FLTCIP* is a group long-term care program available to federal employees, including military personnel.

Two companies were awarded the contract to issue these policies: John Hancock and Met Life. The program is not a guaranteed issue program—underwriting takes place with each application.

We recommend that a person who qualifies for this program ask their financial advisor for their opinion and assistance in determining whether or not this program is a good value for their situation. Many times, a better value can be obtained by purchasing an individually issued policy. *(For more on group LTC insurance, see Chapter 17.)*

QUESTIONS ABOUT PREMIUMS

Q. Explain "Limited-Pay" LTC insurance policies.

A. Limited-pay policies allow you to "pay-up" your LTC insurance coverage in a certain pre-determined number of years. This means that instead of paying your LTC insurance premiums for the rest of your life, you limit the number of years of payments.

Payment options for limited-pay policies are normally offered in these increments:

- Single Pay: one large premium payment
- Pay for 5 years
- Pay for 10 years
- Pay for 20 years
- Pay until age 65

There are advantages and disadvantages to choosing the limited-pay option.

Advantages:

1. You do not have to pay your LTC insurance premiums for your entire life. Perhaps your goal is to retire in 10 years, and you would rather not make premium payments during your retirement years. Paying for coverage during your income-earning years allows you to have coverage with no out-of-pocket premium payments once the coverage is paid-up.

2. If the insurance company has a rate increase after your policy is paid-up, they cannot ask you to pay more premium. Once these policies are paid in full, they remain so for life.

3. If you purchase the inflation-protection rider, the benefits continue to increase on the policy, even after the policy is paid-up. Your coverage continues to increase in value although you are no longer making premium payments.

Disadvantages:

1. The premium on limited-pay policies is much higher than "pay-for-life" policies. For example, the premium for a 10-pay policy is generally between 2 and 3 times higher than a pay-for-life policy.

2. If you are not able to keep your LTC insurance policy in force because your finances change and you can no longer afford the premium, purchasing a limited pay policy would be a more costly financial mistake.

3. If you go on permanent claim while paying premiums and the policy is placed on waiver of premium, you have paid extra premium dollars for no gain in extra benefit.

Limited-pay policies are popular among business owners who plan to retire in a pre-determined number of years. This is because business owners and corporations can enjoy tax advantages by deducting the premium as a business expense. *(This is explained in more detail in Chapter 8: Why People Consider Long-Term Care Insurance and in Chapter 15: Tax Advantages of Long-Term Care Insurance.)* High-income-earning executives, who may be in their last 5 to 20 years of high earnings, are also good candidates for considering limited-pay policies.

Q. *Are there ways to obtain discounts on LTC insurance premiums?*

A. Yes. It's possible to obtain several types of discounts with the same policy. Most insurance companies offer a spousal discount. The spousal discount can be negligible with some companies and substantial with others. A discount of 10 to 20 percent is typical.

Another discount can be offered for a "preferred health rating." Those in excellent health will likely receive a discount of at least 15 percent over a "standard health rating."

But whether or not the company offers a discount, and the discount percentage, is less important than comparing coverage and premium rates among several top-rated insurance companies. One company may offer substantial discounts on a percentage basis, but the overall cost of the premium will be substantially higher than the premium on a policy offered by an insurance company that offers lower percentage discounts.

Q. Do LTC insurance policies offer a grace period for paying the premium?

A. By law, individually issued LTC insurance policies have a grace period of at least 31 days. This means the insured has up to 31 days after the due date to get the premium to the insurance company. After that period, the insurance company can terminate the policy.

Q. Is a policyholder required to continue making premium payments if they go on claim with their LTC insurance policy?

A. It depends. Some policies include a feature known as a "waiver of premium" benefit. It states that if a policyholder is receiving benefits, they are not required to make premium payments for the duration of the claim. Read the policy or outline of coverage for information regarding this benefit.

Q. Can LTC insurance premiums be paid with the funds from an IRA or 401K plan?

A. No. However, LTC insurance premiums can be paid with funds on deposit in MSAs (Medical Savings Accounts) or HSAs (Health Savings Accounts). These programs are similar to IRAs from the standpoint of tax advantages. See your financial advisor or tax specialist for specifics on this strategy.

Q. Is it true that premiums on issued policies can never go up?

A. Unfortunately, this is *not* true but is a common misconception. While rates do not rise with advancing age, deteriorating health, or claims, the carrier may apply for a "class-wide" rate increase, which will affect all policyholders who have the same policy from that particular company. You can reduce your chances of having frequent increases in your premium rate by following the advice offered in *Chapter 12: Choosing the Right Insurance Carrier.*

Q. If an insurance company has a premium rate increase on an LTC insurance policy, does the policyholder have any option other than to pay the higher premium?

A. Yes. If a rate increase is implemented, the insurance company must offer the policyholder the option of reducing the policy benefits instead of paying the rate increase. This allows the policyholder to maintain the same premium amount but with reduced policy benefits.

QUESTIONS ABOUT BENEFITS

Q. Explain the "Reduced Home Care" benefit available on some comprehensive LTC insurance policies.

A. Comprehensive LTC insurance pays for care in any environment: your home, an assisted living community, or a nursing home. As explained in Chapter 10, we recommend comprehensive LTC insurance as opposed to coverage that only covers care in one environment.

Some comprehensive LTC insurance policies allow you to purchase a benefit amount for home care that is less than the benefit amount you purchase for facility care. For example, if you elect a daily benefit amount for facility care of $150 per day, you may be able to choose a reduced home care benefit amount of half that amount, or $75 per day. Choosing the lower daily benefit for home care will save a small amount on the overall premium.

We *do not* recommend choosing the reduced home care benefit option. The savings in premium is negligible and may force you into a facility due to lack of insurance coverage to pay for care at home. We recommend that you always purchase a home care benefit equal to the facility care benefit. Why? Because home care expenses can be just as costly, and sometimes even more expensive, than care in a facility. When the time comes for long-term care services, you want a home care benefit amount that will give you the best odds of staying at home. Choosing an adequate benefit for home care improves your chances of having this choice.

Q. *Explain the "Caregiver Training" benefit of an LTC insurance policy.*

A. When a policyholder needs long-term care services, the family often wants to hire someone they personally know and trust to assist in caring for the loved one. The "Caregiver Training" benefit pays for training that may be needed to assist the policyholder. For example, training may be provided to learn techniques for caring for a patient with Alzheimer's Disease. Or, training could be provided to learn how to use special equipment or administer medications. This benefit is included in most comprehensive LTC insurance policies.

Q. *Explain the "Bed Reservation" benefit of an LTC insurance policy.*

A. There are times when residents of assisted living communities or nursing homes need to be hospitalized for short periods of time. When this happens, there's a chance that the resident could lose their room at the facility. The facility has no reason to "save" the patient's room unless the patient pays for the room during their absence. In response to this problem, the LTC insurance industry designed the "bed reservation" benefit. It is included in almost all comprehensive LTC insurance policies. The benefit states that the insurance company will continue to pay for the room in the facility during the absence of the policyholder. The bed reservation benefit varies by company, but usually pays benefits for 15 to 30 days.

Q. *If a person has minor health conditions, but is issued long-term care coverage, will the insurance company pay a claim caused by one of the existing health conditions if the claim occurs immediately after the policy is issued? In other words, is there a pre-existing condition clause in LTC insurance policies?*

A. No, there are no pre-existing condition clauses. Therefore, the policy will pay benefits if a legitimate claim is submitted immediately after the policy is issued, even if the claim is the result of an existing health condition. However, you must disclose the health condition(s) at the time of application. A misrepresentation on your application could cause a claim to be denied, because it would be an illegitimate claim. It's important to answer all medical questions on the application correctly and truthfully.

Q. *Is it true that it's easier to collect benefits from a non-tax-qualified LTC insurance policy than it is a tax-qualified policy?*

A. To the contrary, benefits may actually be easier to collect with TQ policies, due to the standardized definitions for eligibility mandated by HIPAA. NTQ policies allow too much discretion to the insurance company for deciding whether or not a policyholder is eligible for benefits. Many NTQ policies contain definitions that are vague, unclear, or undefined.

PART SIX

Financial Professionals: Assuring Your Clients' Choice, Independence and Financial Security

Believe one who has proved it.
Believe an expert.

— Virgil (70BC–19BC), Aeneid

PART 6:

Financial Professionals: Assuring Your Clients' Choice, Independence and Financial Security

Long-term care planning is becoming an important issue for financial professionals entrusted with protecting the estates and assets of their clients. If you are a financial professional—a financial planner, estate planning attorney, or CPA—you are in an ideal position to assist your clients with planning ahead for long-term care. You understand your clients' financial situations, their goals, and their philosophies regarding risk management. You are the one they trust for advice and guidance concerning money matters of all kinds, including those that could have a detrimental effect on their financial security.

THE OBLIGATIONS OF A FINANCIAL ADVISOR

If financial professionals fail to address a risk that has a high probability of occurring in the future, can they be held liable for such an omission? What if a client assumes that his or her estate and/or financial plan is complete, but then experiences a long-term care event that effectively drains his or her financial portfolio? Would this be a legitimate case for filing a charge of malpractice?

Two respected journals have published information addressing the potential risk to financial advisors:

- The *Elder Law Journal* (Hayes 1999) published:

  Attorneys who advise clients about future financial security and concerns fulfill their professional obligation when they provide informed counsel in the area of long-term care...if (attorneys) are not informed about the nuances of long-term care insurance, they may be held liable if a client sues them for negligence.

- The *Journal of Financial Planning* (2001) published:

  Harley Gordon, Attorney at Law, identifies two specific areas of concern for financial professionals, including financial planners, estate planning attorneys, and CPAs:

1. Failure to talk about a long-term care plan as a part of the overall financial planning, estate planning, and/or retirement planning process.

2. Failure to talk about the subject of long-term care planning with wealthy clients, who may presume they can self-insure for the high costs of long-term care.

The warning signs point to the need for financial professionals to become familiar with the process of planning for long-term care. This does not mean they need to become an expert. But "due diligence" requires that they raise their clients' awareness of the significant financial risk of long-term care—a risk that has already negatively affected the financial security and future of thousands of families.

FINANCIAL PLANNERS

Financial planners fulfill their professional roles by advising their clients on a variety of financial topics.

Long-term care planning is an integral part of the financial planning process, and a major component of the risk management category of financial planning. *(This is discussed in Chapter 6: Integrating Long-Term Care Planning with Financial & Estate Planning.)*

ESTATE PLANNING ATTORNEYS

As America's population continues to age, the need to integrate long-term care planning into an estate plan cannot be overlooked. Ignoring the crucial financial detail of long-term care planning can result in loss of inheritance and other negative estate transfer consequences.

Estate planning attorneys are learning that estate planning and long-term care planning work hand-in-hand. **Both financial disciplines are related to the same objectives:**
- Protection of Assets
- Preservation of Legacy

CPAs

Many CPAs today are expanding their practice from exclusively being tax experts to including comprehensive financial planning as part of the services they provide.

Many business owners are asking their CPA about the feasibility of offering LTC insurance as an employee benefit *(see Chapter 17: Group and Sponsored Long-Term Care Insurance)*.

CPAs are also in an excellent position to advise their clients of the tax ramifications of long-term care planning and LTC insurance *(see Chapter 15: Tax Advantages of Long-Term Care Insurance)*.

THE CHALLENGE

One major roadblock for financial professionals who want to help their clients with long-term care planning is the availability of resources and tools that competently address this issue. This book provides a foundation for understanding this subject, along with the basic education you need to initiate a discussion about long-term care planning with your clients and offer them initial guidance. We have also developed tools and processes to assist with the entire long-term care planning process using a *comprehensive planning approach*. These tools are available through our training programs and website, **www.superiorltc.com.**

Chapter 18

Long-Term Care Insurance Myths
by Steve Bell, CFP®, MBA

When you get to the fork in the road, take it!
— Yogi Berra

A *comprehensive planning approach* requires that long-term care planning occur within the context of a family's total financial objectives. While LTC insurance is a solution for many families, most financial professionals avoid the issue of long-term care planning with their clients because of long-held myths regarding who should consider LTC insurance. The two most prevalent myths pertain to a person's age before they should consider LTC insurance (most financial professionals believe younger clients should automatically pass on LTC insurance) and a person's net worth (some professionals try to set an upper-end dollar figure at which people should automatically self-insure).

This chapter addresses a few of the commonly held myths about age and net worth, and highlights the importance of discussing long-term care planning with *every* client, and to not automatically disregard LTC insurance as an option, even if you or your clients might have previously considered them too young or too wealthy.

LONG-TERM CARE INSURANCE PLANNING: SIX MYTHS THAT COULD RUIN YOUR CLIENTS' FINANCIAL FUTURE... AND YOURS

Clients rely on you, their trusted financial planner, estate planning attorney, or CPA, to discuss any major risks to their financial and estate plans, and to recommend appropriate preventative measures. *(To simplify this discussion, we will use the term "financial professional" throughout this text, to define a financial planner, estate planning attorney, or CPA.)* This is especially true of insurable risks such as death, disability, fire, theft, accident, and liability. But long-term care, also a real and insurable risk, is often completely overlooked.

When you fail to address your clients' long-term care planning needs, you either encourage them to ignore the issue, or you force them to turn to insurance agents as their sole source for long-term care planning and advice. This does not serve your clients' best interest and could be detrimental to you. Because of your unique relationship with your client, you are in the best position to address long-term care planning and recommend a solution within the context of your client's overall financial situation and goals.

But because so many financial professionals are not addressing this risk, millions of clients who should invest in LTC insurance remain unaware of it. Conversely, thousands who should not invest in LTC insurance purchase it from an insurance agent, as an insurance product, rather than a solution to a financial risk. Why is this? Why are so many financial professionals failing to address the long-term care planning needs of their clients?

I believe it is because of commonly held LTC insurance myths prevailing in our industry—myths that lead financial professionals to avoid long-term care planning.

LONG-TERM CARE INSURANCE MYTHS

Myth 1   If my client is wealthy enough to self-insure, they should automatically self-insure for long-term care.

Myth 2   My younger clients can ignore long-term care planning because they will not need long-term care anytime soon.

Myth 3   My younger clients will pay less if they postpone buying long-term care insurance.

Myth 4   As long as they are willing to pay the higher premiums, clients can wait to purchase long-term care insurance.

Myth 5   My younger clients are better off investing their long-term care insurance premium.

Myth 6   I must be a long-term care insurance expert before I can adequately address this issue with my clients.

Myth 1: If my client is wealthy enough to self-insure, they should automatically self-insure for long-term care.

Many financial professionals want their clients to view them as their primary resource—their first stop—for all financial advice. "Have a question about investments, taxes, insurance, estate planning or lifetime gifting? Come to me first. I can at least point you in the right direction." This level of service is invaluable for all clients, and especially valuable for wealthy clients. Yet, when it comes to addressing the long-term care planning needs of the wealthy client, many financial professionals believe that if clients *can* self-insure, they *should* self-insure.

Is this so different from saying that if a client can pay more taxes, they should pay more taxes? Our wealthiest clients are delighted when we help them with tax planning, and are able to help lower their tax bill; in turn, that money is invested to help reach their financial goals. But we often fail to advise them that by paying insurance premiums, they can potentially avoid hundreds of thousands of dollars in long-term care expenses.

Some advisors might live by a rule such as, "Clients should not consider LTC insurance if their liquid assets exceed $X million." But would your client agree if they knew that even a portfolio as high as $5 million could be depleted several years early if it were used to pay for years of long-term care? The numbers make sense when you realize the national average cost of long-term care is about $58,000 per year, and the cost of long-term care is predicted to rise much faster than the overall rate of inflation in the coming decades.

The *$5 Million Portfolio* chart on the next page shows what can happen to a $5 million portfolio that is required to generate a $208,000 annual income for a 60-year-old client and his spouse. The client plans to spend this income over the next 35 years of retirement. We assumed a 5.3 percent after-tax return on investments, a 3 percent overall rate of inflation and a 5 percent rate of inflation on long-term care expenses.

The **blue line** indicates the best-case scenario: no long-term care event, no money spent on LTC insurance premiums, and a portfolio that lasts through age 95. The **black line** however, shows what will happen if either the client or his spouse requires 10 years of long-term care at an average cost of $58,000 per year beginning one year into retirement.

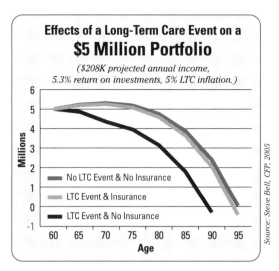

Effects of a Long-Term Care Event on a $5 Million Portfolio

($208K projected annual income, 5.3% return on investments, 5% LTC inflation.)

Legend: No LTC Event & No Insurance; LTC Event & Insurance; LTC Event & No Insurance

Source: Steve Bell, CFP, 2005

This long-term care event causes the portfolio to deplete a full six years earlier than planned. The **gray line** shows that a $5,000 annual investment in LTC insurance premiums restores all but one year of useful life to the portfolio—long-term care event or not.

What should your client do? Most of you will agree that it is not the job of the financial professional to answer this question for our clients. It *is* your job, however, to educate your client about the dangers of failing to plan for their long-term care, to present reasonable alternatives, and then let them decide which planning alternative to implement.

If 10 years of long-term care can shave 6 years off a $5 million portfolio, what do you suppose will happen to a smaller portfolio? It gets much worse. If, for example, your client's starting portfolio and income were half as much ($2.5 million portfolio and $104,000 annual income), their portfolio would be depleted by a full 10 years earlier rather than 6 years—much earlier than planned if the same long-term care event occurred.

The point is this: the acceptability of a catastrophic long-term care risk does not depend on the size of a client's portfolio alone. A *comprehensive planning approach* dictates that we consider:

- the cost of care where the client prefers to receive care
- the client's projected level of spending in relation to their projected resources

- the number of years these resources need to last
- the client's personal tolerance for risk
- the assumptions about after-tax rates of return and inflation

This is the same information financial professionals use with retirement planning software to project a client's capital needs. In fact, financial professionals can use their retirement planning software to quickly quantify and easily communicate the cost of introducing a 10-year long-term care event on a client's otherwise acceptable retirement plan. Simply input $58,000 per year in long-term care expenses (or a more appropriate average cost of care for the client's area) for 10 years with an inflation rate of 5 percent (recent average rate of long-term care inflation). Review the age at which the money runs out and the revised probability of success. Then ask your client, "Is this reduction acceptable to you?" If not, then suggest they consider an alternative to self-insuring as a plan to pay for long-term care, including consideration of passing this risk onto an LTC insurance company.

Give your wealthy clients, who may appear to have the means to pay for long-term care, the advantage of knowing just how their portfolio will be impacted by a long-term care event. This level of service will not go unnoticed by your clients and their families.

Myth 2: My younger clients can ignore long-term care planning because they will not need long-term care anytime soon.

We normally don't hear about young people needing long-term care, but can it happen? What about your younger clients? Could they need long-term care as a result of an illness or accident? Of course they could.

Remember the celebrities who at early ages were disabled by an illness or accident? Annette Funicello was diagnosed with multiple sclerosis at age 45. Christopher Reeve suffered a paralyzing accident at age 43. Michael J. Fox was diagnosed with Parkinson's Disease at age 30.

Your younger clients could find themselves needing long-term care within a few months of leaving your office with their otherwise acceptable estate, retirement, or financial plan in hand, but without your recommendation that they choose a plan to pay for long-term care. It's important to you and them that you warn them of the dangers and recommend an appropriate action. A financial professional once told me: "It's better to advise my clients to plan ahead for long-term care many years too early than one day too late."

Myth 3: My younger clients will pay less if they postpone buying long-term care insurance.

The two premium charts on the next page clearly illustrate that this belief is false. In this example, I use the premium rates from two top-rated carriers to estimate the same policy premium, but for clients of differing ages at the time the policy is issued. The **black bars** represent the annual premiums. The **blue bars** represent the total cumulative dollars in premiums paid to age 85.

Most financial professionals are surprised to see the similarity in total premiums paid over time. In our example, we show policies being issued at various ages. The bars show that cumulative premiums paid to age 85 vary between a low of $80,400 and a high of $89,640. This proves that younger clients never pay significantly higher cumulative premiums than older clients do, and in most cases, younger clients pay less in cumulative premiums.

But you might argue that younger clients will pay more if we consider the time value of money. Intuitively, we know this is not true because the 40-year-old client spreads his payments over more years than our older clients do. For the 40-year-old client, for example, the later years of premium payments will be paid with much cheaper dollars. The *"Today's Dollars"* chart discounts the cumulative dollars in the *"Nominal Dollars"* chart by an overall inflation rate of 3 percent.

The present value of the 40-year-old's 35 years of premium payments to age 85 is $43,367, while the 75-year-old's 10 years of payments to age 85 is $69,795. We have no reason to believe this relationship between older and younger clients will change when your younger client turns 75. This means that at virtually all ages, and factoring the time value of money, the younger a person is when they buy LTC insurance, the lower the premium will be, both on an annual and cumulative basis.

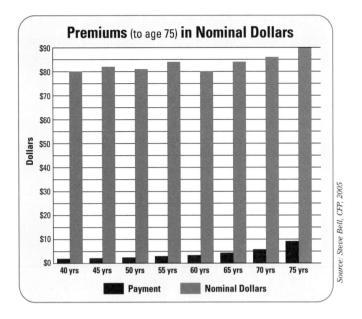

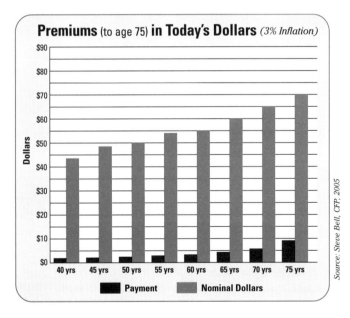

Source: Steve Bell, CFP, 2005

Myth 4. As long as they are willing to pay the higher premiums, clients can wait to purchase long-term care insurance.

While waiting for "the perfect age" to buy, your younger client could suffer a debilitating accident or be diagnosed with a disease that makes her uninsurable. The *"Underwriting Screen Failures"* chart shows the dramatic increases in the percent of applicants who

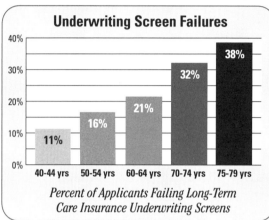

Underwriting Screen Failures

Percent of Applicants Failing Long-Term Care Insurance Underwriting Screens

fail to pass LTC insurance underwriting screens by age group. The number of people who fail to pass LTC insurance underwriting in the 60-64 year-old age group is nearly double that of the 40-44 year-old age group.

To help your client determine eligibility for LTC insurance and to realize how easily they may become ineligible, simply show your client the following list and ask them, **"During the last 12 months did you need any of the following?"**

- Assistance with any Activities of Daily Living (ADLs) including: eating, bathing, dressing, toileting, continence, and transferring
- Home health care services
- Care in a nursing home
- A walker, wheelchair, medical appliance, kidney dialysis machine, or a manufactured source of oxygen
- Treatment for any of the following conditions:
  - Alzheimer's Disease
  - Acute and unspecified renal failure
  - Acute cerebral vascular disease
  - Chronic renal failure
  - Cirrhosis of the liver
  - Chronic memory loss
  - Diabetes Mellitus with complications

- Mental retardation
- Multiple Sclerosis, other bone and musculoskeletal disease
- Paralysis
- Parkinson's Disease
- Schizophrenia and related disorders
- Senility and organic mental disorders
- Transient Ischemic Attack (TIA)

This list includes the most common, but not all, disqualifying health conditions. Long-term care insurance underwriting is performed on an individual basis and the underwriting process and standards vary from one insurance company to another. One carrier may accept your client, but only at a higher-than-preferred or standard premium rate, while another carrier may not accept them at all. While answering "Yes" to any of the above conditions will most certainly disqualify your client for LTC insurance, answering "No" does not necessarily mean they will qualify. After your client submits an application and a more extensive underwriting process is completed, the carrier will determine eligibility *(see Chapter 13: The Application and Underwriting Process).*

Myth 5: My younger clients are better off investing their long-term care insurance premium.

This is only true if the client does not need long-term care for more than a few months during the decades she is investing the insurance premium. Let's compare whether a 40-year-old client should buy LTC insurance or invest the premium for 25 years. For comprehensive coverage and benefits that include inflation protection, her premium will be about $1,788 per year. She believes she can earn a 6 percent after-tax rate of return on her investment. The cost of care in her area is $158 per day. We assume the cost of long-term care will continue to grow at an average annual rate of 5 percent. Let's do the math. In 25 years, the invested premium will grow to $103,984. The cost of care in her area will grow to $535 per day. So at the end of 25 years, when your client is about to turn 65, her investment account will cover 194 days ($103,983/$535) of long-term care. Put another way: after 25 years of investing the premium amount, your client's account will cover less than 7 months of long-term care. And what if she has an accident or develops an illness and requires 10 years of long-term care beginning one year after she starts this investment account? What then? Using national averages and a 5 percent inflation rate, 10 years of long-term care would cost your younger client over $726,000.

What would this kind of catastrophe do to your 40-year-old's retirement plan—the path you drew to her financial goals? Is your 40-year-old client willing to assume this risk? What about her family? You can't know, unless you ask. If she's like most clients at any age, she will automatically assume the risk until you let her know just how big a risk it is and what it can do to her family's financial future. It's up to you to illustrate the consequences of her decision. A proactive education using a *comprehensive planning approach* is the process for helping her select which LTC planning option is best for her.

Should your 40-year-old client postpone purchasing LTC insurance until age 65? **The answer is no unless:**

- She is willing to take the bet that she won't need long-term care for more than 7 months

- She feels she can afford a several-hundred-thousand-dollar setback to her financial goals

- She is willing to bet that she will not have a debilitating accident or won't be diagnosed with a disease that will cause her to fail LTC insurance underwriting requirements before she reaches age 65 *(see Myth 4)*

- She has higher-priority risks that should be considered, and feels she cannot afford the LTC insurance premiums right now *(see Chapter 9: Is Long-Term Care Insurance Suitable for You?)*

Myth 6: I must be a long-term care insurance expert before I can adequately address this issue with my clients.

Do you have to be a CPA to discuss your client's general tax situation? Do you have to be an estate planning attorney to educate your client about the advantages and disadvantages of estate planning alternatives? Do you have to be a licensed insurance agent to recommend planning ahead with life or disability insurance? Of course not! But if you claim to assist your clients with comprehensive financial planning, and unless you clearly limit the advice you give your clients to very narrow and specific financial issues, your clients will justifiably rely on you to address ALL risks to their financial goals, including the risk of long-term care. This is especially true if you are addressing other insurable risks such as disability or early death.

A *comprehensive planning approach* is advocated throughout this book, and allows you to address this important issue with your clients by choosing your own level of expertise and involvement in the LTC planning process *(see Chapter 7: Planning Ahead Using a Comprehensive Planning Approach).*

REPLACE THE MYTHS WITH THE FACTS

Myths can be dangerous when they lead to misinformation and, in the case of long-term care planning, avoidance on the part of financial professionals. The myths surrounding LTC insurance can lead to the demise of a carefully developed financial plan and the collapse of a family's financial security.

In your business, success is not just a matter of delivering responsive service, growing the relationship, and attracting new clients. Success also comes from knowing that a financial plan, estate plan, or retirement plan has addressed all potential risks, including the often overlooked risk of long-term care.

LONG-TERM CARE INSURANCE MYTHS

KEY POINTS

■ Many financial professionals avoid the issue of long-term care planning because of commonly held myths.

■ The two most prevalent myths pertain to age and net worth.

■ Clients rely on their financial professional to identify risks to their portfolios and to make recommendations to eliminate or decrease that risk.

Chapter 19 Interviews

The following interviews provide a variety of perspectives from a diverse range of financial professionals and industry experts.

Many of these financial professionals and experts have been addressing the issue of long-term care planning with their clients for years. You will learn from this well-respected group that there are various reasons for helping clients plan ahead for long-term care. We believe their experiences and stories will provide you with insight that would be difficult to obtain any other way.

PERSPECTIVE FROM A FINANCIAL PLANNER
WHO SPECIALIZES IN HIGH-NET-WORTH INDIVIDUALS
Bob Bingham, CFP ®

*I used to tell my wealthier clients that they
didn't need to include long-term care insurance in
their consideration of long-term care planning options.
But after seeing the true consequences of a long-term
care event, I recommend it to virtually everybody.*

Bob Bingham is a Certified Financial Planner® with more than 20 years of experience. Based in San Francisco, he is an expert on wealth management for high-net-worth individuals. He is widely quoted in the national press, including *The Wall Street Journal*, *Barron's* and *BusinessWeek*. His company has almost $1 billion under management. Bingham, Osborn, and Scarborough serves over 500 clients and employs 22 people in 2 offices. Bingham offers broad-based financial planning, including design and management of investment portfolios, and advice on a wide range of financial planning issues, such as investments, insurance, taxes, and more.

A large percentage of the firm's clients have the means to self-insure for long-term care, even against an extended stay in a first-class long-term care facility. Still, Bingham raises the issue of LTC insurance with all his clients. He feels that even those who could self-insure should do so only after first considering the benefits of LTC insurance, purely from a financial planning perspective.

Q: Your clients are successful and financially savvy. Why do they need a professional adviser to help them make financial decisions?

A: People with substantial assets are confronted and bombarded with multiple financial decisions, choices that they need to make all the time. Even if they are very well informed about one or two areas of investment and financial planning, most do not have the time to become an expert in all areas of planning. I act as a Chief Financial Officer (CFO) for my clients, helping them see a coherent picture that includes all the pieces. My job is to act as a guide, giving them the information and expertise they need to make decisions based on their individual circumstances and objectives. In order to achieve important goals, you need information and guidance. That's where we fit in—we are our client's advocates in planning ahead for their best financial future.

Q: Do you think that LTC insurance is an important part of financial planning?

A: Yes. Long-term care is the biggest uncovered risk in the insurance portfolios of most upper-income people. They have planned ahead by investing in medical insurance, homeowner's insurance, car, life and disability insurance. But in too many cases, they have no insurance for long-term care. It represents a huge risk for all people, whether they have substantial assets or not, because costs can easily run into the hundreds of thousands of dollars. We sometimes find that a new client is insuring a car worth $30,000, and going without insurance that poses a much larger risk of six-figures or more: long-term care. We educate each of our clients about the risks of long-term care.

Q: How do you go about educating your clients?

A: Quite a few clients have given LTC insurance some consideration before we address it. Most are familiar with the concept. In general, people are more and more receptive to the idea that they need to plan ahead for long-term care. One reason is that baby boomers and middle-aged people in their 50s or 60s have often had the experience of caring for their own parents. I've had such an experience with my own father, and it certainly opened my eyes. While it's true that most people are familiar with the topic, we inform our clients by using a process that educates them about the true potential financial risks of long-term care. We heavily emphasize the consequences of not planning ahead and what that could mean to them as an individual or family.

Q: You work mainly with high-net-worth individuals. Don't they have the assets necessary to self-insure against the costs of long-term care?

A: You'd think that people with large portfolios should always self-insure. The conventional wisdom is that the wealthy do not need LTC insurance. But it's not that difficult to be in a situation where you're spending over $250,000 per year on long-term care. That level of expense can quickly consume a portfolio that might otherwise be more productively employed.

We think that assets of two million dollars are the minimum required to comfortably self-insure. But even if you have that amount, you might still want to investigate LTC insurance to mitigate a financial risk that comes at the end of life and may cause consternation among children and heirs. Even if it covers only part of the actual expense, LTC insurance takes a lot of the pressure off people at a difficult time. Additionally, if people purchase coverage at a reasonably young age, and are in good health, LTC insurance is actually a very good economic value, compared to many other types of insurance.

Q. So wealthy people should still investigate coverage even if they can self-insure?

A. I used to tell my wealthier clients that they didn't need to include LTC insurance in their consideration of long-term care planning options. But after seeing the true consequences of a long-term care event, I recommend it to virtually everybody. I carefully explain the risks involved and challenge them to come up with a comfortable scenario without LTC insurance. Very few want to face that challenge, once they're familiar with the risks involved.

I also tell them, "Don't try to insure the full amount." If you estimate costs of $100,000 per year for the quality of care you demand, maybe you should insure for about half of that amount and cover the rest out-of-pocket.

Q: *The long-term care costs you mention are quite high compared to the national average of about $60,000 per year. What accounts for the difference?*

A: I have first-hand feelings about this because of what I went through with my own father. I found it was very easy to rack up costs of over $250,000 if you were arranging care for someone who needed a professional attendant 24 hours a day in order to stay at home.

My father recently died in Cleveland. He had been in an "Assisted Living" apartment for years but eventually came to the point where he needed help with things like dressing or making sure he didn't fall. One option was to move him into a nursing home. Although that was the least expensive choice, we wanted him to be as comfortable as possible during his last years of life.

My father didn't have any exotic debilitating disease, and we decided to pay for his care in the apartment where he had lived for years. We arranged for private caregivers to come in 24 hours a day. In Cleveland, private caregivers charge about $16 per hour. With 24-hour, round-the-clock care, plus rent for his apartment and other medical expenses, we faced costs of $250,000 per year, or close to a million dollars over a period of four years. Although costs like this are far above the average, situations like this are not as rare as most of us think.

Q: *We've talked about high-net-worth individuals. What about people who have less substantial assets?*

A: Long-term care insurance is not cheap, and the hardest decisions about whether or not to purchase coverage are for those who are right on the edge of affordability. The most vulnerable people, in some respects, are couples. A single person can always sell the house to fund years of long-term care. But if one partner in a couple has to go into a facility, the other usually wants to remain at home. That means they can't sell their house and are dependent on money in their investment portfolio. I personally believe that people with average means should at least investigate LTC insurance. The decision to purchase coverage or not will depend on many factors, including their age and health. People of average means who invest in coverage at a young enough age may be able to afford coverage, especially if they are still in good health.

Q: Any other tips for people who are considering LTC insurance?

A: One thing you should look at very carefully with your advisor is the financial strength of the insurance company being considered. There are big differences between companies in this market. Most people have to rely on professionals to keep abreast of the situation. The problem is that there can be a very long period of paying premiums before you receive any benefits. It can easily be 30 years between the time you purchase a policy and the time you need it. You want a company that will be around when you need it. I wouldn't consider buying from an insurance company that is small and unknown, even if their premiums were lower. I would only consider large, highly rated companies with a long history in the LTC insurance industry.

PERSPECTIVE FROM THE PRESIDENT
OF AN INVESTMENT ADVISORY FIRM

Paul C. Pennington, CFP ®

*This story adds to the many reasons why
people buy coverage–so they can enjoy
their retirement years and have peace of mind.*

Paul C. Pennington has been in the financial services field for 35 years, working with individuals, businesses, and financial institutions. Originally in the banking profession, he began his career in financial, estate, and tax planning in 1974. He is a Certified Financial Planner™ Professional (CFP®), and a member of the Financial Planning Association of Northern California (formerly known as the Institute of Certified Financial Planners), serving on several board positions over the past nine years. He is the president and founder of Pennington Financial Group, a registered investment advisory firm providing fee-based asset management services, investment portfolio policy, and financial, estate, retirement, and tax planning services. Paul personally specializes in portfolio management and estate and tax planning. He holds a General Securities Principal license with the National Association of Securities Dealers. Paul attended the University of San Francisco, where he received a bachelor's degree in economics, and the graduate school of business at the University of Colorado, in banking and finance.

*Q. I've heard you say that purchasing LTC insurance can give
you peace of mind. Can you elaborate?*

A. When people get older they become more guarded with their funds. They don't know when and how they are going to need them. I've had clients who have a comfortable nest egg. They have $500,000. They want to protect it. They have the money to travel but don't want to spend it in case they need it for care for either one or both of them. They may not be enjoying their retirement years because they're afraid they may spend the money and then need it for long-term care later. Many times they buy LTC insurance to solve this problem. It frees them to enjoy their retirement years. This puts a personal story behind what LTC insurance can really do. It adds to the many reasons why people buy coverage—so they can enjoy their retirement years and have peace of mind.

Q. *Can you elaborate more on that thought?*

A. Peace of mind is worth a lot. In my 35 years of retirement and estate planning experience, I've noticed that there are two things that can ruin a family's financial plan—health issues and issues with family members, especially children. What I mean by this is, a turn for the worse in a person's health can cause a long-term care need and completely wipe out a family. Additionally, family members and children who either have or can develop financial needs can also hurt a family's financial plan. Long-term care insurance solves at least one of these major problems. It can save the estate when our health declines.

Q. *What else can actually prompt people to look into LTC insurance?*

A. Quite a few times, it is people who have gone through a long-term care event with their parents. The children are middle-aged, and their parents are in their 70s or 80s. The children end up spending their inheritance making arrangements for their parents' long-term care. They don't want to do the same thing to their children. In other words, they want to leave something to the children. It isn't a matter of greed on the part of the children. It is a matter of them seeing their inheritance gone and how expensive long-term care really is. So they become interested in solving the problem for themselves and for their family, and many times they solve the problem by purchasing LTC insurance.

Q. *Where do you see LTC insurance coming into the total financial plan? If you could rank this risk on a list of other insurable risks that families face, where would you rank it in priority?*

A. Well, all types of insurance are risk transfer issues. You wouldn't think of not insuring your home or your car, yet people consider possibly not insuring their estates. I have a client whose husband lived 8 years in a nursing home with Alzheimer's and finally died. At that time you could split the estate. In other words, you would just spend down your spouse's half. You can't do that now. So, I think LTC insurance ranks in the top 2 or 3 for most people and maybe number 1 for people over 60.

Q. *Do most people think about insuring to protect their assets?*

A. Most of my clients with $100,000–$500,000 want to protect those assets for a rainy day, or to give to their children, or to help their children buy a house—things like that. On the other hand, some of my clients that have $2 million or more may decide to self-insure.

Q. *Have you ever worked with clients who had a high level of assets and were still interested in LTC insurance?*

A. Yes, the ones who have a high propensity to keep their estate intact for the children. There are some people who say, "I raised the children, they're fine, they have good jobs, and I educated them. I owe them nothing more." I have other clients who say, "I want to pass along everything to the children." It really depends on their individual value system.

Q. *Do you actively bring up this topic with most of your clients?*

A. Yes, I do. When we are doing retirement and estate planning for our clients, we ask them if there is any possibility that they would be taking care of a parent in their old age. Or, we ask them if they would have any financial responsibility to assist their parents. Many times the answer we get back is, "No, they're well off." But, the problem is, parents don't usually open up to their children until they are around 70. They should have opened up when they were younger and more likely to be insurable. I have a lot of clients who would love to have LTC insurance, but they are just not insurable. They waited too long. They may have diabetes, need their knee replaced, or need hip replacement. We have clients on Kaiser's waiting lists for these types of things. They are just not eligible for LTC insurance coverage.

Q. *So if your clients have the assets to protect, do you have a certain age that you really think people should be taking a look at LTC insurance?*

A. There is no ideal age, but they have to be educated about the potential need for long-term care. Many times this comes from direct experience with a friend or family member in need of long-term care. We show them that if they buy at a young enough age, LTC insurance can be a good economic value because they lock in a low premium rate. The average LTC insurance client is probably around 60.

Q. *How do you approach the subject of long-term care with your clients?*

A. Asking about the client's parents—if they are comfortable, well off or well positioned. This is usually a good way to open up the conversation to questions. We've told lots of people that their parents should apply for LTC insurance. If the clients are around 55, they think their parents are fine and will be healthy forever. But, back to the insurability issue, if you take the average 75 year old, probably half of them would be declined for LTC insurance. They don't have to have anything catastrophic, but based on the trend of tight underwriting standards, they're simply not insurable.

Q. *Do you have very many of your clients actively ask you about LTC insurance?*

A. More and more. Quite frankly, the CALPERS program has brought it to the forefront. But many times they can get a better LTC insurance value in the private market.

Q. *Because you are a leader in your industry and very involved with the FPA (Financial Planning Association), do you find that financial planners are as aware of this subject as they should be?*

A. Yes, I think they generally are. Financial planners have so much on their plates, but we realize the importance of educating clients about long-term care planning and insurance. Some planners believe it's important to get their clients to at least look into LTC insurance so that the children don't hold the planner responsible legally, since they covered other insurable risks with mom and dad, but not long-term care. There are actually planners who educate their clients about LTC insurance and then ask the client to sign a waiver.

PERSPECTIVE FROM AN ESTATE PLANNING AND TAX ATTORNEY
James Phillips, Estate Planning Attorney

> *Unfortunately, in my practice I've had to personally help clients whose children had become more concerned for their inheritance than they were for mom or dad's care. Long-term care insurance can help to guard against this greed/fear factor.*

James Phillips is an attorney who has been specializing in estate planning, trusts and related matters since 1980. In addition to his law degree, he has a Masters in Law Taxation. His family has a two-generation legal tradition in Northern California. His father was Alameda Superior Court Judge George W. Phillips. James grew up with an elderly grandmother who had a profound influence on his values, especially his interest in issues relating to older people and long-term care.

Q: Is LTC insurance an important aspect of estate planning?

A: It's on the list of areas that I discuss with all new clients who come to me for estate planning. I ask how they plan to pay for long-term care in a nursing home, assisted living community, or their own home. Most people have not thought the matter through. But since people who come to me are in a planning ahead mode of thinking, I think it's important to make them aware of this issue. Long-term care planning is something that my clients are usually glad we covered.

Q. Do you go over the various options available to them in planning ahead for long-term care?

A. I think every client should make an informed and analytical decision about planning for the payment of long-term care services. So, yes, I explain the four planning options available to them: self-insure, rely on family, rely on Medicaid (the welfare program), or purchase LTC insurance.

Q. How do your clients choose the right option?

A: We talk about how each option fits in. To self-insure, clients need sufficient assets and income to provide comfortably for home health care or long-term care in a nursing home or assisted living community. Only the fortunate few fall into this category. Most of my clients, even those with significant wealth, do not want to spend their after-tax income on a prolonged need for long-term care.

Medicaid, or MediCal as we call it in California, does pay for long-term care in a nursing home, but rarely includes home health care. I make sure that my clients understand that the safety net offered by Medicaid provides for long-term care only in Medicaid-certified facilities and in a non-private-room type environment. To qualify for government assistance, clients must pass three tests: an income test, an asset test, and a wealth-transfer test. Most of my clients would flunk the income and asset test because they own more than Medicaid allows. If they pass assets over to their heirs, they will fail the transfer test that defines the time period and the manner in which assets can be transferred in order to qualify for government aid.

In addition to these issues, most of my clients would rather choose the non-welfare options available to them. If they do not want to self-insure or rely on their family, LTC insurance becomes the option of choice. The Medicaid option is simply a "problematic solution" for most of my clients.

If clients don't have sufficient wealth to self-insure, and own too much estate for Medicaid, I actively recommend the third option —LTC insurance—rather than relying on their family to provide their care.

Q. How should they go about investigating coverage?

A. I tell healthy, insurable clients that they should work with a certified, independent long-term care specialist who will provide them with quotes for LTC insurance from several top-rated carriers, not just one. With those quotes and a detailed explanation of the benefits, they have the information they need to decide whether or not coverage makes sense for them as a solution for planning ahead for long-term care.

Q: Is LTC insurance a good value from an estate planning perspective?

A: If clients can afford the premiums, there are three compelling reasons to buy LTC insurance. The first is to avert the risk of significant economic harm from uninsured costs. I've seen handsome estates decimated by the cost of long-term care where there was no LTC insurance in force. Second, for married couples there is enormous emotional stress associated with worrying about payment and the quality of available services for the care of a spouse in need of care. Owning LTC insurance allows a family to significantly reduce both the economic stress of a long-term care event, as well as the emotional stress. Third, there is always the risk that whoever is in charge of your finances will be so consumed by fear or greed about their future inheritance that they may not be willing to allocate your funds for the high quality of care that you had planned on receiving. Unfortunately, in my practice I've had to personally help clients whose children had become more concerned for their inheritance than they were for mom or dad's care. Long-term care insurance can help to guard against this greed/fear factor.

PERSPECTIVE FROM A CPA WHO WORKS WITH INDIVIDUALS ACROSS THE ECONOMIC SPECTRUM

Larry Pon, CPA

The tax break is not the first benefit people look for when it comes to long-term care insurance. Most of the people we work with who buy coverage do so to keep from becoming a burden to their children.

Larry Pon is a CPA with a solo practice in the heart of Silicon Valley, California. His clients include individuals and small business owners. A typical service might involve a Silicon Valley entrepreneur whose company is being bought out and who seeks help in calculating and/or minimizing the tax bill from the sale of the business. Other common situations include reducing the tax bill on the sale of real estate. Recognizing that tax planning is just one piece of a larger puzzle, Pon likes to work collaboratively with the other professionals involved in his clients' financial planning.

Q: Long-term care insurance is sometimes called a "tax-favored form of insurance." As a CPA, do you agree with that assessment?

A: The tax benefits of LTC insurance can be good for some people, especially for business owners. Starting in 2003, companies with employees were able to write off 100 percent of their LTC insurance premiums as an above-the-line deduction. Even individual taxpayers can deduct premiums if their total medical expenses are above 7.5 percent of their adjusted gross income. In contrast, the premiums for many other types of individually issued insurance aren't tax deductible at all.

Q: What about the benefits a policyholder receives if she needs long-term care? Are they considered taxable income?

A: The benefits in tax-qualified LTC insurance policies are generally tax-free. So while business owners who purchase coverage for their employees are able to enjoy a tax deduction, the employee is not required to report the coverage as a benefit because it is a tax-free benefit. And the benefits received from an LTC insurance policy are not subject to taxes if and when they collect on the policy. It can be a very big incentive for many employees, and can help employers retain good employees by offering a benefit that most companies do not offer. Of course, each person's tax situation should be reviewed by a tax professional since tax issues related to long-term care can be complex.

Q: *Do you recommend that your clients buy policies because of the tax advantages?*

A: That depends on a cost-benefit analysis that varies for each individual. But for the majority, the tax break is not the first benefit people look for when it comes to LTC insurance. Most of the people we work with who buy coverage do so to keep from becoming a burden to their children. Another common scenario is when a client's children decide to buy coverage for their parents. The children pay the premium, with the objective of having their parents remain at home, or at least move to a facility where they feel comfortable, rather than relying on the welfare program, Medicaid (MediCal in California).

Q: *Have you had any personal experiences with clients who actually used their LTC insurance coverage?*

A: About two-thirds of the people I have had personal experiences with are still either very healthy, or have passed away without ever using the policies they purchased. But I had an experience just recently that shows the value of the coverage when it is used. A client purchased LTC insurance at the age of 80. She purchased two years of facility care coverage. She later needed care and went into a facility and stayed for about two years before she died. Even though she purchased at such an advanced age, she still received benefits that were far greater than the premiums paid.

Fortunately, my clients have purchased LTC insurance policies with high-quality companies and for those who have had claims, I have only heard positive feedback regarding the customer service and claims process. It is very important to understand how to work with the insurance company and providers. Claims go smoothly if you understand the process.

PERSPECTIVE FROM ONE OF THE LEADERS OF THE FOUNDATION THAT LAUNCHED THE PUBLIC/PRIVATE PARTNERSHIPS FOR LONG-TERM CARE INSURANCE

Dr. James Knickman, Ph.D.

> *Long-term care insurance, an example of a private sector solution, is working, but we need more government education about the issue of long-term care.*

Dr. James Knickman, Ph.D., is Vice President of Research and Evaluation at the Robert Wood Johnson Foundation, which launched the respected program for public/private partnerships in LTC insurance called the "Partnership Programs." An economist by training, Dr. Knickman was the Regents Lecturer at the University of California.

Long-term care insurance Partnership Programs match private contributions with public funds on a dollar-to-dollar basis to pay for long-term care costs. Only four states offer Partnership programs at this time, including two of the nation's most populous states, California and New York. The Partnership Program is explained in *Chapter 16.*

Q: Are our current systems for long-term care finance and delivery doing a good job?

A: Our current systems are not exactly a national embarrassment but they let too many people fall through the cracks. They are also too confusing. Many people can't figure out how to get the services they need. In about 45 of the 50 states, we are a humane society in that you will get care, even if you run out of money. The tough question for public policy is how will the system develop in coming years? Will we expand services for the truly poor, or try some universal system that gives coverage to the middle class and even the wealthy?

Q. Please elaborate on the options for financing long-term care.

A. There are two revenue streams for financing the cost of long-term care: public and private. The public stream is Medicaid, our backup system for the truly poor, or for middle-class people who become impoverished due to the high cost of long-term care. Most people start out as private-pay, paying for the costs of long-term care out-of-pocket. Once they "spend-down" their assets, they go on Medicaid. If you have no resources and start off as a Medicaid patient, it may be hard to get into a good nursing home. The better homes are hoping you'll be private-pay for at least a year or two prior to going on Medicaid. These nursing homes use a strategy of servicing a blend of Medicaid and private-pay patients, so that they are able to remain fiscally solvent.

In terms of private financing for long-term care services, we have a decentralized delivery system which is very private-sector oriented. Even the non-profits in the field act like for-profit corporations. That kind of market-oriented delivery system has a negative and a positive side. The negative side is that the system is not as "touchy-feely" or as humane as some might want. On the positive side, it is an efficient system in that it responds quickly to the market.

Long-term care insurance, an example of a private sector solution, is working, but we need more government education about the issue of long-term care. This would create more innovative responses from the industry and more interest from consumers.

Q: Where are the costs of long-term care heading?

A: The costs of nursing homes and home care will continue to rise sharply, and in some years, much greater than the rate of inflation. It's been difficult in both the public and private sector to keep a solid lid on costs. A high rate of inflation will create real problems if it compounds over twenty or thirty years. But, as an economist by training, I don't see that trend continuing indefinitely.

For example, my brother recently bought a house in Florida and told me enthusiastically, "Real estate prices are up 15 percent per year, and maybe that will last for the rest of our lives!" But prices can't go up like that forever. Mitigating factors come into force. The upward trend will slow at some point, normally due to supply and demand issues, and average out to a much lower percentage.

In other words, the market works. We are going to see technologies and innovations in long-term care services and delivery that keep the costs from escalating beyond control. In my opinion, it will not be so much a matter of controlling costs as it will be transforming the delivery system. Instead of making the cost of beds in a skilled nursing home go way down, we'll see new communities of care evolve to offer enriched services at a lower cost. That's what people want. It's already beginning to happen. The decline in use of nursing homes is a mirror image of the rising popularity of assisted living communities.

Technology will also play a major role in helping elders stay independent. Surveillance technology for monitoring vital signs could reduce the cost of care, and high-tech wheelchairs with onboard computers to help with stability could make disabled people much more mobile.

Q: Who faces the greatest financial risk from the high cost of long-term care?

A: The people in the middle are most at risk. The poor can be taken care of by Medicaid. The wealthy can pay for their own care even if they don't purchase LTC insurance. It's the people in the middle who are caught short.

Take a couple with a modest amount of assets, say $100,000. They don't want to spend money on LTC insurance because they have other financial responsibilities that seem to take precedence. They have medical bills and maintenance on the home. Important questions are ahead of them, such as "What will the wife do if she outlives the husband?" They don't know how long they'll live, or how many years of long-term care services they might need. And because of all these uncertainties, and the fact that LTC insurance premiums represent such a large percentage of their income and assets, they decide not to buy coverage.

Q: Are the baby boomers really a demographic time bomb as some experts say?

A: Yes, they are a time bomb. From a macro-economic perspective, 76 million boomers are going to challenge the long-term care system. They will really drive Medicaid crazy. The whole issue of who is and is not being taken care of will gain prominence as the boomers move further into retirement and old age. The salience of the issue in the media will increase. As a nation, we have the resources to care for the baby boomers, but we have not yet made the tough choices about how to marshal these resources.

An interesting demographic change is taking place. If you define dependents as people who don't work, we will have no more dependents as a percentage of population in 2030 than we did in 1960. In the 1960s, we had more children and fewer elders. But that ratio will be reversed in coming years.

The boomers will face three economic shocks as they turn 65. One is the cost of prescription drugs, which recently created a huge national debate. The second area is the continually rising cost of health care services not covered by Medicare, including doctor and hospitalization care. And the third, by far the biggest shock, will be the cost of long-term care.

When it comes to long-term care, the debate will be (1) do you want to force baby boomers to pre-fund their own care, through some sort of mandatory contribution into a private account or (2) do you rely on the current system—a public, pay-as-you-go system where each generation finances care for its elders?

*Q: **Which method of funding long-term care seems most viable?***

A: Personally, I think pre-funding is the only realistic answer. I just do not see the government stepping in and funding a multi-billion dollar entitlement for long-term care. We are running deficits now, but even in times of surplus there are competing priorities. I am not sure that most Americans are eager to be taxed at higher and higher rates for public services. If you ask, "Do you want lower taxes now or public long-term care benefits thirty years from now?" most people are going to want lower taxes. That's just the way it is.

One solution might be mandatory savings accounts for long-term care. If everyone was required to put a certain percentage of income, say 1.5 percent, into a private, personal, unshared account, and if they began contributing in their 20s, most people would have enough money accumulated to buy their own paid-up LTC insurance policy as they reached their middle age years. You might cap contributions at a maximum of $600 per year.

By forcing people to contribute, in effect, you are raising their taxes. But even relatively conservative people, such as Pete Peterson (author of *Gray Dawn* and a very influential voice in the long-term care debate), recommend mandatory pre-funding. It's a way of forcing people to put away a little each week. Those who oppose tax increases on principle are willing to consider mandatory pre-funding because the funds invested stay private. They go into your personal account, not into a common fund.

Q: *Where do the Partnership Program policies fit into this debate?*

A: Our feeling was that we already have some share of Medicaid dollars going to support long-term care for middle-class people who were independent until they became old and frail. Why not try to blend these public dollars with what people now spend out-of-pocket to develop more comprehensive LTC insurance and create some incentives for people to pre-fund? We came up with one idea: "quid pro quo," or dollar-for-dollar matching. Whatever dollar amount of insurance benefits you use up front, you automatically get to keep, and receive Medicaid benefits after your private long-term care coverage runs out. There are probably lots of other ways to blend public and private funding more efficiently than we do now, but this was a good start. The point is to use public dollars as an incentive to encourage middle-class people to invest in their own long-term care financing.

Q: *How successful have the Partnership Programs been?*

A: The Partnerships are alive and healthy. But they reach only a small percentage of the elderly. They are doing well, but not reaching down into the levels of the middle class we really hope to engage.

Q. Are they going to grow beyond the four states that already have them?

A. There is much interest in other states. However, the federal government needs to pass a law to authorize states to blend Medicaid and private revenues before new states can start Partnership Programs. There have been some hints that this may happen. Our model has not completely solved the problem, but we're still convinced that some variant of our approach, some way to combine and leverage public and private spending, is the way to go.

Right now, we seem to be in a dysfunctional stalemate. Half the people hate the idea of using public funds for long-term care, and the other half hate spending their own private dollars for long-term care services. Our view is that even a public solution will require some out-of-pocket premiums for the middle class. And even people who are opposed to public funding will have to agree that we can get more leverage from Medicaid money by using some portion of it to encourage private pre-funding by the middle class.

PERSPECTIVE FROM A FINANCIAL PLANNER
Heidi Estroff, CFP ®

> *I believe it is shortsighted to make*
> *recommendations without the full*
> *awareness of all aspects of a client's*
> *personal and financial situation.*

Heidi founded Estroff Wealth Management in 2003, bringing more than 14 years of professional experience to the firm. She entered the financial services industry in 1987, spending the majority of her career with national brokerage firms. Most recently, she was Vice President, Operations and Planning Services for the Wealth Management affiliate of a large regional CPA firm. Heidi lives with her family in the Augusta, Georgia area.

Q: Heidi, please tell us briefly about your philosophy when it comes to financial planning.

A. I decided to open my own financial practice for several reasons, the strongest reason being that I like to work with clients in a comprehensive planning manner. I believe it is shortsighted to make recommendations without the full awareness of all aspects of a client's personal and financial situation.

Q. Why did you attend our long-term care workshop at the National FPA Convention in 2003? In your financial planning practice, do you have very many clients who ask you about LTC insurance?

A. I attended your workshop because a large number of my clients bring up LTC insurance. Just in the last two weeks I've had two clients ask about it. It's a subject that is on people's minds more and more. I think many of the baby boomers are seeing what their parents are going through and have started to think about it themselves. One couple I worked with recently not only bought coverage for themselves, but also purchased policies for their parents.

Q. Do you find that a lot of these people who bring up LTC insurance have had personal experiences with this issue?

A. Many clients bring it up just because so many other people are making them aware of the need. They are asking themselves, "Is this something that is appropriate for me?" But, yes, a large number of people have relatives who would have been better off if they had planned for the possibility of needing long-term care— now they are planning ahead for themselves.

Q. Is LTC insurance a part of your planning checklist?

A. Yes. We always bring up the subject. We ask them how they plan to pay for long-term care. It is one of the main points in the planning process with our clients.

Q. Do you feel that most financial planners are familiar with this topic and are bringing it up with their clients?

A. Yes, more now than two or three years ago. When I left my previous firm, the carriers were just starting to educate us about LTC insurance. Some financial planning practices are even setting up in-house planners to help specifically with LTC insurance. But a few years ago, most financial consultants didn't take the time to understand it themselves. Fortunately, more and more financial planners are getting involved in actively addressing long-term care planning.

Q. When it comes to a hierarchy of risks, where would you place LTC insurance from the standpoint of importance?

A. I believe it is very important, especially for women. The odds are much higher that a woman will need long-term care. In a typical marriage, the female is probably going to outlive the male. She is going to be around to take care of her husband, but then no one will be around to take care of her. So for women, I'd say LTC insurance should rank as number 1 or 2.

Q. Do you think there is an ideal age for people to be taking a look at LTC insurance?

A. I think it varies from situation to situation. I like to talk to people about it at fairly young ages because the premiums are less. Fifty seems to be the age when most people can consider coverage, especially if they have good incomes. It's smart to lock in a lower premium during your income-producing years.

Q. *When it comes to income, do you have a ballpark income that you think people should have to be able to afford LTC insurance?*

A. No. I really look at it within the context of their overall objectives, and whether or not the premium is comfortable for them. I believe that if people can qualify for the coverage and afford the premium without changing their lifestyle, then they should invest in LTC insurance.

Q. *Do you have any thoughts on the amount of assets a person should have before they should self-insure?*

A. Again, the answer is no. It has more to do with their risk tolerance philosophy and goals. Some wealthy people believe LTC insurance is a good economic value. Long-term care planning should be completely customized, and the amount of assets is less important than the client's overall objectives.

Q. *From a personal standpoint, is LTC insurance something that you believe in? Have you had any personal experiences with relatives or friends that needed long-term care?*

A. Yes. My stepfather is receiving home care right now. He has both dementia and Parkinson's. And my grandmother ended up needing care after living with one of my uncles for quite a while. Because she did not have any long-term care coverage, my mother and her siblings had to step in and take care of her. It was both a financial and emotional strain on the family. So, yes, I personally have a strong belief in LTC insurance.

PERSPECTIVE FROM A CERTIFIED FINANCIAL PLANNER
Louise Schroeder, CFP®

I look at long-term care insurance premiums as a gift of peace of mind to my children that they will benefit from while I am still living, and not something that reduces what they will receive after I'm gone.

Louise Schroeder is a Certified Financial Planner™ professional and owner of Personal Financial Solutions, Inc. in Stillwater, Oklahoma. She provides financial planning and investment advice to clients for an hourly fee. Louise is a member of the Garrett Planning Network and is a contributor to their recently published book, "Just Give Me The Answer$: Expert Advisors Address Your Most Pressing Financial Questions." She holds a B.S. degree from Iowa State University, and M.S. and M.B.A. degrees from Oklahoma State University. Before establishing her own practice in 1998, she served on the OSU faculty for 10 years and was Assistant Director of Planned Giving at the OSU Foundation for 4 years. Louise serves on the Board of Directors of Citizens State Bank located in Stillwater and Morrison, Oklahoma. She is a member of the Financial Planning Association.

Q. Do you actively bring up the subject of LTC insurance with your clients?

A. I believe it is an intricate part of financial planning. For younger couples, starting in their 40s, if all of their major needs are met, we discuss the potential for long-term care needs for either them or their parents. I give them preliminary information on LTC insurance and some people will decide right then and there to take care of this need to secure their peace of mind. For anyone over 50, the topic is automatically covered.

Q. Do you think most financial planners are addressing LTC insurance with their clients?

A. It depends on their comfort level. Most financial planners don't want to sell LTC insurance, but they still need to understand the importance of long-term care planning and when LTC insurance is appropriate.

Q. Do you currently have a needs-analysis process for long-term care planning that you go through with your clients?

A. Yes, I include long-term care planning as an integral part of my client's retirement planning and/or estate planning. Some clients want to use their assets entirely for retirement and are concerned about running out of money; others want to keep certain assets to pass along to their children. For these people, LTC insurance can be an important part of their overall financial plan to protect those assets. For almost all of my clients, protecting their independence is extremely important to them. They do not want to interrupt the lives of their children or other relatives or friends with a potential long-term care need for themselves.

Q. Where do you rank LTC insurance in importance?

A. The importance many times is age-based. With a younger person, I would make sure their medical, life, and disability insurance needs are met first before discussing LTC insurance. But, many people buy LTC insurance in their 40s if they have their other insurance priorities covered. With an older person, depending on their financial situation, LTC insurance is often one of the top priorities.

Q. What is your opinion of life insurance policies with LTC insurance riders?

A. I believe that life insurance should be considered as life insurance and LTC insurance should be considered as LTC insurance. Why diminish life insurance benefits that you may need? And if you don't need life insurance, why buy it when better LTC insurance policies are available? I don't believe that this concept of bundling more than one insurance product is a good value. I look at LTC insurance premiums as a gift of peace of mind to my children that they will benefit from while I am still living, and not something that reduces what they will receive after I'm gone.

Q. *Do you think the government does a good job of educating people that they are not going to receive long-term care services from government programs?*

A. The government could do a much better job of educating consumers. The Department of Insurance in each state normally has an insurance counseling program that includes some information on LTC insurance, but the states could also do more to inform consumers about the need to plan ahead.

Q. *Do you have a certain amount of assets in dollars that you think a person should have before they do not need LTC insurance?*

A. No. It depends on your financial and emotional objectives. You may have a $5 million estate, but if you want to pass that on to your children or to causes you care about, LTC insurance may then be a very good value for you. Also, I have worked with one too many widows who were very comfortable financially before their husbands died, but for various reasons found themselves in financial trouble after their husbands were gone. Sometimes the hardship is due to the cost of the husband's illness and/or care needs; sometimes it's due to inexperienced financial management of the remaining assets. It's important to plan for the future: a long-term care need that may cost tens of thousands of dollars per year today may very easily cost hundreds of thousands of dollars twenty years in the future.

Q. *Have you had any personal experiences with long-term care needs?*

A. We're going through a need with my family right now. My brother and sister-in-law just moved in with my mother, who is having some memory problems. Mom has no LTC insurance. Even though this situation is working for now, my sister-in-law is in her 60s and would not be able to handle any physical care if my mother needed it. My brother is still working. The future holds uncertainty for us.

But, let me tell you a very personal story. A while back my husband and I applied for LTC insurance once I became aware of the importance of coverage. When we were ready to submit the applications, I developed severe back muscle spasms and had to have physical therapy. The insurance company would not even consider coverage on me until after the physical therapy was completed. We were very concerned about something more serious being diagnosed and me not being able to qualify for coverage. We were finally issued coverage, but that experience taught me to strongly encourage clients to apply for LTC insurance while they are healthy.

PERSPECTIVE FROM THE PRESIDENT OF THE CENTER FOR LONG-TERM CARE FINANCING
The Coming Challenge of Long-Term Care
Stephen A. Moses

> *If the baby boom is the Titanic,*
> *long-term care is the iceberg.*

Stephen A. Moses is President of the Center for Long-Term Care Financing, a 501(c)(3) charitable, nonprofit, nonpartisan think tank and public policy organization dedicated to "ensuring quality long-term care for all Americans." For published articles, reports and speeches, see the Center's website at *www.centerltc.org.*

Q: How would you describe the challenge of long-term care?

A: If the baby boom is the Titanic, long-term care is the iceberg. Nearly 40 years of easy access to Medicaid nursing home benefits and, more recently, long-term home care from Medicare, have lulled the American public into a false sense of security about long-term care. Today, Medicaid is on the verge of bankruptcy and suffers from a dismal reputation for problems of access, quality, reimbursement, discrimination, and institutional bias. Medicare's fiscal crisis is closing like a vise and the program has already cut back on home care costs with draconian vigor. Can you imagine what these programs are going to look like, if they even exist, in 20 or 30 years when the boomers start to need long-term care? It will not be pretty!

Q: How do you see your organization, the Center for Long-Term Care Financing, helping with the problem of long-term care?

A: Our only hope to prepare for the demographic onslaught of exponentially greater long-term care needs is to wean the public off the expectation that Medicaid, Medicare or any future publicly financed program is going to pay for long-term custodial care. We must offer a better and affordable alternative to people when they are still young, healthy, and affluent enough to qualify for it. That is the mission of the Center for Long-Term Care Financing.

We promote universal access to high-quality long-term care by encouraging private financing and discouraging welfare dependency for most Americans. We pursue this objective by warning the public about the risks of Medicaid Planning (artificial self-impoverishment) and by pointing out the benefits of good LTC insurance and home equity conversion alternatives.

Q: *How did America's long-term care service delivery and financing system become so dysfunctional?*

A: Medicaid was originally an afterthought, a tag-on to Medicare in 1965. Advocates for the elderly had huge political clout so they got a big, new social insurance program (Medicare). Advocates for the poor were much weaker politically, but they argued successfully that the needy should not be left out entirely. They prevailed, but achieved only a smaller, welfare-based program (Medicaid). The focus of both programs was acute care. But Medicaid contained a kicker, a provision authorizing payment for nursing home care for the elderly. No one thought this portion of the program would cost very much, because formal fee-for-service long-term care was still relatively rare.

The rest is history. The nursing home industry exploded in size to take advantage of this new source of money. Lax eligibility rules allowed families to place their frail elders in nursing homes on Medicaid at little or no expense. Home care, assisted living and private LTC insurance languished for decades for lack of demand and financial oxygen. Why pay out-of-pocket or buy insurance when nursing home care was virtually free? Medicaid long-term care costs skyrocketed even as the program acquired a reputation for inferior access and quality. Consequently, America finds herself at the start of the twenty-first century with a fragmented long-term care system suffering from institutional bias, an underdeveloped home and community-based services infrastructure, inadequate public financing, and market penetration by private LTC insurance of less than 10 percent.

As Medicaid nursing home expenditures shot up in the 1970s and 1980s, our government began to clamp down on eligibility. Restrictions on asset transfers began in 1981 with the Boren-Long

Amendment. Authorization for liens and estate recoveries came in 1982 with the Tax Equity and Fiscal Responsibility Act. Congress tackled trust abuses with the Omnibus Budget Reconciliation Act of 1985. The Medicare Catastrophic Coverage Act of 1988 made transfer of assets restrictions mandatory and longer. The Omnibus Budget Reconciliation Act of 1993 closed many loopholes and made estate recoveries mandatory. As soon as the government started restricting eligibility, however, the private Elder Law Bar began to offer "Medicaid Planning" to help prosperous seniors get around the new rules and qualify for public financing of their long-term care without having to spend down their assets. Beginning in the early 1980s, the rapidly expanding Medicaid Planning bar succeeded in opening many new eligibility loopholes to replace each one the government closed.

Finally, Congress and President Clinton became exasperated. They criminalized Medicaid asset transfers in the Health Insurance Portability and Accountability Act of 1996. This law came to be known as the "Throw Granny in Jail Law." It attracted a lot of opposition. Consequently, in the Balanced Budget Act of 1997, Congress let Grandpa and Grandma off the hook and targeted the real culprits with the criminal penalty. Anyone who, for a fee, recommended a transfer of assets to qualify for Medicaid became vulnerable to a $10,000 fine and/or one year in jail. But President Clinton's Attorney General, Janet Reno, concluded that it would be unconstitutional to enforce such a penalty. How could lawyers and other financial professionals be held legally culpable for recommending a practice that became legal again when the "Throw Granny in Jail Law" was repealed? Ecstatic Medicaid Planners quickly returned to marketing their artificial impoverishment schemes and the government went back to searching half-heartedly for new means to control these abuses.

Q: Isn't Medicaid an entitlement program like Medicare? Why shouldn't people manipulate their income and assets to qualify?

A: Medicaid is a means-tested public assistance program. It is welfare. Medicaid was intended to be a safety net for our nation's neediest. One is not entitled to Medicaid as one is entitled to Medicare, which is social insurance, not welfare. People qualify for Medicaid if they meet certain income and asset limitations. The intent of Congress and the expectation of taxpayers is that people should spend down their wealth paying for their own care before they look to Medicaid for assistance.

Medicaid Planners short-circuit the spend down process. They encourage seniors (or more often, their heirs) to impoverish themselves artificially in order to take advantage of Medicaid benefits without following the intent of the rules. As a direct consequence, genuinely needy people have a harder time gaining access to beds in quality nursing homes; heirs get early inheritances at the expense of the taxpayers; nursing home owners receive less than the cost of providing the care from Medicaid (according to the accounting firm BDO Seidman), and America's beloved World War II generation has largely died in nursing homes on welfare instead of aging in place at home.

While Medicaid Planners line their pockets with big fees, agents struggling to sell LTC insurance to a nation in denial have to be altruistic, masochistic geniuses to make a decent living. Is it any wonder private LTC insurance has penetrated less than 10 percent of the senior market and only very few of the baby boomers have purchased it?

Q: What is the likelihood that we'll ever see a government-financed model for long-term health care that provides for the middle class?

A: Social Security is in dire straits and will probably have to be at least partially privatized soon. Medicare has been bailed out by general tax revenues for many years, but it still faces bankruptcy in the foreseeable future. Managed care, long presumed to be the savior of Medicare and Medicaid, has undergone a severe backlash against inferior access and quality. Long-term home health care financed by Medicare was brutally curtailed in 1997. Medicaid's fiscal problems are legion and its reputation for access and quality is dismal and still declining.

In the meantime, private financing of long-term care has declined drastically even as public financing has skyrocketed. America spent $103.2 billion on nursing home care in 2002. The percentage of nursing home costs paid by government (mostly Medicaid and Medicare) has been going up for the past 14 years (from 49.6 percent in 1988 to 64 percent in 2002, up 14.4 percent of the total) while out-of-pocket costs have been declining (from 38.5 percent in 1988 to 25.1 percent in 2002, down 13.4 percent of the total). (*Source: www.cms.hhs.gov/statistics/nhe/historical/t7.asp*)

The situation with home health care financing is very similar to nursing home financing. According to the Centers for Medicare and Medicaid Services (CMS), America spent $36.1 billion on home care in 2002. Medicare and Medicaid paid 55.4 percent of this total and private insurance paid 18.6 percent. Only 18 percent of home health care costs were paid out of pocket. The remainder came from several small public and private financing sources. (*Source: www.cms.hhs.gov/statistics/nhe/historical/t9.asp*)

It does not take a demographic or economic genius to see what is happening here. The baby boomers are moving through American society like the proverbial pig through a python. When their generation approached adulthood, America got drugs, sex, and rock and roll. When the boomers arrive at senescence, America faces an equally dramatic cultural impact, but this time it will not be fun and it will be very expensive. With the major social insurance programs imploding already, having struggled only with income security and acute health care, what hope does the public have that government programs will survive to confront the much bigger future problem of long-term care? Answer: none!

The smart money is already preparing to take personal responsibility for long-term care planning. If enough of the smart people plan ahead, save or insure, it is still possible that some remnant of a publicly financed safety net for the long-term care of genuine indigents may survive. But don't count on it!

Q: *If the government isn't going to pay for long-term care, where can we turn? Many experts say LTC insurance is unafford-able, so our only hope is "social insurance."*

A: Experts like that still cling to an anachronistic social insurance model and ignore the massive empirical evidence that disproves it. Their argument boils down to this: widespread catastrophic nursing-home spend down and the unaffordability of private LTC insurance make publicly financed long-term care inevitable. Neither of these premises is true. Few people spend down their life savings before qualifying for Medicaid. Therefore, the public has little financial incentive to buy LTC insurance. That is what makes the premiums seem "unaffordable."

We used to think that 50 to 75 percent of all people in nursing homes on Medicaid spent down their savings to qualify. We now know the truth is that only 15 to 25 percent begin as private pay and convert to Medicaid. As low as these figures are, they include everyone who does artificial impoverishment to qualify for Medicaid as well as those who spend down the old-fashioned way, by paying for their own care. Actually, 78 percent of all peo-ple who enter nursing homes are already eligible for Medicaid and Medicaid pays for nearly 80 percent of all patient days in America's nursing homes. Medicaid eligibility rules are so gener-ous that the average senior, in terms of income and assets, qual-ifies for nursing home care without fancy legal planning. Virtually anyone else, irrespective of wealth, can qualify easily and quickly given the right legal advice. These facts, not its cost, account for the low market penetration of private long-term care insurance. People only buy insurance against a genuine risk.

Private LTC insurance is not cheap. If every tenth house burned down, fire insurance would not be cheap either. This does not mean, however, that LTC insurance is unaffordable. Purchased when one is young and healthy, say between the ages of 45 and 65, good private coverage is available at affordable rates. Even for a person over 70, premiums are nominal compared to the cost of a catastrophic long-term nursing home stay. You could argue reasonably that no one could afford not to insure privately if the financial risk were real. The problem is that easy availability of Medicaid financing after the insurable event occurs has anesthetized the American public to the risk of long-term care. Consequently, people do not think about private insurance until they are too old to obtain it or too sick to qualify medically.

Q: *All right, so how would you change public policy to meet the challenge of long-term care?*

A: The solution to the problem is clearly not more government financing. That would be like trying to put out a fire by dousing it with gasoline. Rather, the answer is to invite the public to look realistically at the risk of long-term care while they are still young, healthy and affluent enough to afford and qualify for private LTC insurance. To get them to take this danger seriously, we must advise people no later than when they apply for Medicare and Social Security that Medicaid will not pay for long-term care while they retain significant assets, that they will genuinely have to spend down to qualify, and that Medicaid only pays for nursing home care, not the preferred choices of home care or assisted living. Faced with a real risk, the public will buy private insurance to avoid the consequences of Medicaid spend down and to assure access to home care, assisted living, and higher quality private nursing homes.

Affordability of LTC insurance will no longer be an issue as people begin to purchase policies at earlier ages. Recognizing the need, seniors will consider reverse annuity mortgages as a means to supplement their incomes in order to afford coverage. Faced with the loss of their inheritances, adult children of seniors will help their parents afford private insurance to protect the estate. Between the nearly $2 trillion in home equity held by seniors today and the $10 trillion their baby boomer children will inherit, there is more than enough wealth in America to solve the long-term care financing crisis with private insurance in a free market. If the government stopped destroying the market for private insurance by indemnifying upper middle class heirs for the cost of their parents' long-term care, we could unleash private insurance and save Medicaid for the genuinely needy.

Q: How should smart consumers plan for long-term care?

A: As one of the all-time-great LTC insurance agents once told me, "Denial is not a river in Egypt." Most people fail to plan for long-term care by purchasing private insurance, because they think, "It will never happen to me. I'll never go to one of those places." What they don't realize is that most people who need expensive long-term care are cognitively impaired. Half of all people over the age of 85 already have Alzheimer's Disease.

The fact that people are in denial about long-term care is not the most important point. Of course, no one wants to think about the possibility of becoming frail and incapacitated. Who wants to live in an institution? What interests me is the question, "How is it that people can be in denial about the long-term care risk when nine percent of all seniors will spend five years or more in a long-term care facility at $30,000 to $80,000 per year?" If Americans really faced a one in ten chance of being wiped out by a catastrophic long-term illness, they would not have the luxury to be in denial and they would plan ahead to insure against the risk.

That is the primary point I want to make. Medicaid financing of long-term care has enabled the American public's denial of the long-term care risk. Because Medicaid, with all its faults, has been there for the last four decades paying the bills after the insured event occurs, most Americans do not feel a sense of financial urgency about the risk of long-term care expenses. The solution is to encourage our fellow countrymen to take long-term care more seriously by assuring that Medicaid only goes to the genuinely needy. Anyone else who receives the welfare program's benefits while retaining exempt assets must pay the system back out of his or her estate. Once heirs cannot get a free ride at the taxpayers' expense, they will encourage and help their parents to buy LTC insurance. More importantly, they will buy it themselves!

If we don't change public policy in this way, baby boomers will pay the price. Their income security is at risk because of Social Security's insolvency. Their acute health care is at risk because of Medicare's impending bankruptcy. And their long-term care will be entirely their own responsibility because Medicaid is already collapsing. If the boomers don't buy insurance, they will pay for their long-term care out of their home equity. Their children, the echo boomers, are too small a population cohort to support Social Security and Medicare, much less Medicaid. The front cusp of a generation that will overwhelm America's long-term care service delivery and financing system is already approaching seniority.

Bottom line: we have faint hope that politicians and bureaucrats will fix these problems in time. The only good news is that individuals and families can protect themselves. The tools to do so are LTC insurance, for those who qualify, and home equity conversion, such as reverse mortgages, for others who will not qualify and own homes. If enough people pay privately for long-term care, we can hope that some kind of safety net will survive for the poor.

APPENDIX

ACRONYMS

AAHSA	American Association of Homes and Services for the Aging
AARP	American Association of Retired Persons
ADLs	Activities of Daily Living
BBA	Balanced Budget Act of 1997
CCAC	Continuing Care Accreditation Commission
CCRC	Continuing Care Retirement Communities
CFP	Certified Financial Planner
CPA	Certified Public Accountant
ERISA	Employee Retirement Income Security Act
FLTCIP	Federal Long-Term Care Insurance Program
HIPAA	Health Insurance Portability and Accountability Act
IADLs	Incidental Activities of Daily Living
LPN	Licensed Practical Nurse
LTC	Long-Term Care
NADSA	National Adult Day Services Association
NAIC	National Association of Insurance Commissioners
NCOA	National Council on Aging
NTQ	Non-Tax Qualified
OBRA	Omnibus Budget Reconciliation Act
TQ	Tax-Qualified

STATE TAX INCENTIVES FOR LONG-TERM CARE INSURANCE

* States not listed may not currently offer a tax advantage.

STATE	INCENTIVE	DESCRIPTION
Alabama	Deduction	A deduction is allowed for the amount of premiums paid pursuant to a qualifying insurance contract for qualified long-term care coverage. Code of AL. 40-18-15(27)(1996)
California	Deduction	A deduction is allowed, beginning in taxable years on or after January 1, 1997, for qualified long-term care insurance premiums to the extent that amount does not exceed the limitation allowed for certain attained ages. CA. Rev. & Tax Code §17213 (1996)
Colorado	Credit	A credit is allowed in taxable years on or after January 1, 2000 for 25 percent of premiums paid for long-term care insurance. The credit will be available only to individual taxpayers with taxable income of less than $50,000 or two individuals filing a joint return with taxable income of less than $100,000. C.R.S. 39-22-122 (1999)
Hawaii	Deduction	A deduction is allowed for premiums paid for long-term care insurance to the extent such premiums are deductible in determining federal taxable income beginning in taxable years after December 31, 1998. HRS Sec. 235-2.4 (1999)
Idaho	Deduction	For taxable years commencing on or after January 1, 2001, 50 percent of the premiums paid during the taxable year by a taxpayer for long-term care insurance as that term is defined in section 41-4603, Idaho Code, which long-term care insurance is to be for the benefit of the taxpayer, a dependent of the taxpayer or an employee of the taxpayer, may be deducted from taxable income. Effective July 1, 2001. Idaho Code, 63-3022P

Iowa	Deduction	A deduction is allowed for tax years beginning on or after January 1, 1997, for premiums for long-term care insurance for nursing home coverage to the extent the premiums for long-term health care services are eligible for the federal itemized deduction for medical and dental expenses. IAC Chapter 40, §701-40.49(422);IAC§422.7(1997)
Kentucky	Deduction	A deduction is allowed for any amount paid during the taxable year for long-term care insurance premiums from adjusted gross income applied to taxable years beginning after December 31, 1997. KRS 140.010 (Sec.1)(1998)
Maine	Deduction	A deduction is allowed for an amount equal to the total premium spent for insurance policies for long-term care that have been certified by the Superintendent of Insurance as complying with Title 24-A, Chapter 68. Title 36, Part 8, Chapter 805, Sec. 5122 (1989)
	Credit	For employers, a credit is allowed against the tax imposed for each taxable year equal to the lowest of the following: (A) $5,000; (B) 20 percent of the costs incurred by the taxpayer in providing long-term care policy coverage as part of the benefit package; or (C) $100 for each employee covered by an employer-provided long-term care policy. Title 36, Part 4, Section 2525, Chapter 357 (1996)
Maryland	Credit	A credit is allowed against the state income tax for employers providing long-term care insurance up to an amount equal to 5 percent of the costs incurred by the employer during the taxable year for providing long-term care insurance as part of the employee benefit package. The credit may not exceed $5,000 or $100 for each employee covered by long-term care insurance under the employer benefit package and it is applicable to all taxable years beginning after December 31, 1998, Ins. Art. 6-117, Chapter 7 (1998)

Minnesota	Credit	A credit is allowed for long-term care insurance premiums during the taxable year equal to (1) 25 percent of premiums paid to the extent not deducted in determining federal taxable income or (2) $100. Sec. 21, Sec. 290.0672 subdivision 2 (2000)
Missouri	Deduction	A deduction is allowed for a resident from state taxable income for an amount equal to fifty percent of all non-reimbursed amounts paid by an individual for qualified long-term care insurance premiums to the extent such amounts are not included in the individual's itemized deductions for all taxable years beginning after December 31, 1999. Section 8 of R.S. MO 334660 (1999)
Montana	Deduction	A deduction is allowed for all premium payments made directly by the taxpayer for long-term care insurance policies or certificates that provide coverage primarily for any qualified long-term care services as defined in 26 U.S.C. 7702B(C) beginning after December 31, 1994 or of the taxpayer's parents, grandparents, or both for taxpayers beginning after December 31, 1996. Chapter 111 (1997)
New York	Credit	A credit is allowed equal to 10 percent of the premium paid during the taxable year for long-term care insurance approved by the Superintendent of Insurance pursuant to Section 1017 of the insurance law and applicable to taxable years beginning on or after January 1, 2002. Chapter 407 (2000)
North Carolina	Credit	A credit is allowed for premiums paid on long-term care insurance in an amount equal to 15 percent of the premium costs the individual paid during the taxable year for the individual, spouse, or dependent. The credit may not exceed $350 for each qualified long-term care insurance contract for which credit is claimed. Part 2, Article 4, Chapter 105, §105-151.28 (1998)

North Dakota	Credit	A credit is allowed to be applied against an individual's tax liability in the amount of 25 percent of any premiums paid by the taxpayer for long-term care insurance coverage for the taxpayer or the taxpayer's spouse, parent, stepparent, or child. The credit may not exceed $100 in any taxable year. Title 57, Chapter 57-38 (1997)
Ohio	Deduction	A deduction is allowed for individual policy premiums paid for qualified long-term care insurance effective for taxable years beginning January 1, 1999. Ohio Rev. Stat. Section 5747.01 (1999)
Oregon	Credit	A credit is allowed for amounts paid or incurred for long-term care insurance by an individual on behalf of himself, dependents or parents and for amounts paid or incurred by an employer on behalf of employees. Limits credit to lesser of 15 percent of premiums or $500. Effective October 23, 1999. Chapter 1005, (1999)
Utah	Deduction	A deduction is allowed from federal taxable income of a resident or nonresident individual for tax years beginning on or after January 1, 2000, of any amounts paid for premiums on long-term care insurance policies to the extent the amounts paid were not deducted under Section 213 of the Internal Revenue Code in determining federal taxable income. Chapter 60, §59-10-114 (1999)
Virginia	Deduction	A deduction is allowed from federal adjusted gross income for taxable years beginning on or after January 1, 2000 for the amount an individual pays annually in premiums for long-term care insurance, provided the individual has not claimed a deduction for federal income tax purposes. Chapter 298, §58.1-322 (1999)

West Virginia	Deduction	A deduction is allowed for taxable years beginning on or after January 1, 2000 for any payment during the taxable year for premiums for a long-term care insurance policy that offers coverage to either the taxpayer, spouse, parent, or dependent, only to the extent the amount is not allowable as a deduction when arriving at the taxpayer's adjusted gross income. Article 21 §11-21-12C, Chapter 11 (2000)
Wisconsin	Deduction	A deduction is allowed for 100 percent of the amount paid for a long-term care insurance policy for the person and his or her spouse beginning on or after January 1, 1998. Wis. Stat. §71.05(6)(b)26 (1997)

Source: The Corporation For Long-Term Care Certification, Inc., www.ltc-cltc.com
The above information is not to be construed as tax or legal advice.
Seek advice from your financial professional.

GLOSSARY

– A –

Accelerated Benefits: A clause in a life insurance policy that allows payment of benefits for long-term care services.

Accumulation Period: The amount of time an insured is given to accumulate the number of days of care needed to satisfy the elimination period of a long-term care insurance policy.

Activities of Daily Living (ADLs): Physical functions that are performed on a daily basis such as bathing, dressing, eating, transferring, toileting, and continence. The ability or inability to perform these functions often determines whether an individual is capable of living independently. Long-term care insurance policies use the inability to perform ADLs as a criteria for determining eligibility for benefits.

Acute Care: Medical care received from licensed health professionals and/or hospitals with the aim of full restoration or rehabilitation of physical functions. Acute care usually refers to a treatment period of 100 days or less, which we define as short-term care.

Adult Day Center: A facility in which services and care are provided to individuals who are unable to remain at home alone during the day. These services might also include social and recreational events to alleviate the social isolation that a person living alone might experience. Caretakers who are regularly employed during the day frequently utilize these programs during working hours. Senior centers and community centers often offer adult day programs.

Adverse Selection: The disproportionate number of people who are likely to submit claims in an "insurance pool," resulting in a higher rate of claims than expected with the potential to have inadequate premium reserves to cover the costs of the claims unless premium rates are increased.

Alzheimer's Disease: A progressive, irreversible form of dementia that causes severe intellectual deterioration that eventually results in complete dependency. It affects 5 percent of those over 65 and 20 percent of those over 80. The cause of the disease is unknown at this time. Symptoms begin with loss of memory and rational thinking, with progressive deterioration over the course of several years.

Ambulatory: The ability to move about, generally without any type of assistance.

Ambulatory with Assistance: The ability to move about with the aid of a cane, crutch, brace, wheelchair, or walker.

Ancillary Services: Personal care services such as podiatry, dentistry, and hair care that are needed by a nursing home or assisted living resident, but not typically included in the basic costs charged by the facility.

Assisted Living Facility/Community: A residential facility for those individuals who may need help with activities of daily living. These facilities usually include private units (apartments or rooms), two to three meals a day, laundry services, transportation, activities, and housekeeping. In most facilities, a 24-hour staff is available to meet residents' needs.

– B –

Bed Reservation Benefit: Allows a facility to receive payment for a bed being held for a resident who requires temporary hospitalization. This is a covered expense in most long-term care insurance policies.

Benefit Amount: A set dollar amount of benefit per day, week, or month that a long-term care insurance policy will pay for long-term care costs.

Benefit Period Maximum: The maximum amount a long-term care insurance policy will pay for covered services in a lifetime. The benefit can be expressed in length of time, or a dollar amount. This benefit may be payable to the owner of the policy or to a third party, such as the facility or home care provider.

Benefit Triggers: The criteria used by insurance carriers to determine eligibility for long-term care insurance benefits. The best policies "trigger" benefits when a policyholder is unable to perform two or more ADLs without assistance.

Board and Care Homes: "Homes" that provide limited supervision and care to their residents. Medical personnel are usually not on staff and the administration of medications is not usually available.

Bundled Products: Policies that combine life insurance or some other financial product with long-term care insurance.

– C –

Care Coordination: Assistance with the development and implementation of the plan of care including helping people identify appropriate services and making arrangements to receive care.

Caregiver: A person giving assistance to another. Assistance is usually required due to medical reasons, inability to perform activities of daily living, or cognitive impairment.

Caregiver Training Benefit: A benefit in a long-term care insurance policy that pays for someone to learn the best methods to use in caring for the policyholder who is on claim.

Certification: A certificate given to a facility that is in compliance with a set of federal standards on staffing, cleanliness, and maintenance of records, etc. Nursing homes must be certified before they are reimbursed for care provided to Medicaid recipients.

Chronic Illness: An illness characterized by the following: permanency and/or residual disability requiring a long period of care.

Cognitive Impairment: Deficiency in short- or long-term memory; orientation as to person, place, and time; abstract reasoning; or judgment as it relates to safety awareness.

Co-insurance: The process of paying for a portion of the cost of care out-of-pocket.

Community-Based Services: Services designed to help older people stay independent and in their own homes.

Comprehensive Planning Approach: A process of considering long-term care planning within the context of your financial situation and goals.

Comprehensive Long-Term Care Insurance Policy: A long-term care insurance policy that covers care in any environment, including facility care and home care.

Conditionally Renewable: A policy that can be canceled at any time for any reason, including excessive claims history. No longer allowed in currently issued long-term care insurance policies.

Conservatorship: If a court determines that a person is unable to manage his/her property due to mental illness or deficiency, physical illness or disability, drug abuse, chronic intoxication, advanced age, confinement, disappearance, detention by a foreign power; and if that property will be wasted or dissipated without being properly managed or if funds are needed to care for the individual or those supported by him, a "conservator" may be appointed by the court.

Continuing Care Retirement Community (CCRC): Also called "Life Care Communities," these communities offer the full spectrum of living and care arrangements, from independent living to nursing home care, without having to leave the community.

Custodial Care: Care to help an individual meet their personal needs such as bathing, dressing, and eating.

– D –

Delayed Word Recall (DWR): A memory exercise that is used to screen for short-term memory or primary memory loss.

Dementia: Deterioration of intellectual faculties.

– E –

Elimination Period: The time period during which a policyholder pays for covered services before a long-term care insurance policy will begin to pay for those services.

Estate Recovery: When a Medicaid recipient dies and leaves an estate, Medicaid may seek to recover from the estate the money it spent on care for the recipient.

Estate Planning: Addresses tax-efficient ways to acquire, preserve, and transfer a person's financial wealth to other parties, both during and after life.

– F –

Facility-Care-Only Policy: A long-term care insurance policy that only covers care in a facility such as a nursing home or assisted living community. Care in the home is not covered with these policies.

Financial Planning: The overall process of setting financial goals, evaluating where you are with respect to those goals, laying out a plan to achieve them, implementing the plan, and modifying the plans and actions as your current situation and goals change.

Formal Care Provider: Caregivers who are trained specialists and provide long-term care services for a living.

Free-Look Period: Also called the "Right to Return" provision. A newly insured long-term care insurance policyholder has the right to return the policy to the company within 30 days of issuance for a full refund of any deposits or premium payments made.

– G –

Grace Period: A length of time after the premium due date during which the coverage remains in force although payment has not been made. This period is normally 31 days.

Group Long-Term Care Insurance: Coverage offered by employers or other groups that is normally issued on a Guaranteed Issue or Modified Guarantee Issue basis. This means that the applicant could be accepted for coverage without full underwriting.

Guaranteed Issue: A policy issued without any underwriting requirements. Coverage may be obtained regardless of current or past health conditions.

Guaranteed Purchase Option: A provision giving the insured the right to purchase additional coverage at set intervals without having to reapply and health-qualify for coverage. The premium for the additional coverage will be based on the policyholder's age at the time of benefit increase.

Guaranteed Renewable: A policy that can only be canceled because of non-payment of premium. Adjustments in premium may be made, but only for a whole class of insureds and not just the individual.

– H –

Health Insurance Portability and Accountability Act (HIPAA): An extensive piece of legislation passed by Congress in 1996. Resulted in the standardization of long-term care insurance policies and clarified the tax treatment of benefits and premiums for long-term care insurance.

Home Care: Personal care services provided by trained but not skilled personnel. Does not require the supervision of a physician.

Home-Care-Only Policy: A policy that does not cover care in any type of facility. Typically, covers home health care, home care, adult day centers and some homemaker services.

Home Health Agency: A private or public agency that specializes in providing skilled nurses, homemakers, home health aides and therapeutic services (e.g., physical therapy) in an individual's home.

Home Health Care: Care or services received from skilled personnel in your home. The treatment or plan of care is supervised by a physician or registered nurse.

Homemaker Services: Activities that focus on managing a household such as laundry, housekeeping, and meal preparation.

Hospice Care: A special way of caring for the needs of a terminally ill patient and his or her family. This care addresses physical, spiritual, emotional, psychological, social, financial, and legal needs while enhancing the dying person's quality of life.

– I –

Incidental Activities of Daily Living (IADLs): Activities such as cooking, cleaning, shopping, laundry, managing money, administering medications, and providing transportation.

Inflation Protection Rider: An option on a long-term care insurance policy that provides for automatic increases in benefit levels to hedge against expected increases in long-term care service costs.

Informal Caregivers: Caregivers who care for a patient out of love or a sense of duty rather than as a profession.

Institutionalization: To admit a person into a facility, such as a nursing home, where they will have an extended or indefinite stay.

Intermediate Care: Provided when recovery and rehabilitation are the primary goals and 24-hour-a-day physician supervision is not needed.

– L –

Lapse: Termination of a policy when a premium is not paid.

Life Care Arrangement or Life Care Contract: Typically, a financial arrangement utilized by Continuing Care Retirement Communities. The resident pays an initial lump sum of money when they move in, and then a predetermined monthly amount thereafter.

Lifetime Policy: A long-term care insurance policy in which there is no maximum limit on the cumulative benefits collected.

Lifetime Maximum Benefit: The term used to describe the total dollar amount that can be collected from a long-term care insurance policy. Choices in the lifetime maximum range from as short as one year to unlimited coverage, which has no cumulative dollar or time limit.

Limited Pay: Long-term care insurance policies in which premiums are paid for a limited time period instead of over the life of the policy. Common periods include single payment, five-year pay, ten-year pay, and twenty-year pay.

Long-Term Care: Medical and social care given to individuals with a chronic illness, disability, or cognitive disorder over a period of time, defined by the author as longer than 100 days. This care may take place in a skilled nursing facility, assisted living community, adult day center, the home of the person receiving care, or someone else's home. Care can be administered by medical professionals or nonprofessional personnel.

– M –

Meals-On-Wheels: A program that delivers meals to people who are homebound.

Medicaid: A welfare program administered by the federal and individual state governments that helps pay for certain medical care given to needy and low-income people. A nursing home must be certified by Medicaid in order to be reimbursed for care provided to a Medicaid recipient.

Medi-Cal: The Medicaid program in California.

Medicare: A federal health insurance program that pays for health care for people over 65 and some under 65 who are disabled. Part A is Hospital Insurance and Part B is Medical Insurance. Medicare pays for limited short-term care in a skilled nursing facility but only under certain conditions. Medicare DOES NOT pay for long-term care.

Medicare Supplement Insurance: Private insurance policies that cover health care costs not fully covered by Medicare. Medicare supplement insurance DOES NOT pay for long-term care.

Medigap Insurance: Another name for Medicare supplement insurance.

Modified Guaranteed Issue: People who are in poor health but can certify that they are currently not needing long-term care services, or do not have a condition that will result in the need for long-term care in the near future, may qualify for coverage under this type of issue.

– N –

National Association of Insurance Commissioners (NAIC): A membership organization of state insurance commissioners. One of its goals is to promote uniformity of state regulation and legislation related to insurance.

Nonforfeiture Benefit: Usually available as an option, it allows the policyholder to receive some type of benefit if the policy lapses. The benefit usually is in the form of a paid-up maximum benefit equal to the cumulative premiums paid at the time of the lapse.

Non-Tax-Qualified Policies (NTQ): Policies that do not conform to HIPAA's requirements and do not receive the same tax treatment as Tax-Qualified policies.

Nursing Home: A licensed facility that provides general nursing care to those who are chronically ill or unable to take care of daily living needs.

– O –

Outline of Coverage: A description of the coverage and benefits of a long-term care insurance policy. Includes a statement of principal exclusions; limitations in the policy; a statement of the terms under which the policy may be returned and the premiums refunded; and a description of the policy benefits.

– P –

Partnership Policy: A type of policy that allows you to protect some of your assets if you apply for Medicaid after using your policy's benefits. Currently available in 4 states: California, New York, Indiana, and Connecticut.

Plan of Care: An organized schedule of treatment or care for a patient, usually developed by physicians, nurses, or discharge planners at hospitals.

Planning Gap: A shortfall between the resources allocated to meet long-term care costs and the estimated cost of that care.

Power of Attorney: A written agreement that authorizes a relative, attorney, business associate, friend, or another person to sign documents and enter into transactions on behalf of the individual.

– R –

Respite Care: The in-home care given to a chronically ill beneficiary in order to give the regular caregiver(s) a break.

Restoration of Benefits Rider: When you buy a policy with less than an "Unlimited Benefit Maximum," and you use a portion of your policy benefits, the entire pool of benefits in the policy will be restored if your health returns and you go without care for a specified period of time.

– S –

Sandwich Generation: Members of the baby boom generation who are raising children and caring for an aging parent at the same time.

Senility: Mental deterioration that sometimes accompanies aging.

Senior Center: A community-based facility that provides seniors with activities such as recreation, education, cultural, and social events.

Short-Term Care: Care that is required for less than 100 days.

Single Sales Approach: Addressing one aspect of insurance or financial planning in a vacuum instead of looking at all aspects within the context of the overall financial situation and goals of the individual, family or company.

Skilled Care: Care provided by a trained medical person and under the supervision of a doctor or other qualified medical person.

Skilled Nursing Facility (SNF): A facility providing skilled care by licensed staff.

Sponsored Long-Term Care Insurance: Offered by an employer or other "group," but unlike true group insurance, sponsored programs use the same strict underwriting guidelines as individually issued policies.

Spousal Discount: If husband and wife, or partners, purchase coverage from the same insurance carrier, they may receive a premium discount on both policies.

Survivorship Benefit: Offered as a rider, this provision says that if one spouse dies after paying premiums for a certain period of time, the spouse still living is no longer required to pay premiums on their own policy. Requires both spouses to have coverage with the same insurer, and normally requires that both policies be claim-free for a certain number of years.

– T –

Tax-Qualified Policy (TQ): Long-term care insurance policies created by HIPAA legislation in 1996. Resulted in the standardization of long-term care insurance policies and the clarification of tax consequences.

Third Party Notification of Lapse: Requires insurers to send a notice to an individual designated by the insured before a policy is canceled due to nonpayment of premium.

– U –

Underwriting: The process of examining, accepting, or rejecting insurance risks, and classifying those accepted to charge the appropriate premium for each.

Uninsurable: Individuals who are not eligible for insurance due to the presence of a health condition that requires them to already receive care, or who may have a high probability of needing care in the future. Examples would be those who have already been diagnosed with Alzheimer's Disease or Parkinson's Disease.

– W –

Waiver of Premium: A provision that states the insured is not required to continue paying premiums while he or she is receiving long-term care insurance benefits.

REFERENCES

American Association of Retired Persons (AARP). 2003. "Beyond 50.03: A Report to the Nation on Independent Living and Disability." Available as a download from **www.aarp.org.**

American Health Care Association. 2004. News release: "New BDO Seidman Analysis of Nation's Medicaid Program," February 4. Available as a download from **www.ahca.org.**

Congressional Budget Office. 2000. "Options to Expand Federal Health, Retirement, and Education Activities," *CBO Memorandum,* June. Prepared by the Health and Human Resources Division. Available as a pdf download from **www.cbo.gov.**

Douglas, Jennifer. 2001. *Long-Term Care Insurance: Trends and Outlook,* LIMRA International.

Employee Benefits Research Institute (EBRI). 2004. "Will Americans Ever Become Savers?" *The 14th Retirement Confidence Survey,* April. Retrieved from **www.ebri.org.**

Harper, Sarah. 2004. "Aging Society," *The Oxford Magazine,* March.

Hayes, Robert D., Nancy G. Boyd, and Kenneth W. Hollman. 1999. "What Attorneys Should Know About Long-Term Care Insurance," *The Elder Law Journal,* Vol. 7, No. 1.

Health Care Financing Administration (see The Centers for Medicare and Medicaid Services). **www.cms.hhs.gov.**

Health Insurance Association of America (HIAA). 2001. "Who Buys Long-Term Care Insurance in the Workplace?" October. Available as a download from **www.hiaa.org.**

Hewitt Associates. 2004. Press release: "Hewitt Study Shows U.S. Employees Sluggish in Interacting with 401(k) Plans," May 24.

Journal of Financial Planning, February 2001. "Coming of Age: The Shifting Dynamics of Elder Care" by Jacqueline M. Quinn.

Long-Term Care Financing Strategy Group. 2004. "A Vast Majority of Americans Over Age 45 Unprotected Against the Risk of Needing Long-Term Care, According to Second Annual Study." From *The Index of Long-Term Care Uninsured,* Washington, D.C., May 17.

LTCi Sales Strategies. Vol. 3, No. 2. Reprinted with permission. Available through **www.LTCSales.com.**

Merlis, Mark. 2003. Medical Expenditures Panel Survey cited in "Private Long-Term Care Insurance: Who Should Buy It and What Should They Buy?" March. Available as a download from **www.kff.org.**

Metropolitan Life Insurance Company. 2004. Press release: "Caring for an Aging Loved One at a Distance Costs Much in Time, Money, and Hours on the Job," MetLife Mature Market Institute.

Metropolitan Life Insurance Study. 1999. "The MetLife Juggling Act Study: Balancing Caregiving with Work and the Costs Involved," November. Available as a download from **www.metlife.com** (search Mature Market Institute for pdf report).

Metropolitan Life Insurance Study. 2001. "The MetLife Study of Employed Caregivers: Does Long-Term Care Insurance Make a Difference?" Findings from a national study by the National Alliance for Caregiving and LifePlans, Inc., March. Available as a download from **www.metlife.com** (search Mature Market Institute for pdf report).

National Alliance for Caregiving and AARP. 2004. "Caregiving in the U.S." Funded by the MetLife Foundation. Available as a download from **www.caregiving.org.**

National Association of Insurance Commissioners, **www.naic.org.**

National Council on Aging. Definition of "senior center" by the National Institute of Senior Centers. Retrieved from **www.ncoa.org.**

National Council on the Aging. 1999. "Americans Look to Employers and Government for Help with Long-Term Care," March 23.

O'Neil, John. 2004. "Easing the Burdens of Care." *The New York Times,* May 11. Available for purchase from **www.nytimes.com.**

Parker-Pope, Tara. 2004. "Health Matters," *The Wall Street Journal,* June 28.

Prenda, Kimberly M. and Margie E. Lachman. 2001. "Planning for the Future: A Life Management Strategy," *Psychology and Aging,* Vol. 16, No. 2, pp. 206-216.

Rush University Medical Center. 2004. "Diabetics at Significantly Higher Risk for Alzheimer's Disease," May 17. Available as a download from **www.rush.edu.**

Slome, Jesse R. 2002. Paraphrased interview reprinted with permission from *Long-Term Care Insurance Sales Strategies,* Vol. 4, No. 4. **www.LTCSales.com**

U.S. Department of Health and Human Services. 2003a. "A Profile of Older Americans: 2003," *Administration on Aging.* Retrieved from **www.aoa.gov.**

U.S. Department of Health and Human Services. 2003b. "Family Caregivers: Our Heroes on the Frontlines of Long-Term Care," December 16. Retrieved from **www.hhs.gov.**

U.S. Department of Health and Human Services. 2005. *Medicare and You 2005.* Available as a download from **www.medicare.gov/publications/pubs/pdf/10050.pdf.**

U.S. Department of Labor. 2001. *Report of the Working Group on Long-Term Care,* November 14. Retrieved from **www.dol.gov.**

U.S. General Accounting Office. 2001. "Baby Boom Generation Increases Challenge of Financing Needed Services," Statement of William J. Scanlon, Director, Health Care Issues, GAO Report No. GAO-01-563T, March 27. Available as a download from **www.gao.gov.**

University of California. The Institute for Health and Aging. Retrieved from **www.nurseweb.ucsf.edu.**

University of Pittsburgh Medical Center. 2004. Press release: "University of Pittsburgh Finds That People Would Trade Longevity for Quality End-of-Life Care," May 19. Retrieved from **www.eurekalert.org.**

RESOURCES

Administration on Aging (AoA)
Department of Health and Human Services (DHHS)
330 Independence Avenue, SW
Washington, DC 20201

Public Inquiries: 202-619-0724 • 202-619-7501
Eldercare Locator: 1-800-677-1116 (toll-free)
Fax: 202-401-7620
Website: **www.aoa.gov**

- Caregivers information and support
- Alzheimer's Resources
- Local Aging Agencies Services for Seniors
- Eldercare locator.

Working in close partnership with its sister agencies in DHHS, the AoA is the Federal agency dedicated to policy development, planning and the delivery of supportive home-and community-based services to older persons and their caregivers. The AoA works through the national aging network of State and Area Agencies on Aging. Tribal and Native organizations, and thousands of service providers, adult care centers, caregivers and volunteers.

Alzheimer's Association
919 North Michigan Avenue, Suite 1100
Chicago, IL 60611

Phone: 1-800-272-3900 (toll-free) • 312-335-8700
TTY: 312-335-8882
Fax: 312-335-1110
Email: **info@alz.org**
Website: **www.alz.org**

The Association is a nonprofit organization offering information and support services to people with Alzheimer's Disease (AD) and their families. Contact the 24-hour, toll-free telephone line to link with local chapters and community resources. The Association funds research to find a cure for AD and provides information on care giving. A free catalog of educational publications is available in English and Spanish.

Alzheimer's Disease Education and Referral (ADEAR) Center
PO Box 8250
Silver Spring, MD 20907-8250

Phone: 1-800-438-4380 (toll-free) (English, Spanish) • 301-495-3334
Email: **adear@alzheimers.org**
Website: **www.alzheimers.org**

The ADEAR Center, funded by the National Institute on Aging, distributes information about Alzheimer's Disease (AD) to health professionals, patients and their families, and the public. Contact the Center for information about the symptoms, diagnosis, and treatment of AD; recent research; and referrals to State and other national services. On its website, the Center offers searchable publications and databases, including the AD Clinical Trials Database of studies accepting volunteers.

American Association of Homes and Services for the Aging (AAHSA)
2519 Connecticut Avenue, NW
Washington, DC 20008-1520

Phone: 202-783-2242
Fax: 202-783-2255
Email: **inform@aahsa.org**
Website: **www.aahsa.org**

AAHSA is a national, nonprofit organization providing older people with services and information on housing, health care, and community involvement. Visit the AAHSA website for information for seniors and caregivers.

American Parkinson's Disease Association (APDA)
1250 Hylan Boulevard, Suite 4B
Staten Island, NY 10305

Phone: 1-800-223-2732 (toll-free)
Fax: 718-981-4399
Email: **info@apdaparkinson.org**
Website: **www.apdaparkinson.org**

A nonprofit organization, APDA funds research to find a cure for Parkinson's Disease. APDA's toll-free line refers callers to local chapters for information on community services, specialists, and treatments. Publications and educational materials are available on Parkinson's Disease, speech therapy, exercise, diet, and aids for daily living.

American Stroke Association (ASA)
7272 Greenville Avenue
Dallas, TX 75231

Phone: 1-888-4STROKE (478-7653) (toll-free)
Fax: 214-706-5231
Email: **strokeassociation@heart.org**
Website: **www.strokeassociation.org**

ASA, a division of the American Heart Association, provides the Stroke Family Warmline, a toll-free information and referral service offering lists of certified doctors who are stroke specialists and volunteer stroke survivors or family members. Callers receive support and can request free information. ASA publishes *Stroke Connection,* a priced subscription magazine for survivors and families.

Assisted Living Federation of America (ALFA)
11200 Waples Mill Road, Suite 150
Fairfax, VA 22030

Phone: 703-691-8100
Fax: 703-691-8106
Email: **info@alfa.org**
Website: **www.alfa.org**

ALFA represents over 5,000 for-profit and nonprofit providers of assisted living as well as a diverse range of organizations involved in the assisted living industry. With more than 40 state affiliates, ALFA promotes the philosophy of consumer choice and quality of life for seniors.

Children of Aging Parents (CAPS)
1609 Woodbourne Road, Suite 302A
Levittown, PA 19057

Phone: 1-800-227-7294 (toll-free) • 215-945-6900
Fax: 215-945-8720
Website: **www.caps4caregivers.org**

CAPS is a nonprofit organization that provides support services to caregivers of older people. It serves as a clearinghouse for information on elder care resources and issues, including Instant Aging workshops to help communities understand the needs of older people. Send a self-addressed, stamped envelope to receive publications on aging or information about support groups.

Continuing Care Accreditation Commission (CCAC)
2519 Connecticut Avenue, NW
Washington, DC 20008-1520

Phone: 202-508-9459
Fax: 202-220-0022
Email: **afinnega@ccaconline.org**
Website: **www.ccaconline.org**

CCAC helps consumers identify quality retirement options. CCAC also accredits aging services that meet or exceed industry-generated standards of excellence in three areas: governance and administration; financial resources and disclosure; and resident life, health, and wellness.

Elderweb
1305 Chadwick Drive
Normal, IL 61761

Phone: 309-451-3319
Fax: 866-422-8995
Email: **ksb@elderweb.com**
Website: **www.elderweb.com**

Elderweb is a research website for older people, professionals, and families seeking information on elder care and long-term care. Visit Elderweb for news and information on legal, financial, medical, and housing issues for older people and links to other websites.

The Centers for Medicare and Medicaid Services (CMS)
7500 Security Boulevard
Baltimore, MC 21244

Phone: 1-800-MEDICARE (633-4227) (toll-free) (Medicare hotline)
410-786-3000
Fax: 202-690-7675
Website: **www.cms.hhs.gov**
www.medicare.gov (Medicare information)

The 10 regional offices of CMS work with the contractors who administer the Medicare program. Also works with the states that administer the Medicaid, SCHIP, HIPAA, and provide certification of health care providers. CMS works closely with the Social Security Administration (SSA) to provide information about Medicare to beneficiaries applying for, or currently receiving, retirement or disability benefits at local SSA district offices.

National Academy of Elder Law Attorneys, Inc. (NAELA)
1604 North Country Club Road
Tucson, AZ 85716

Phone: 520-881-4005
Fax: 520-325-7925
Website: **www.naela.org**

NAELA is a nonprofit association assisting lawyers, bar associations, and others who work with older people and their families. Contact NAELA for information on lawyers specializing in issues pertinent to older people, resources to legal information, assistance, and education. A list of publications is available.

National Adult Day Services Association (NADSA)
722 Grant Street, Suite L
Herndon, VA 20170

Phone: 1-866-890-7357 (toll-free)
Fax: 703-435-8631
Email: **info@nadsa.org**
Website: **www.nadsa.org**

NADSA provides community based group programs, designed to meet the needs of functionality and/or cognitively impaired adults through an individual plan of care, usually during regular working hours five days a week at adult day centers. Some programs are available in the evenings and on weekends.

National Alliance For Caregiving
4720 Montgomery Lane, Fifth Floor
Bethesda, MD 20814

Email: **info@caregiving.org**
Website: **www.caregiving.org**

A nonprofit coalition of national organizations that focuses on issues of family caregiving across the life span. The Alliance was created to conduct research, do policy analysis, develop national programs and increase public awareness of family caregiving issues. The mission of the Alliance is to be an objective national resource on family caregiving with the goal of improving the quality of life for families and care recipients.

National Association for Home Care and Hospice (NAHC)
228 7th Street, SE
Washington, DC 20003

Phone: 202-547-7424 (Agency Locator)
Fax: 202-547-3540
Website: **www.nahc.org**

NAHC promotes hospice and home care, sets standards of care, and conducts research on aging, health, and health care policy. Association publications include How to Choose a Home Care Provider and other free consumer guides on home care and hospice care.

National Association of Area Agencies on Aging (N4A)
927 15th Street, NW, 6th Floor
Washington, DC 20005

Phone: 1-800-677-1116 (toll-free) (Eldercare Locator) • 202-296-8130
Fax: 202-296-8134
Website: **www.n4a.org**

N4A is the umbrella organization for the AoA-funded Area Agencies on Aging. The Association administers the AoA-sponsored Eldercare Locator, a toll-free number linking older adults and their family members with local aging resources. N4A publishes the National Directory for Eldercare Information and Referral.

National Association of Professional Geriatric Care Managers (NAPGCM)
1604 North Country Club Road
Tucson, AZ 85716-3102

Phone: 520-881-8008
Fax: 520-325-7925
Email: **info@caremanager.org**
Website: **www.caremanager.org**

NAPGCM is a nonprofit organization representing the interests of elder care practitioners and advocating for older peoples' independence, autonomy, and quality of health care. Contact NAPGCM for resources, referrals to local Association chapters, and information on counseling and treatment programs. Publications and referrals to professional care managers are available through the website.

National Institute on Aging (NIA)
National Institutes of Health (NIH)
Office of Communications and Public Liaison
Bethesda, MD 20892-2292

Phone: 1-800-222-2225 (toll-free) (NIA Information Center – NIAIC)
1-800-438-4380 (toll-free) (Alzheimer's Disease Education and
Referral Center-ADEAR)
301-496-1752
TTY: 1-800-222-4225 (toll free) (NIAIC)
Fax: 301-589-3014 (NIAIC) • 301-495-3334 (ADEAR)
Email: **niainfo@ibs1.com** (NIAIC)
adear@alzheimers.org (ADEAR)
Website: **www.nih.gov/nia** • **www.alzheimers.org**

The Institute produces the Age Pages – a series of fact sheets for consumers on a wide range of subjects including nutrition, medications, for-
getfulness, sleep, driving, and long-term care. Information, publications,
referrals, resource lists, and database searches on Alzheimer's Disease
are available through the Institute-funded ADEAR Center.

National Resource Center: Diversity and Long-Term Care (NRCDLTC)
The Heller School for Social Policy & Management
Brandeis University
PO Box 9110
Waltham, MA 02454-9110

Phone: 1-800-456-9966 (toll-free) • 781-736-3965
Fax: 781-736-3965
Website: **www.sihp.brandeis.edu**

NRCDLTC, a partnership between Brandeis University and San Diego
State University, provides information on methods, resources, systems,
and services for caring for older people. The Center provides referrals
to health resources and information on issues of diversity in aging,
including disabilities, race, ethnicity, gender, generations, and chronic
diseases. A list of publications is available on request.

Parkinson's Disease Foundation (PDF)

833 West Washington Boulevard
Chicago, IL 60607

Phone: 1-800-457-6676 (toll-free) • 312-733-1893
Fax: 312-664-2344
Website: **www.pdf.org**

PDF is a nonprofit organization providing research funding, information and supportive services to people with Parkinson's Disease. Contact the Foundation for referrals to specialists. Publications are available.

The Parkinson's Institute

1170 Morse Avenue
Sunnyvale, CA 94089-1605

Phone: 1-800-786-2958 (toll-free) • 408-734-2800
Fax: 408-734-8522
Website: **www.parkinsoninstitute.org**

The Institute is an independent, not-for-profit organization conducting patient care and research activities in the neurological specialty area of movement disorders. The goal of the Parkinson's Institute's Outreach program is to offer education, help, and support to those who are dealing with a movement disorder. Services are provided to patients, caregivers, family, friends, and health care professionals. Outreach staff is normally available for phone calls Monday through Friday from 9:00 am to 5:00 pm.

SPRY Foundation

10 G Street, NE, Suite 600
Washington, DC 20002

Phone: 202-216-0401
Fax: 202-216-0779
Email: **spryfoundation@nepssm.org**
Website: **www.spry.org**

SPRY – Setting Priorities for Retirement Years – is a nonprofit foundation that develops research and education programs to help older adults plan for a healthy and financially secure future. The website links consumers to national health resources.

United Seniors Health Council (USHC)
409 3rd Street, NW, Suite 200
Washington, DC 20024

Phone: 1-800-637-2604 (toll-free) (orders only) • 202-479-6973
Fax: 202-479-6660
Email: **info@unitedseniorshealth.org**
Website: **www.unitedseniorshealth.org**

USHC is a nonprofit organization dedicated to helping older consumers, caregivers, and professionals. The Council produces publications on topics such as financial planning, managed care, and long-term care insurance. The Council pioneered a Health Insurance Counseling Program, which helps consumers understand their many insurance options. Its Eldergames program is a comprehensive series of materials designed to stimulate the imagination and memories of older people.

Well Spouse Foundation (WSF)
30 East 40th Street
New York, NY 10016

Phone: 1-800-838-0879 (toll-free) • 212-685-8815
Fax: 212-685-8676
Email: **wellspouse@aol.com**
Website: **www.wellspouse.org**

WSF is a not-for-profit association of spousal caregivers. It offers support to the wives, husbands, and partners of chronically ill or disabled people. The Foundation has lists of support groups nationwide and sponsors recreational respite opportunities.

ADDITIONAL EDUCATIONAL RESOURCES
FOR CONSUMERS

A Shopper's Guide to Long-Term Care Insurance
National Association of Insurance Commissioners (NAIC)
2301 McGee Street, Suite 800
Kansas City, MO 64108-2604
Phone: 1-816-842-3600
Website: **www.naic.org**

How to Protect Your Life Savings from Catastrophic Illness
Harley Gordon, Corporation for Long-Term Care Certification (CLTCC)
188 Needham Street, Suite 230
Newton, MA 02464
Phone: 1-877-771-2582
Website: **www.ltc-cltc.com**

Terry Savage, **Terry Savage Talks Money,** WBBM-TV (CBS)
Terry Savage Productions, Ltd.
676 N. Michigan Ave., Suite 3610
Chicago, Ill 60611
Phone: 1-312-266-1717
Website: **www.TerrySavage.com**

United Seniors Health Council
300 D Street
Washington, D.C. 22024
Phone: 1-800-373-4906
Website: **www.ncoa.org**

ADDITIONAL EDUCATIONAL RESOURCES
FOR FINANCIAL PROFESSIONALS

Certified Senior Advisor Designation,
Society of Certified Senior Advisors
1777 S. Bellaire Street, Suite 230
Denver, CO 80222
Phone: 1-800-653-1785
Website: **www.society-csa.com**

Corporation for Long-Term Care Certification
233 Needham Street, Suite 230
Newton, MA 02464
Phone: 1-877-771-2582
Website: **www.ltc-cltc.com**

Long-Term Care Professional Designation
601 Pennsylvania Ave., NW, Suite 500, South Bldg.
Washington, D.C. 20004
Phone: 1-202-778-8471
Website: **www.ahip.org**

Superior LTC Planning Approach™ Certification
1024 Serpentine Lane, Suite 118
Pleasanton, CA 94566
Phone: 1-800-400-0577
Website: **www.superiorltc.com**

WEBSITE RESOURCES

Alzheimer's Association: **www.alz.org**

American Association of Homes and Services for the Aging: **www.aahsa.org**

Assisted Living Federation of America: **www.alfa.org**

Center for Long-Term Care Financing: **www.centerltc.com**

ElderWeb Online Eldercare Sourcebook: **www.elderweb.com**

Federal Administration on Aging: **www.aoa.gov**

National Association for Home Care
HOMECARE Online: **www.nahc.org**

Medicare: **www.medicare.gov**

National Alliance for Caregiving: **www.caregiver.org**

National Senior Citizen's Law Center: **www.nsclc.org**

National Family Caregivers Association: **www.nfcacares.org**

National Adult Day Services Association: **www.ncoa.org/nadsa**

Senior Alternatives: **www.senioralternatives.com**

Senior Care Resources, Nursing Home Report Cards Online: **www.seniorcarehelp.com**

Superior LTC Planning™ Services, Inc.: **www.superiorltc.com**

The Administration of Aging's Adult Day Center Resources: **www.aoa.dhhs.aoa/webres/adultday.htm**

Visiting Nurse Associations of America: **www.vnaa.org**

INDEX

M

material change, 169

maximum lifetime benefit, 117-118

Medicaid, 36, 41, 49-54, 59, 176-179, 195, 253-261

Medicaid planning, 52-54, 254-255

Medi-Cal, 48

Medicare, 56-57, 81-82, 253-255

Medicare Supplement Insurance, 57

modified guaranteed issue basis, 184

N

National Adult Day Services Association (NADSA), 26

National Aging Services Network, 27

National Association of Insurance Commissioners (NAIC), 98, 143

National Council on Aging (NCOA), 27, 91

New York State Partnership Program, 102, 177

non-cancelable LTC insurance, 196

nonforfeiture benefit rider, 122

non-skilled care, 22

non-tax-qualified policies (NTQ), 169, 205

O

Omnibus Budget Reconciliation Act of 1993 (OBRA), 175, 255

P

paid-up survivor benefit, 123

Parkinson's Disease, 99

Partnership Programs, 175-179, 240, 244-245

personal care, 24

plan of care, 35, 156-157

pre-existing condition, 204